CELTIC

DAILY LIGHT

A SPIRITUAL
JOURNEY THROUGH
THE YEAR

COMPILED BY
RAY SIMPSON

Hodder & Stoughton
LONDON SYDNEY AUCKLAND

British Library Cataloguing in Publication Data.
A record for this book is available from the British Library.

ISBN 0 340 69488 2

Typeset by Hewer Text Composition Services, Edinburgh
Printed and bound in Great Britain by
Mackays of Chatham plc, Chatham, Kent

Hodder and Stoughton Ltd
A Division of Hodder Headline PLC
338 Euston Road
London NW1 3BH

I dedicate this book to
Christ the Sun of suns
and

to the peoples of the Commonwealth
and to all other peoples
who made welcome Irish pilgrims
from America to Russia.
May it bless you.

August 31: Here I am, lord, is it I, lord

CONTENTS

Preface by David Fitzgerald

Introduction

Daily readings through the year

Index of People

Index of Subjects

Index of Bible Texts

Sources and Acknowledgments

Map

PREFACE

Here is the perfect travelling companion for all who seek a deeper understanding of Celtic daily life, prayer and meditation. These words, drawn from centuries of written text, offer to us a daily contemplation of the shared experiences of all generations, of our pilgrimage through this life and of our contemplation of the life to come.

There is much talk of Celtic spirituality currently, as many are seeking answers to their questions within our pagan culture (which is now rooted in today's earth religions). Although the words of this book are saturated with references to the past, and speak of 'that great cloud of witnesses' who have gone before us, they have very real significance today. These readings will have a profound relevance for all who read them as they respond to our shared Celtic Christian heritage.

Through our daily reading of Celtic Daily Light, the early saints: Cuthbert, Aidan, Columba, Hilda, Brendan reach down to us and share what has been their own experience of their relationship with God and with His creation around them. Ray is one who has chosen actually to live the life of one of these early saints, and not just contemplate what once was. God has called him to be one of His 'voices' into this present age where so many are yearning for Light to shine into their daily experience.

God told the prophet Jeremiah that He would 'make my words in your mouth a fire' (Jeremiah 5:14). In the Bible, fire has always been used in reference to the Holy Spirit. And, although past traditions and religious practices and beliefs are often accused of being irrelevant, ancient fossils best forgotten, these words affirm that tradition is not dead, it is very much alive and has power to penetrate our being and to transform us. As a dear Orthodox Priest once said to me, 'David, tradition is not dead, tradition is Fire!'.

These daily readings offer to us the Light of centuries, the Light that continues to reach into the lives of all who seek to find it. These readings speak to me of the Light of the World, Jesus Christ, the Son of the Living God.

David Fitzgerald

INTRODUCTION

This book offers us the best of our birthright to take us into a new millennium.

Often readings are from Celtic pilgrims, poets or saints, but the book also includes sayings of people from many lands who seem to be natural soul friends to our Celtic Saints; the entire book breathes a Celtic spirit.

In order to help you make the most of the book, a number of indexes have been included, and a map of the British Isles:

* **Index of People**
  so that you can find material on a favourite Celtic Saint, particular author or specific source

* **Index of Subjects**
  to help you find readings particularly linked to areas of interest or need such as anger, healing, depression, evangelism

* **Index of Bible Texts**
  identifying which particular Bible passages are used on which day

* **Map**
  shows key places mentioned in the book and shows the positioning of the Celtic Saints (St Petroch in the South West and St Mungo in Scotland and so on)

REACHING OUT

Following God is a pilgrimage of faith. The road ahead is only revealed as
we step out in trust, with God the Father, the Son and the Spirit
(represented by the central triangular knot) before us.

Forgetting what is behind, and reaching towards what is ahead, I press towards the goal of the high calling in Christ.
Philippians 3:13–14

A new year. New resolutions. Yet, if we just go forward into this year with nothing but our own flimsy resolutions, they are likely to come to nothing. There is so much more that we can go forward in, as this Celtic call makes plain:

> Let us go forth
> In the goodness of our merciful Father
> In the gentleness of our brother Jesus
> In the radiance of the Holy Spirit
> In the faith of the apostles
> In the joyful praise of the angels
> In the holiness of the saints
> In the courage of the martyrs
>
> Let us go forth
> In the wisdom of our all-seeing Father
> In the patience of our all-loving Brother
> In the truth of the all-knowing Spirit
> In the learning of the apostles
> In the gracious guidance of the angels
> In the patience of the saints
> In the self-control of the martyrs
> Such is the path of all servants of Christ
> The path from death to life eternal.
> > *In* Celtic Fire *Robert Van der Weyer (Unattributed)*

Whatever our regrets about last year, it is important to put them behind us; to release them into the hands of Christ, and to place everything that lies before us into his sure hands.

> Go before us
> In our pilgrimage of life.
> Anticipate our needs
> Prevent our falling,
> And lead us to our destiny.

Turn to God from whom you have deeply revolted, for in the coming day everyone will throw away their self-made idols.
Isaiah 31:6,7

A Church of Scotland minister has suggested that the Reformers of the 15th. century made a mistake when they abolished the Christmas festival in Scotland. For this created a vacuum which was filled, he suggests, with the now dominant pagan celebration of Hogmanay. Whatever the truth of that, we can all glean something from the approach of Samson.

Samson arrived in Guernsey in the 5th century at the time of the New Year anniversary, which, his anonymous 6th century biographer tells us, the islanders used to celebrate 'according to a vile custom of their forbears'. Samson made friends of these pagans, he took an initiative, which included everyone, and he exuded a spirit of love, not blame. He was always crystal clear about right and wrong.

'Prudent in spirit' his biographer tells us, 'to soften their hardness he called them all together in one place and, God showing the way, a discussion took place for the removal of so great evils. Then all these folk, truly loving him, forswore these evils for his sake and truly promised to unreservedly follow his guidance'.

The children tended to run wild at this season, so Samson called them together also, gave each a little present and told them in Jesus' name to change their ways.

His method was one of meeting, not denunciation. Before his dedicated love their hardness melted away and the pagan customs of generations were abandoned for something better.

> Lord of the years
> May we celebrate the good life past
> And not forget the Giver of that life.
> God of the call
> May we contemplate the good road ahead
> And walk along it,
> With love in our hearts, hand in hand with you.

The Lord said to Abram, 'Leave your country, your people and your household, and go to the land I will show you.'
Genesis 12:1

Europe was changed by the pilgrims for the love of God
David Edwards

Home is not a place, it's a road to be travelled, we say,
Our only defence is the armour of God,
With the Gospel of Peace our feet are shod;
So alone, alone,
We walk into the great unknown.

Mightier than fear is the Shield of Faith we bear;
Our task is to lighten another's load,
And home for us is the great high road,
So alone, alone,
We walk into the great unknown.

Righteousness our Breastplate, the Belt of Truth we wear;
We go where conquering armies have trod,
But we carry the Sword of the Word of God;
So alone, alone,
We walk into the great unknown.

The seed of God's love in the hearts of folk we sow;
And stronger and taller that seed will grow,
That all creation the truth may know;
Then alone, alone,
It will conquer the great unknown.
From the play with music – Columba

Lord, be within me to give me strength
Over me to protect me
Beneath me to support me
In front of me to be my guide
Behind me to prevent me falling away
Surrounding me to give me courage
So that alone, alone
I may walk into the great unknown.

Some wandered in trackless wastes, finding no way to a city to stay in.
Hungry and thirsty, their soul fainted within them. Then they cried to
the Lord in their trouble, and the Lord delivered them from their
distress, and led them by a straight way.
Psalm 107:4–7

Therefore let us live by this principle, that we live as travellers on the
road, as pilgrims, as guests of the world . . . singing with grace and
power 'When shall I come and appear before the face of my God?'

Columbanus

Many prayers for journeys were collected in the nineteenth century by
Alexander Carmichael, some of which went back to the times when
Celtic Christians such as Brendan travelled the seas in coracles. When
he wrote there were still many small prayer places where men went to
pray before and after their voyages.

This spirituality continues in the different circumstances of modern
life. It is reflected, for example, in this prayer, written and displayed in
an airport chapel:

> Home!
> Relaxed, warm-welcomed,
> Full of ease, embraced and nourished.
> Newly arrived from far away, yet home.
> The words that sped me on my way
> Still echo in this foreign place.
> The hands that held me there
> Now greet me here
> And I am home
> With that same God who knew and loved me then.
> This end of journey too is but a staging post
> On another journey
> From this on to another home.
>
> *Anon*

> May Father aid me
> May Son aid me
> May Spirit aid me
> On sea and land
> In the shielding of the City everlasting.
>
> *Carmina Gadelica*

I am sending you out like lambs among wolves.
Luke 10:3

The famous sculpture of St. Aidan on Holy Island has four features
which have much to say to us as we begin another year. The four
features are: his face, his torch, his staff and his Celtic cross.

Aidan's face looks out to the future, and south, to the unevangelised
regions, with faith-filled vision. Which places does Christ want us to
give our attention to this year? Aidan takes with him from the past the
torch of the Faith to hand on to others as a living flame. To whom
does God want us to hand on the flame of faith in the coming year?
Aidan carries everywhere with him his pastoral staff, a sign of gentle
love and compassion for all. Where do we need to grow in gentleness
and compassion?

There is something else in this sculpture which we must never
forget. Behind and above Aidan, as a shield wherever he goes, is a cross
with a circle. For Aidan had a sacrificial mission – to plant a cross in
the soil of a new land, and in the soul of its people. The circle meant
that the message of the cross was to encompass all. It was not just to be
a message but an experience of the cross to be lived and applied in
every area of life, every moment of every day.

No gain without pain. No false triumphalism. No words divorced
from humble service. Only so will our dreams and resolutions survive
the rocks of cruel human nature. Only so will setbacks be surmounted
and the serene strength of Christ still be ours as we journey on in faith.

> God be with you at every leap;
> Christ be with you on every steep;
> Spirit be with you in every deep;
> Each step of the journey you go.
>
> All that I do
> All whom I'll meet,
> All that I'll ever be I offer now to you.

The three magi rejoiced when they saw the star. They entered the house and saw the child with Mary his mother, and they knelt and worshipped him. They offered him gifts of gold, frankincense and myrrh.
Matthew 2:10, 11.

At a new year we step out afresh on virgin ground. Let us learn from the wise kings of the long journey how our journey should be.

The first king stands for gold, something we all want, something good in itself. It stands for prosperity, and all the things money can buy. Hopefully many of us will have times of prosperity. But gold cannot buy love, truth, eternity; it cannot fill the heart. The wisdom of this king was that he knew this, and he came to find that which would fill his heart, that for which he could give his life. In this wise person money was put in perspective, and he was willing to kneel and offer it as a gift.

The second king brings incense; he is at home with the routines of religion, of scholarship. These things, too, can be good. But, just as the pocket cannot satisfy the heart, neither can the brain. Perhaps this man came to realise that. He was drawn onwards by a sense of mystery. As he knelt, he was filled with a sense of wonder that no amount of theory could have produced. When the heart is right, we have a sense of wonder at the smallest thing, and all life becomes a sign of God's Presence.

The third king is a sad person; it is unusual for an adult to talk about death in front of a new-born baby. This wise man had an intuitive understanding of the suffering and early death that was to mark Jesus's life. He shows us how to accept and be dignified in the times of loss, disappointment or downturn.

High King of the universe
We offer you our possessions, make them all your own.
We offer you our mind-sets and we place them at your feet.
May we be filled with your Presence as incense fills a holy place.
We offer you the shadows of our lives, the things that are crushed;
Our little deaths and our final death.
May these be like the straw in the out-stable.
May something beautiful for you be born in all this straw.

Being warned in a dream not to return to King Herod, the visitors
who studied the stars returned home another way.
Matthew 2:12

> After the star, the dim day.
> After the gifts, the empty hands.
> And now we take our secret way
> Back to far lands.
>
> After the cave, the bleak plain.
> After the joy, the weary ride.
> But journey we, three new-made men
> Side by side.
>
> Came we by old paths by the sands.
> Go we by new ones this new day,
> Homewards to rule our lives and lands
> By another way.
>
> *Author unknown*

> I beg assistance, God of my journey
> To accept that all of life is only on loan to me
> To believe beyond this moment
> To accept your courage when mine fails
> To recognise the pilgrim of my heart
> To hold all of life in open hands.
>
> *Joyce Rupp OSM, A Pilgrim at Glendalough*

> Be a smooth way before me,
> Be a guiding star above me,
> Be a keen eye behind me,
> This day, this year, for ever.

The Lord said to Moses . . . 'I will make you and your heirs into a great nation.'
Exodus 32:10

One frosty night I meditated under the stars on the hill overlooking Edinburgh known as Arthur's Seat. Our lands seemed to be sinking under a sea of troubles, and those who were meant to give a lead seemed to be blighted by small-mindedness. I sensed that God was wanting to release the potential for great leadership that lies untapped in so many people, and that the spirit that animated that great leader, Arthur, can animate us, too.

Unlike the well-known Celtic saints, the life of the great Celtic war hero Arthur is shrouded in the mists of legend. Yet, wherever he may have lived, and whatever the actual details of his life, we can be grateful that here was a man who dared to give a lead, to stand up to the tyrant, to rally the forces of good, and to live out Christian values.

The legends give a sense of Arthur's Christ-centred strategy for the nation during the period after the Roman troops left, when brutal Saxon invaders were taking over. Arthur built a chain of defended towns to protect the Britons from the invaders, and so secured, for a period, what is known as 'Arthur's Peace'. Arthur was thwarted by quarrelling Celtic kings, yet 'he was beginning to display that rarest of qualities: a joy inspired by hardship, deepened by adversity, and exalted by tragedy'. He was given a vision for Britain: 'A land shining with goodness, where each man protects his brother's dignity, where war and want has ceased, and all races live under the same law of love and honour . . . a land bright with truth, where a man's word is his pledge . . . where the True God is worshipped and his ways acclaimed by all'. *Stephen Lawhead* Arthur, *an historical novel*

Some nation must produce a new leadership, free from the bondage of fear, rising above ambition, flexible to the direction of God's Holy Spirit . . . Some nation must give a lead. Some nation must find God's will as her destiny, and God-guided people as her representatives at home and abroad. Will it be your nation?

Frank Buchman

> Lord, give to us that inner dynamic
> Which calls out and combines
> The moral and spiritual responsibility of individuals
> For their immediate sphere of action.

This is what the Lord God, the Holy One, says to you . . . 'In
quietness and trust shall be your strength.'
Isaiah 30:15

Arthur may have looked out from that hill named 'Arthur's Seat'
towards the defended cities he had established at Dunedin, Dundonald,
Dunbarton, Stirling and Dunpelder. These were the result of leadership
of great activity. Yet, if the kingdom of God is to be established in the
heart of a people, the leadership of action needs to be complemented
by leadership of a different kind that cultivates the inner life.

A fine example of such leadership, working hand in glove with
Arthur, is Monenna. She had been inspired by St Brigid to found a
monastery in her native Ireland. Such was its quality that crowds
flocked to her. They encroached too much upon her calling to the
inner life, so she moved away to Scotland where she had space for a
daily discipline of contemplation.

Monenna's real name was Edana, to which was added the affectionate
prefix 'Mo'. At the summit of the high rock where Edinburgh castle
now stands she built herself a prayer cell. The hill became known as
Edana's Hill, later as Dunedin, and much later as Edinburgh. Arising
out of her contemplation God led her to match Arthur's strategy by
founding a community of prayer in each of his five defended towns.
These two types of leadership ensured that both the outer and the inner
life of society was looked after.

Monenna's type of leadership is still as needed as Arthur's. We need a
brain drain in reverse, a constant stream of people who are ready to
leave behind the whirlpool of business and concentrate on the
contemplative life. In fact we need both kinds of leadership – the active
and the contemplative – as never before. In which direction is God
calling you?

> Holy Three
> Help me to live at the still centre
> Of the world's whirring wheels
> Where everything is led by you.

You, my child, will be called a prophet of the Most High God; you will go ahead of the Lord to prepare his road for him, to tell his people that they will be saved, by having their sins forgiven.
Luke 1:76–77

A new year is a time for new beginnings and of new births. The above prophecy over his baby by John the Baptist's father is echoed in the lives of many of the Celtic saints. Such prophecies were signs that God was doing something new from the very beginning of their lives.

Take, for example, the parents of St Samson, Anna and Amon. They were court officials in neighbouring kingdoms of 5th century Wales. Anna was infertile. She took to fasting, to charitable giving, and to churchgoing in order to get God to give her a child. One day when they were in church they overheard an animated discussion about a man in North Wales who could foretell with uncanny accuracy what would happen to people.

So Amon and Anna undertook a three day journey to see this man, Librarius, who gave them overnight accommodation. Next day Librarius surprised Amon twice. First, he told them, before they had spoken of it, he knew they had come because Anna was barren and they wanted him to prophesy that they would have a baby. Second, he asked Amon, not just to give him payment, but to have made a silver rod the same length as his wife and to give this to God. A rod is a symbol of a ruler's control. It seemed God wanted both Amon and Anna to put God first, before power, before one another, and even before their longed-for baby. Amon was so keen to respond that he made not one, but three rods, and handed them all over.

That night an angel told Anna in her dreams that she would indeed have a baby who would be holy, profitable to many, seven times brighter than the silver her husband had given to God, and that 'of the British race there has not been or will be anyone like him'. The angel encouraged Anna to trust God and to name the baby Samson, after the biblical Samson, who was so strong for God. Few who read the *Life of St Samson* can doubt that all that was prophesied has indeed come to pass.

> Holy God, holy and mighty
> You can bring a holy child to birth in a barren womb
> You can bring a new thing to birth in a barren land
> Bring to birth in me that new thing that is your will.

Abraham 'is the spiritual father of us all. As the Scripture says: I have made you a father of many peoples.'
Romans 4:16, 17

Is the faith community to which you belong like a museum or a nursery? Museums are painless, but also lifeless. Nurseries are messy, but they foster life. Ever since Abraham God has been in the business of nurturing people of faith.

This is how a nursery of saints began in Ireland. The day before St Comgall was born Mac Nisse of Connor heard a horse and carriage passing by and said to the people around him, 'That carriage carries a king.' However, when they all went outside to have a look they could see only two occupants, neither of them royal, Sedna and his pregnant wife Birga. Had Mac Nisse got it wrong? He insisted that his first 'seeing' had not been mistaken. 'It is the baby that woman is carrying who shall be a king,' he said, 'he will be adorned with all sorts of virtues and the lustre of his miracles will light up the world.'

So it proved to be. Comgall was to establish the famous community at Bangor at which, it was said, some four thousand monks were under the grace of God. Among the famous missionaries who trained there and went on to win countless disciples on the continent were Columbanus and Gall. The service book of the monastery, *The Antiphonary of Bangor*, survives in the Ambrosian Library in Milan.

Bangor became known as 'The Vale of Angels', and later Bernard of Clairvaux described it as being 'truly sacred, the nursery of saints'.

Sometimes individuals develop their own little nurseries. St Ita, who died in January 570, was originally named Deidre. She adopted her new name as a pun which reflected her 'hunger for divine love'. As a result of her great love and her powers of healing and prophecy she became known as 'the foster mother of the saints of Ireland'. When Comghan was dying in a monastery he felt God tell him that if Ita laid hands upon him in prayer he would go straight to heaven. This she did.

> Lord, I would like to be part of a nursery of saints.
> Show me what needs to happen for this to be.
> May my life be a seed-bed of prayer and of friendship
> Lived out in fellowship with others of like mind.

For this is God's plan: to make known his secret to his people, this rich
and glorious secret which God has for all peoples.
Colossians 1:27

Glimpses of God's plan were given when Columba's birth was foretold
to elders of Ireland in visions and dreams. Columba's mother Eithne
dreamed she was given a great cloak that stretched from Ireland to
Scotland and contained every colour of the rainbow. A youth took this
radiant cloak from her, which made her extremely sad. Then the youth
returned to Eithne and said, 'You have no need of grief but rather of
joy and delight. The meaning of this dream is that you will bear a son,
and Ireland and Scotland will be full of his teaching.'
    It was through a dream that sabotage to God's plan for Samson was
averted: Lest the part destined by God for Samson should be
contaminated in any details during his childhood 'divine providence
wrapped him round and preserved him uninjured'. Later Samson's
father turned against the plan to send his son to a Christian school
which God had revealed at Samson's birth. However, after a powerful
dream, Amon said to his wife, 'let us lose no time in sending our son,
rather God's son, to school, for God is with him and we ought to do
nothing against God.' *The Life of St Samson of Dol*

I believe that God has a Divine Plan for me. I believe that this plan is
wrapped in the folds of my being, even as the oak is wrapped in the
acorn and the rose is wrapped in the bud. I believe that this Plan is
permanent, indestructible and perfect, free from all that is essentially
bad. Whatever comes into my life that is negative is not a part of this
God–created Plan, but is a distortion caused by my failure to harmonise
myself with the Plan as God has made it. I believe that this Plan is
Divine, and when I relax myself completely to it, it will manifest
completely and perfectly through me. I can always tell when I am
completely relaxed to the Divine Plan by the inner peace that comes to
me. This inner peace brings a joyous, creative urge that leads me into
activities that unfold the Plan, or it brings a patience and a stillness that
allow others to unfold the Plan to me.

Glenn Clark

Lord, help me to relax into your plan for me.
Unfold it for me as the acorn unfolds into the oak.

Before you were born I chose you.
Jeremiah 1:4

Some of us find it hard to believe that God really wants to use us to
carry out the Divine Plan. Perhaps you were unwanted as a baby, and
therefore assume that nobody, not even God, wants you? If so, the
story of Tannoc's baby may help you.

King Loth of Dunpelder, in Lothian, was a petty and pagan ruler,
but he sent his daughter Tannoc to a convent founded by Monenna.
There she gave her life to God. One day her father offered her in
marriage to the Prince of Rheged in the hope of forging an alliance.
The untactful fifteen-year-old Tannoc informed Rheged's Prince Owen,
'I am already promised to a King far greater than you will ever be.'

A furore ensued, and Tannoc was exiled to live among some
peasants. The outraged Owen tracked her down and raped her before
returning to his home at Carlisle. Alone in the woods, Tannoc must
have felt all the rage and humiliation that every raped woman feels.
Abandoned by her father, scorned by her own privileged class, she was
friendless. Was this the end of the bright hopes she had had at the
convent? With all her heart she had tried to choose God's way, yet
what would become of her? Had God abandoned her? The peasants at
the farm were Christians, and offered her support, especially when she
realised she was pregnant.

Did Tannoc rebel against this uninvited life inside her? Perhaps she
realised that the baby was as much a victim as she was herself, with no
one to turn to for help, and she cherished it with the full passion of her
love. In so doing she found her own destiny. With a touch of courage
and wry humour, Tannoc named her baby Kentigern, which in her
tongue meant 'Big Chief'. Her Christian friends fetched the village
priest from nearby Culross; he christened the child 'Mungo', which
meant 'my beloved', and adopted them both. Mungo became a
shepherd of souls, the founder of Glasgow, an inspiration to millions,
and a saint. Perhaps some readers are carrying an unwanted baby. You
are in anguish as to what to do. You will have to go through the cycle
of anger and denial. But it need not end there. For you are carrying a
baby who is called to become a saint. Whenever you doubt this, think
of Mungo.

> Blessed are you, King of the universe
> For the precious gift of life
> Which, even in the most ghastly circumstances, is beyond price.
> May I always honour and cherish every human life.

God waters the world

After all the people had been baptised, Jesus also was baptised.
Luke 3:21

Christ is baptised and the whole world is made holy. He wipes out the
debt of our sins; we will all be purified by water and the Holy Spirit.
An Orthodox antiphon

'For as the rain and the snow come down from heaven, and do not
return there, but water the earth and make it blossom, so shall my
word be, says the Lord.' Christians understand that Christ is the Word
of God made flesh, and through the power of his Incarnation is present
in all creation. Yet creation is disordered. It is not only humankind that
is infected with a disoriented relationship with the Creator, the whole
creation shares the same fate of being unfulfilled without the Redeemer.
So how can Christ be everywhere present in it?

Although he was without sin, Jesus Christ came in a body as physical
as any sinful human body. He became like us in all things except sin.
At his baptism in the river Jordan, Jesus received a vision as he came
out of the water. He saw the Spirit in the form of a gentle dove and
heard his Father declare from on high, 'You are my dearly loved Son
with whom I am deeply pleased.' Jesus's baptism had a cosmic
significance: The sinless Saviour enters the streams of the Jordan,
therefore cleansing the waters and imparting divine redemption to the
entire material creation. As he comes up out of the water, he carries the
created world up with him. He sees the heaven open, which the first
human being had closed against himself and posterity, when Adam
caused the gates of paradise to be shut with a flaming sword. Now they
are opened, the waters of the sea are made sweet, the earth is glad. As
the water falls over his human body, so the love of the Father for his
loved Son cascades over him, covering him with glory. God and matter
become one in the Son . . . The world is charged with the grandeur of
God.

Adapted from Brendan O'Malley A Pilgrim's Manual: St David's

> Lord, water the world.
> Revive our dryness
> Soak our soreness
> Refresh our tiredness
> Wash our filthiness
> Bathe our woundedness
> Immerse us in your love.

The child Jesus grew and became strong; he was full of wisdom and
God's blessings were upon him.
Luke 2:40

As Mungo grew up he learned some invaluable lessons from his mother
Tannoc. She belonged to the generation that still cherished the healthy
and pleasant Roman practice of a daily hot bath; she taught her son to
enjoy this cleanliness and he practised it to the end of his long life.

Another lesson he learned from Tannoc was the sensitivity of Celtic
Christians to the wild creatures of nature. Long walks with his mother
by the river and the forests were his college. He learned the names of
flowers and their seasons, the feeding and mating habits of birds and
beasts and how to win the confidence of the furred and feathered
creatures. No one who has a loved family dog can doubt an animal's
ability to love, understand and communicate in wordless language with
humans. It is not only domestic animals that have the gift, but people
rarely allow a relationship of trust to develop with wild creatures.
Mungo learned to understand animals, fish and birds with his heart. All
through his life this gift came to light, as it does in the first story of his
boyhood.

At Culross one day some robins were pecking on the ground for
scraps. Village boys, as boys will, started throwing stones at them. One
bird was hit and fell to the ground. The boys ran away. But Mungo
ran to the fallen bird, smoothed and caressed its feathers and prayed,
'Lord Jesus Christ, in whose hands is the breath of every creature, tame
or wild, give back to this bird the breath of life, that your name may
be glorified.' After a little while the bird revived and flew away. The
villagers said it was a miracle. That robin flew right into Glasgow City's
coat of arms where it now proudly perches on the top of the oak tree.
                    Based on The Beloved St Mungo *Reginald B. Hale*

Many of us have missed out, in one way or another, on the
'developmental process'. Perhaps there are areas of our lives that have
not grown in wisdom, strength or sensitivity as they were meant to.
We can learn from Mungo the wisdom of the long walks; we can open
ourselves today to observe the breath of God in the little things we
encounter. As we learn from them, we shall grow.

> Help me to grow today
> In understanding and sensitivity
> In patience and prayerfulness.

The God of gods shall be seen in Zion.
Psalm 84:7

A boat landed on the East Anglian shore near Burgh Castle, the site of
the last fort the Romans built before they left Britain. From the boat
stepped three brothers, two priests and other Christians, who had come
from Ireland to share the faith with the pagan Anglo-Saxons. Perhaps
they had heard that East Anglia's King had found a true faith while in
exile in Gaul, and had recently brought a Bishop Felix over from
Burgundy to spread the Faith from the south of his kingdom. Whatever
the reason, it was certainly the wind of the Spirit that had blown them
to this place.

The leader of this faith-sharing team was Fursey. As a boy in Ireland
he had devoted all his energy to the study of the Bible and to the
disciplines taught by the monasteries. He had preached the word of
God to such effect that he could no longer endure the crowds who
flocked to hear him, for he had become renowned for the power of his
words, for his deeds, and for his life. His supreme aim in life was to do
wholeheartedly whatever God gave him to do; that is why he had
taken this opportunity to follow the life of a pilgrim for the Lord's sake
in a strange land. The king welcomed him; his persuasive teaching and
way of life won many unbelievers to Christ, and confirmed many
believers in their faith. Soon the King gave them some land at Burgh
Castle on which to establish a Christian community.

After some years at Burgh Castle, Fursey felt God call him away to
the hermit life where, as well as prayer and study, he did manual work
every day. At one point he became ill and had an out-of-the-body
experience; he heard angels singing: 'The saints shall go from strength
to strength' and 'The God of gods shall be seen in Zion'.

The time came when Fursey sensed that pagans from a neighbouring
kingdom would soon invade, so our intrepid pilgrim sailed for Gaul,
where he was welcomed by Clovis II, the Christian king of the Franks.
He established a monastery at Lagny, where he died on 16 January 649.

> God of gods, establish your presence among us
> God of gods, may your fire purge the wastelands.
> May your people advance from one virtue to another
> And may the kingdoms of this world
> Become the kingdom of our God.

The Lord says, 'You must leave them and separate yourselves from them. Have nothing to do with what is unclean.'
2 Corinthians 6:17

Celtic Christians drew inspiration from the example of the 4th and 5th century believers who fled the false, comfortable ways of the cities, to live for God alone in the Egyptian and Syrian deserts. These believers became known as the Desert Mothers and Fathers. The movement began with Paul the Hermit and Antony, who founded desert communities. They are depicted together on many high crosses that still stand in Ireland.

When the Roman Emperor Constantine made Christianity the official religion of the Roman Empire in the 4th century, churches were built with public money, people who put career before calling became clergy, and there were no more martyrs to inspire faith. The church became respectable, part of a culture which talked about Christian goals but overlaid the Gospel simplicities. The result was that people began to ask whether it was possible any longer to live a truly Christian life while tied to the structures and possessions of such a greedy society. Many, inspired by the example of Antony and Paul, and later Pachomius, went out to the deserts to live out the Gospel.

By the time Antony died, aged 105, on 17 January 356, there were monastic communities in many parts of the Empire, each touched in some way by his example. It was said that Antony went into the desert with nothing but a cloak, and left behind a desert full of Christians.

Shortly after this Pachomius, the other great founder of communities, established more highly organised monasteries in the south of Egypt, but with similar goals. Pachomius first met Christians when he was a miserable conscript in the army at Thebes. Some Christians brought him food as an act of love. Pachomius was so touched by this that he asked who these people were. He was told that Christians 'are people who bear the name of Christ, the only Son of God, and who do all manner of good things for everyone'. This so struck Pachomius that he vowed that when he was released from the army he would become a Christian. After his release his call to the desert came through a voice which told him three times: 'The Lord's will is to minister to the human race in order to reconcile them'.

Lord, if possible, take me from environments that are unclean.
But wherever I am take from me all that is false.

Unity

Be of the same mind. Have the same love. Be in full accord.
Philippians 2:2.

The spread of Christianity to diverse cultures posed this question: How do Christians remain united?

St. Paul gave the advice above. Cyprian, a 2nd century church leader, urged Christians to think of themselves as members of a choir, whose conductor was the bishop.

Antony was sought out for advice by Christians of very different backgrounds – peasants and politicians, army officers and teachers. His secret of unity was to live the simplicity of the Beatitudes – the beautiful attitudes which Jesus recommended in Matthew 5. We learn that so many people followed Antony's way of life in the desert that their cells in the hills were like tents filled with divine choirs – people chanting, studying, fasting, praying, rejoicing in the hope of future boons, working for the distribution of alms, and maintaining love and harmony among themselves. It was as if one truly looked on a land all its own – a land of devotion and righteousness. For neither perpetrator nor victim of injustice was there, nor complaint.

The Life of Antony *by Athanasius*

One secret of unity for Celtic Christians was to make themselves one with the Trinity – Father, Son and Holy Spirit – and to make themselves one with the people among whom they lived. In this way they experienced unity in diversity, unity without uniformity. When we make ourselves one we want what is good for the other. In order to make ourselves one we must empty ourselves, as Jesus emptied himself. This brings about a universal love. The attitude of making ourselves one in all things except sin should be the basis of our relationship with everyone, with those in authority and with those who have nothing.

Perhaps you are sometimes caught speaking disparagingly of Christians of another church? Remember, you do not have to agree with them to be of the same love. Whenever you find yourself doing this, decide to make yourself one.

> Father, I make myself one with you
> Jesus, I make myself one with you
> Spirit, I make myself one with you
> Christians of every church, I make myself one with you.

'Stand at the cross-roads,' says the Lord, 'and look for the ancient way; ask for the good way and take it; so shall you be safe and prosper.'
Jeremiah 6:16

> How wonderful it is to walk with God
> Along the road which holy men have trod.
> *Theodore H. Kitching*

Picture Branwalader sailing into the sweeping, golden bay. He and his monks beach the boat, walk to an incline, and there kneel in prayer. Some local Jersey fishermen, who share with them the perils and skills of the sea, become believers, and a place of prayer is built on that hill beside what is now St Brelade's Bay.

Branwalader, whose name in Welsh means Raven Lord, is known in French as Brelade. He was said to be the son of Kenen, a Cornish king. Renowned as 'a star', he forsook his fame and fortune for the life of a wandering missionary monk. He most likely trained at the Welsh monastery at Llantwit Major where Samson was a fellow pupil. These two were to work together in Ireland, Cornwall, the Channel Isles and Brittany. To this day there is a church of St Samson in Guernsey and of St Brelade in Jersey. When the North men laid waste the Breton church where the earthly remains of these two saints were kept, King Athelstan brought them for safe keeping, still together, to his monastery at Milton Abbas, on this day in 935.

The Channel Islands have attracted people of prayer in all ages. Many pilgrims come to the Fisherman's Chapel where Branwalader first prayed, and sense a return to ancient ways. In contrast to much of fragmented Christendom, the different strands of the church – biblical, catholic, charismatic, mystical, socially concerned, ecumenical – are being woven together in a holy Celtic pattern and prayer. The wonderful thing is that we can become part of such a weaving too.

> God's love is around us like the sea round an island
> And we stand secure on the rocks of our faith.
> He has given his word like a beacon to guide us
> His love is a harbour in which we are safe.
>
> All glory to God our leader and captain
> All praise to the Son, our guide and our light
> All praise to the Spirit – the wind and the power
> All honour and praise and glory and might.
> *Susan Halliwell and Jenny Cornwall of St Brelade*

I pray that they all may be one, father! May they be in us, just as you
are in me and I am in you.
John 17:21

For all we Irish, inhabitants of the world's edge, are disciples of Saints
Peter and Paul and of all the disciples who wrote the sacred canon (of
the New Testament) by the Holy Spirit. We accept nothing outside the
evangelical and apostolic teaching. None of us was a heretic . . . no one
a schismatic; but the Catholic Faith, as it was first transmitted by you,
successors of the holy apostles, is maintained unbroken . . . For among
us it is not who you are but how you make your case that counts.
Love for the peace of the Gospel forces me to tell all in order to shame
both of you who ought to have been one choir. Another reason is my
great concern for your harmony and peace. 'For if one member suffers
all the members suffer with it' . . .

Therefore, my dearest friends, come to an agreement quickly . . . I
can't understand how a Christian can quarrel with a Christian about the
Faith. Whatever an Orthodox Christian who rightly glorifies the Lord
will say, the other will answer Amen, because he also loves and believes
alike. 'Let you all therefore say and think the one thing' so that both
sides 'may be one' – all Christians.

Jesus has gathered us, is gathering us, and will gather us out of all
regions, till he should make resurrection of our hearts from the earth,
and teach us that we are all of one substance, and members of one
another.

> *Columbanus' letter to Pope Boniface 1V in 613,*
> *at a time when there were two power-hungry*
> *rivals for the 'Chair of Peter'.*

Thrice Holy God, eternal Three-in-One
Make your people holy, make your people one.
Stir up in us the flame that burns out pride and power
Restore in us the love that brings the servant heart to flower.
Thrice holy God, come as the morning dew;
Inflame in us your love
Which draws all lesser loves to you.

How wonderful it is, how pleasing, for God's people to live together in
unity.
Psalm 133:1.

Barinthus, grandson of Ireland's famed King Niall, loved to share his
experience of how unity between a father and son can be restored. His
son Mernoc rebelled and ran away from home. Mernoc back-packed
until he found an island on which some monks had settled. Here he
put things right with God, with himself, and with his fellows. In his
heart he even forgave and grew to love his father. This released in him
prophetic and healing gifts which God greatly used.

Barinthus heard about this, and set out to visit his son. Although
there was no physical communication between them, God's Spirit
revealed to Mernoc in his prayers that his father was on his way to visit
him. Mernoc did not just sit back, he took a step for unity. While his
father was still three days' journey away, Mernoc set out to meet him.
They warmly embraced and Mernoc introduced his father to his island
friends, the monks.

The monks lived separate lives in cells that were some distance from
each other; from Night Prayer until dawn they neither saw nor spoke
to one another. Yet, as Barinthus was later to recount to Brendan, he
was greatly struck by their togetherness. 'The brothers came to greet us
out of their cells like a swarm of bees,' he recounted. 'Though their
dwellings were divided from one another, there was no division in their
conversation, their counsel or their affection.' Barinthus and Mernoc left
for a fortnight's boating trip together, and it was clear to all that what
was true of the monks was now true of them. Father and son were one
– and it gave such pleasure.

Dear Father
What pleasure it gives you when we reflect in our relationships
The love you and Jesus and the Spirit have for one another and for
    us.
I know that I am as near to you, Father,
As I am to the person from whom I am most divided.
I pray for those persons I am furthest from.
In my heart I reach out to them.
And you are pleased
And I am pleased.

Though we are many . . . we are joined to each other like different parts of one body.
Romans 12:5

The founders of the churches were all bishops, three hundred and fifty in number, famed and holy and full of the Holy Spirit. They had one head, Christ. They had one leader, Patrick. They maintained one Eucharist, one liturgy . . . one Easter . . . what was excommunicated by one church was excommunicated by all.
Catalogue of the Saints of Ireland 6th to 9th century

Always be of one mind.
David's final message to his followers in Wales

Always keep God's peace and love among you, and when you have to seek guidance about your affairs, take great care to be of one mind. Live in mutual goodwill also with Christ's other servants, and do not despise Christians who come to you for hospitality, but see that you welcome them, give them accommodation, and send them on their way with friendship and kindness. Never think you are superior to other people who share your faith and way of life.
Cuthbert's last words as noted by Bede

Keep the peace of the Gospel with one another, and indeed with all the world.
The last words of Hilda to her sisters at the Whitby monastery

There is only one true flight from the world . . . the flight from disunity and separation, to unity and peace in the love of other people.
Thomas Merton

The walls of separation do not reach heaven.
Cornerstone Community, Belfast

> Peace between believers
> Peace between neighbours
> Peace between lovers
> In love of the King of Life.
>
> Peace between person and person
> Peace between wife and husband
> Peace between parents and children
> The peace of Christ above all peace.

In your sight my lifetime seems nothing . . . I am only your guest for a
little while.
Psalm 39:5, 12

Once Antony was conversing with some brothers when a hunter came
upon them. He saw Antony and the brothers enjoying themselves and
disapproved. So Antony said to him, 'Put an arrow in your bow and
shoot it.' The hunter did this. 'Now shoot another,' said Antony, 'and
another, and another.' Then the hunter said, 'If I bend my bow all the
time it will break.' Abba Antony replied, 'It is like that in the work of
God. If we push ourselves beyond measure, the brothers will soon
collapse. It is right therefore, from time to time, to relax.'

Someone once asked Antony, 'What shall I do?' Antony replied, 'Do
not presume your own righteousness; do not grieve over something
that is past; control your tongue and your belly.'

Here are two other sayings of Antony:

The spaces of our human life set over against eternity are most brief
and poor.

The time is coming when people will be insane, and when they see
someone who is not insane, they will attack that person, saying 'You
are insane, because you are not like us.'

Finally, we recall the occasion when someone asked Antony, 'What
shall I keep in order that I may please God?' Antony advised this
person to keep these three things: 'Always keep God before your eyes;
always keep the example of the holy Scriptures; and wherever you stay,
keep yourself there long enough not to move on in a rush.'

Keeper of eternity
Help me keep you ever before me.
Help me keep the example of your saints ever before me.
Help me keep sufficient sense of proportion to relax when needed,
To savour the blessings of hospitality
With ever grateful poise.

An honest answer is a sign of true friendship.
Proverbs 24:26

If you have a chest full of clothing, and leave it for a long time, the clothing will rot inside it. It is the same with thoughts in our heart. If we do not carry them out by physical action, after a long while they will spoil and turn bad.

Abba Pastor

When someone wants to return evil for evil, they are able to hurt their neighbour's conscience even by a single nod.

Abba Isaiah

As wax is melted before a fire, so is the soul enfeebled by praise, and loses the toughness of its virtues.

Amma Syncletica

Unless a person says in their heart, 'I alone and God are in this world' they shall not find quiet.

Abba Allois

Abba Arsenius was taking counsel with an old Egyptian man. Someone said to him, 'Abba Arsenius, how is it that you, such a great scholar of Latin and Greek, should take counsel from this countryman?' Arsenius answered, 'It is true I have acquired the learning of the Greeks and the Latins, as this world goes; but the alphabet of this countryman I have not yet been able to learn'.

We do not go in to the desert to escape people but to learn how to find them.

Thomas Merton

> Infinite One of the wise heart
> Saving One of the clear sight
> Knowing One of the hidden deeps
> May I learn from you as an eager pupil
> May I learn from life as a humble child
> May I learn from night, may I learn from day
> May I learn from soul friends, may I learn from the stillness.

The God of our forbears has chosen you that you should know God's will.
Acts 22:14

So often we miss God's will for us because we spend our lives like actors, acting out a script that others have written for us. This may consist of the expectations that parents or peers have put upon us, or perhaps, because of our insecurity, we ourselves are trying to copy others. We need to learn to follow, not our conditioning or our compulsions, but what our soul desires according to God.

Someone asked Abba Nisteros, a friend of Antony, 'What good work shall I do?' He replied, 'Not all works are alike. For Scripture says that Abraham was hospitable and God was with him. Elijah loved solitary prayer and God was with him. And David was humble before God and God was with him. Therefore, whatever you see your soul desire according to God, do that thing and you shall keep your heart safe.'

Sometimes God uses circumstances to draw out our true calling. Mungo grew to manhood and was ordained a priest in his home area. No doubt he had dreams of being called to some glorious, sacrificial task. Instead, he was called to visit an ailing old priest, Fergus, who lived seven miles upstream. He was shocked to find how the old man was failing; he stayed with him, cooked supper, and listened to the old man's memories of his home on the river Clyde, where the great missionary Ninian had established a church. About midnight Fergus had a fatal seizure, and died in Mungo's arms. His last words were, 'Promise you will bury me at the old church hallowed by Ninian.'

So Mungo, with the oxen pulling Fergus' body, went a day's journey to the little church by the Clyde. Neighbours gathered. They looked forlorn; they had not seen a priest for several years. Next day, at the funeral, as Mungo looked at these sad faces, and as he looked at the large Druid centre four miles away which threatened to replace the faith to which they had held, he knew that he could not return, as he had planned. For God's plan was that he build up a community of faith here. Soon his mother joined him. She called the community 'Eglais Cu' (the loved church) meaning the people as a family. Today it is pronounced Glasgow.

> Lord, we propose, but you dispose.
> Teach me that your plan unfolds
> As I follow the desire you put in my soul,
> As I follow the way of unselfish service
> And as I let one thing lead to another.

How can I blaspheme my King who saved me?

They kept on stoning Stephen as he called out to the Lord, 'Lord Jesus, receive my spirit!'
Acts 7:59

Celtic Christians had heard of the beautiful martyr's death of Polycarp, the disciple of the apostle John, who became a bishop in the east of the Roman Empire. Polycarp was led before the proconsul who urged him to change his mind saying, 'Have respect for your age. Swear by the genius of Caesar and say, "Away with the atheists."' The proconsul thought of atheists as people who would not worship the Roman gods, including the Emperor. Then Polycarp looked sternly at the noisy mob in the stadium, and waving his hand at them said, 'Away with the atheists'. But the proconsul went on, 'Swear, and then I will release you; curse the Christ.' Polycarp said, 'Eighty-six years have I served him and he has done me no wrong. How then can I blaspheme my king who saved me?'

Now it was the turn of Mungo's generation to face persecution. Mungo had developed a close friendship with King Rhyderch of Strathclyde, but in the 540s Morcant, a pagan ruler, raided the farms of Christians in Rhyderch's territory; then pagans threw out the Christian ruler and church leaders in the Carlisle area, and one disaster followed another. A violent mob swept through the town of Falkirk, and its Bishop, Nevydd, who may have ordained Mungo, died a martyr's death, his place of worship being burnt over him. Mungo, deeply grieved, soon also suffered the death of his dear mother. Then he learned that the priceless library at Whithorn had gone up in flames, and the members of its Christian community had fled to Gaul. Worse, there was now no Christian bishop in the entire north, and no one to ordain new priests.

Rhyderch conferred with Mungo, and they agreed to ask an Irish bishop to come over and consecrate a bishop of the north. Then Rhyderch insisted that, although the minimum age for becoming a bishop was thirty, the twenty-five-year-old Mungo was the man to be consecrated. This was not Mungo's idea, but how could he, in this crisis, deny his King who saved him? 'Be to the flock of Christ a shepherd. Hold up the weak, bind up the broken, bring again the outcast, seek the lost', was the charge to Mungo. With all his soul Mungo answered, 'I will, with the help of God.'

Lord, do not lead me into a time of such trial
But in whatever trials I have to face
Help me to remain true to you,
My King who saves me.

Use every opportunity you have, because these are evil days.
Ephesians 5:16

We should never delude ourselves that the Christian way is all roses. There is much that is bad and ugly in the world, and there is no guarantee that Christians will not become victims of it. We can, however, learn to discover God in the ugliest of situations, and to use evil days as an opportunity for good.

Not long after Mungo's consecration as a bishop an ugly crowd, headed by Morcant, arrived. 'Your royal friend Rhyderch,' he crowed, 'has sailed away into exile, and now I am king of Strathclyde.' Riding with him was a young man, a distant relative of Mungo, who was decidedly unfriendly. He lashed out with his stirruped foot and kicked Mungo in the chest, knocking him down. 'You bastard bishop,' he shouted as he rode away.

The writing was on the wall. It seems that Mungo set out to join David in Wales, so that a new mission might move north from a sound base in the south. But in order to get to Wales, he had to go on a difficult journey.

As Mungo and his companions trudged through the dales they found, not only a different, craggy landscape, but a hostile population. They reached the headquarters of the Christian Prince Urien, who conducted his government in exile near Penrith. The Prince was the most statesmanlike of the Christian leaders of that generation. They discussed the sad situation of the region. Perhaps Mungo had intended to pass quickly through on his way to Wales, but when he realised the swift growth of pagan influence in the mountain areas he turned aside, and with God helping him, won many from strange beliefs. As he journeyed from well to well, crowds gathered. Some jeered, but others were healed and some accepted Christ. The Christian Faith revived. At Crosthwaite, in 533, a crowd worshipped God as a large cross was erected opposite a pagan stronghold.

So once again we see that, in an ugly situation, God can bring good out of the bad.

> Lord,
> Help me to face the things
> That are ugly in our situation today.
> Show me how you want to bring good out of the bad.

Good and faithful servant

'Well done, you good and faithful servant', said his master . . . 'Come on in and share my happiness.'
Matthew 25:21

In Wales Mungo was known by his formal name, Kentigern. He developed teamwork with a number of Wales's vibrant Christian leaders, one of whom was Asaph. These two established the large Christian community at Llanelwy.

Six hundred years later Joceline of Furness wrote the story of its founding: Kentigern had set his heart on building a monastery to which the scattered sons of God might come together like bees from East and West, from North and South.

Young men, scattered throughout a hostile countryside, heard by bush telegraph the news of the founding of the monastery. Many slipped quietly away from home to wend their way through the forests. Like the early Christians they were an underground movement. But they came by the hundreds, every sort of Briton, farm labourers and men of noble rank.

Joceline continued: After prayer they manfully set to work. Some cleared and levelled land, others built foundations, carried timber, erected with skill a church of planed woodwork after British fashion, enclosing it all in a *llan* or rampart and named it Llanelwy. Nine hundred and sixty five people moved in. One third laboured on the land. One third looked after the buildings, cooking and workshops. One third were responsible for worship, teaching, and scribing.

In 573 the pagans in the north suffered a mighty defeat, and the Christian Rhyderch received back his throne, though the Christian religion had been virtually wiped out. He asked his friend Mungo to lead a mission to his kingdom. Mungo spent eight years leading a mission from a half-way base at Hoddam, and then moved back to Glasgow.

He was to have heart to heart meetings with Columba from Iona, and with Bishop Gregory in Rome. These men perhaps discussed a common plan for the conversion of the English people. Mungo's dying words were, 'My children, love one another . . . be hospitable . . . keep the laws of the church . . .she is the Mother of us all.'

> Help me to be faithful in things both great or small
> In setback or success,
> Faithful to the church, faithful to my call.

Foxes have holes; birds have nests, but the Child of Humanity has nowhere to lay his head.
Luke 9:58

A young housewife cried. She felt so weak, needy, small. But then she thought of her baby. He was all those things, too. He was so dependent upon others, so vulnerable – yet that was precisely why she loved him so much!

When people are hard, prickly, proud, defensive, no feeling can flow. They cannot reach out and touch. Whereas when people are vulnerable it draws out our love for them. Is this why God made us with a capacity to be hurt, so that we can love and be loved more deeply? God needs us and wants us to be lovable. By being vulnerable we are being considerate to God, we are being human.

Celtic Christians were vulnerable. They had no riches stored up, no protected stone mansions – they were vulnerable to the elements, to predators, to visitors. And how they were loved – loved by the people and loved much by God. We know this because people saw special guards of honour sent from heaven to welcome them when they died. How lovely to be vulnerable!

Yet it is all too easy to adopt an 'I'm all right Jack' attitude. How can we overcome this? This is how members of the Northumbria Community try to do it:

We are called to intentional, deliberate VULNERABILITY.
We embrace the vulnerability of being teachable
expressed in a discipline of prayer
in exposure to Scripture
in a willingness to be accountable to others
in ordering our ways and our heart in order to effect change . . .
by making relationships the priority and not reputation . . .
living openly amongst unbelievers and other believers in a way that
the life of God in ours can be seen, challenged or questioned.
                    The Rule of Life of the Northumbria Community

            Take from me, O Lord:
            Pride and prejudice
            Hardness and hypocrisy
            Selfishness and self-sufficiency
            That I may be vulnerable, like you.

God makes me strong . . . sure-footed as a deer . . . keeps me safe on the mountains . . . trains me for battle.
Psalm 18:32–34

The endless adventure of the Desert Christians was described like this:

> Not that they beggared be in mind, or brutes,
> That they have chosen a dwelling place afar
> In lonely places: but their eyes are turned
> To the high stars, the very deep of Truth.
> Freedom they seek, an emptiness apart
> From worthless hopes: din of the market place
> And all the noisy crowding up of things,
> And whatever wars on the Divine,
> At Christ's command, and for his love, they hate.
> By faith and hope they follow after God,
> And know their quest shall not be desperate,
> If but the Present conquer not their souls
> With hollow things: that which they see they spurn,
> That they may come at what they don't see,
> Their senses kindled like a torch that may
> Blaze through the secrets of eternity.
>
> *Paulinus of Nola*

Life is meant to be an adventure; change is a gift that we have to learn to use aright. In Celtic folk tales a curse that could happen to a person was to enter a field and not to be able to get back out of it. To be stuck in that place for ever. It was seen as a definite curse to be unable to venture or change . . . The open gate is the opposite to this. It is the invitation to venture and to grow, the call to be among the living and vital elements in the world. The open gate is the call to explore new areas of yourself and the world around you.
David Adam The Open Gate

True religion is betting your life that there is a God
Donald Hankey

> You who are heroic Love
> Have built adventure
> Into each day and into every life.
> Help me to explore, to overcome, and to step out
> Towards this day's horizons
> In the spirit of Christ the Endless Adventurer.

In the beginning was the Life Force . . . The Life Force was the source
of life, and this life brought light to humanity.
John 1:2, 4

The Greek word *Logos* was used in the Bible, and in Greek writings of
the time, to describe the life force that people believed lay behind the
material things of the universe. Science fiction films often reflect a
similar belief. 'The Force be with you' was a saying in an early science
fiction film, *Star Wars*. This idea of the Life Force, which was strong in
the eastern part of the world, was taken up by the apostle John, who
brought many people in eastern parts to faith. John, who had such
'flow' with Jesus, helped people understand that this Life Force was
channelled, in an almost unbelievable way, in one man, Jesus Christ.
Once you grasp this amazing truth, your hopes and your horizons are
transformed.

> I muse on the eternal Logos of God, and
>   all creation is lit up:
> I muse on the eternal Light, and
>   every person is lit up:
> I muse on the eternal Life, and God's
>   heaven is lit up:
> I muse on the beloved disciple at the Last Supper
>   and God's sacrament is lit up:
> I muse on the loved mother and apostle at the cross
>   and Christ's church is lit up:
> I muse on the risen Christ at Lake Galilee
>   and all our Easters are lit up:
> I muse on the eternal Lamb of God
>   and eternity's tenderness is lit up:
> I muse on the radiance of the eastern light
>   and pray that it becomes the transforming glory of the west.

> Grant to me, O Lord,
> That tender love, that deathless vision, that flowing life
> Of John the loved disciple
> Until the Logos, the Lamb, and I
> Your little loved one
> Flow together as one.

Never forget these commands that I am giving you today . . . write
them on your door posts and on your gates.
Deuteronomy 6:6, 9

St Brigid's Day falls on the day of Imbolc, the Celtic season that marks
the coming of light after the dark days of winter, the time of the
suckling of the ewes.

On St Brigid's Day each year a cross is blessed and placed in homes and
outhouses as an extended prayer – to repel the dark powers of evil and
hunger that may have got a hold during the winter, and to invite in the
light and provision of God. This custom stems from the account of
how Brigid nursed and witnessed to a pagan chief. To help make the
Gospel clear to him she made a cross from the rush matting, and he
subsequently became a Christian. Those who observe this custom take
rush crosses to their homes, and to outhouses and places that were not
used much in winter but which will be needed in the warmer days of
the growing season. Perhaps, in your life, a greenhouse or shed, a
week-end caravan or boat, a business or sporting location will soon
come back into use. Why not, physically or in your mind, bless these
places? Indeed, why not look ahead and make sure that there will be
no 'no-go' areas for God in your life? Here are some prayers to use in
any of these places:

> Dear Lord, may all that is here reflect the harmony and
> Wholeness that you want for your creation.
> Bless the moon that is above us
> The earth that is beneath us.
> May the pets be happy and healthy.
> Bless the hard work to be done here
> The seedlings that shall grow here
> The neighbours we shall greet here
> And all who overlook here.

> Circle this place by day and by night
> Keep far from it all that harms
> Bring to it all that is good
> May this place be fragrant with the presence of the Lord
> God's peace be always here
> And in those who dwell here.

God is light and in God there is no darkness at all.
1 John 1:5

Forty days after his birth Jesus was presented to God in the temple,
according to Jewish law. In the 6th century eastern churches began to
celebrate this occasion as a thanksgiving for the ending of the plague.
This was known as 'The Meeting', to mark the meeting in the temple
between the infant Jesus and Simeon, who recognised that Jesus was the
true light of the world. Later this became popular in the Western
Church as Candlemas. The blessing of the candles to symbolise Christ,
the true light of the world, has become the distinctive feature, and is a
fitting thing to do near the start of Imbolc, the Celtic season of light.

The strongest attraction of Candlemas is the 'bitter-sweet' nature of
what it celebrates. It is a feast day, and the revelation of the child Jesus
in the temple, greeted by Simeon and Anna, calls for rejoicing.
Nevertheless, the prophetic words of Simeon, which speak of the falling
and rising of many and the sword that will pierce, lead on to the
passion and Easter . . . It is as if we say, on 2 February, 'One last look
back at Christmas, and now, turn towards the Cross.'

The Promise of His Glory

> Christ as a light illumine and guide me
> Christ as a shield overshadow me
> Christ under me
> Christ over me
> Christ beside me on my left and my right
> This day be within and without me
> Lonely and meek yet all powerful
> Be in the mouth of each to whom I speak
> In the mouth of each who speaks to me
> Christ as a light illumine and guide me.
> *John Michael Talbot, after* St Patrick's Breastplate.

Your Holy Spirit rested on Simeon and he recognised your coming.
May we recognise you in our lives.
Simeon recognised in you the true light that brings light to the
world.
Help us to receive and radiate that light.
Simeon foresaw that your mother would be pierced to the heart.
Give us the faithful love she showed at the cross.

The kingdom of God is like a woman who takes some yeast and mixes it with flour until the whole batch of dough rises.
Luke 13:20, 21

Brigid was the spiritual midwife who helped bring to birth Christian Ireland, and she is a potent symbol of womanhood. Through her flowed compassion, energy, and healing powers, and everything she set her hand to increased. Her large monastery at Kildare, in the central plain of Ireland, came to replace the influence of pagan kings.

> Her heart contained no poison, no snake lurked within her breast
> She nursed no grudges, harboured no resentments.
> In the spiritual field where she sowed, the weather was always right.
>
> When she sowed the seeds of the Gospel in people's hearts,
> the soft rain would fall so the seeds would sprout.
>
> When she taught Christians how to grow in the image of Christ,
> the sun shone in the day, and the rain fell at night,
> so the fruits of good works would swell.
>
> When she welcomed the sick and the dying
> the weather was warm and dry
> to prepare their souls for God's harvest.
>
> Now in heaven she intercedes for us
> sending upon us the gentle dew of God's grace.
>
> *A medieval Irish hymn to Brigid*

> You who put beam in moon and sun,
> You who put fish in stream and sea,
> You who put food in ear and herd,
> Send your blessing up to me.
> Bring forth the warmth, the tears, the laughter
> From our repressed and frozen ground;
> Bring forth loving, healing, forgiving,
> To our fretting, festering wound.
> Bring in light and truth and singing after dark and frigid years.

Put me to the test and you will see that I will open the windows of heaven and pour out upon you in abundance all kinds of good things. *Malachi 3:10*

Brigid was born about AD455, the daughter of Leinster's pagan King Dubtach and his slave woman, Broicsech, who was a Christian. After Brigid was conceived two Bishops from Scotland prophesied great things for her over her mother. Dubtach's infertile, jealous wife forced him to sell Broicsech as a slave to a druid priest.

Brigid used to throw up the food provided by the priest, so a good local woman was allowed to feed her from her own stock. Brigid wanted to be holy and from her earliest days she rejected anything that was not wholesome. She grew strong and bold, and liberally fed the sheep, the birds and the poor. She then returned to her father's house, where she exasperated Dubtach by her habit of giving away his food and goods. She constantly took the initiative. Once when she was travelling with her father her attendant was taken ill. Brigid fetched water from a well, prayed over it, and gave it him to drink; it tasted like ale and he recovered.

Brigid's mother continued as a hard-working slave, and Brigid often returned to help her. A song she sang as she churned the butter for her mother and their many visitors is recorded in *Lives of the Saints from the Book of Lismore*, 'Mary's Son, my friend, come to bless this kitchen. May we have fullness through you.' Through Brigid the Lord multiplied the butter as he once multiplied loaves and fishes. Eventually this faith-filled way of life won the heart of the druid, who became a Christian, and he gave Brigid's mother her freedom.

> Mary's Son, my friend, come and bless the kitchen.
> May we have fullness through you.
>
> Mary's Son, my friend, come and bless the school.
> May we have fullness through you.
>
> Mary's Son, my friend, come and bless the soil.
> May we have fullness through you.
>
> Mary's Son, my friend, come and bless the work.
> May we have fullness through you.

Barrels full

Give to others, and God will give to you. Indeed, you will receive a
full measure, a generous helping, poured into your hands – all that you
can hold. The measure you use for others is the one that God will use
for you.
Luke 6:38

Dubtach, despairing of Brigid's generosity with his goods, arranged a
marriage of his beautiful daughter to a member of a noble family.
Brigid refused; Dubtach allowed her to become a nun and gave her a
dowry. When Brigid took the veil an old bishop was so awe-struck by
the holy fire he saw above her, that he unintentionally read the words
of the consecration of a bishop over her. He told a colleague who
objected, 'I have no power in this matter; this dignity has been given
by God to Brigid.'
  Brigid resolved to establish a community where women could work
and pray together. The king in Kildare refused her request for a grant
of land, but relented when she said she would accept a plot of land as
small as the size of her cloak. Once Brigid had a foothold, however, the
area of land never seemed to stop growing. The church was built in a
place that had been set aside for pagan worship, where a sacred flame
was always kept alight. So the nuns, too, kept a fire of resurrection
burning outside the church, night and day, and this was not
extinguished for a thousand years.
  Brigid needed priests to perform the sacraments, so she chose Bishop
Conleath to govern with her, but there was no doubt who was in
charge! Through Conleath there came monks and many skilled
craftsmen, and a double monastery of men and women was established
under Brigid's leadership. Sick people came to the monastery and were
healed, lepers were given barrels full of apples, bishops, kings, and
saints, such as Finnian, came for advice.

God wants to prosper our work, too; but our attitude is all important.
It must be done God's way. In the following prayer, let the lumps stand
for something that you contribute to the world through your work.

> Come, you rich lumps, come!
> Come, you rich lumps, come!
> Come, you rich lumps, masses large,
> Come, you rich lumps, come!
> *Carmina Gadelica*

Do not store up for yourselves riches here upon earth, where moths and rust destroy, and robbers break in and steal. Instead, store up riches for yourselves in heaven, where moths and rust cannot destroy, and robbers cannot break in and steal.
Matthew 6:19, 20

Brigid's monastery brewed ale for the churches round about and, as Christianity spread, Brigid's faith-sharing teams went out to churches far and wide. Easter was an opportunity to minister to the increased numbers who came, and in one church a blind person, a consumptive, a leper and a mentally ill person were healed through Brigid's ministry

Once Brigid visited a place where the Christians feared to preach God's Word because a madman was about. Brigid challenged the madman to preach the Word of God himself, which he did! She told nuns who saw the Devil, 'Make Christ's Cross on your face and on your eyes.'

Her unknown biographer writes, 'Her heart and mind were a throne of rest for the Holy Spirit. She was simple towards God; compassionate towards the wretched; she was splendid in miracles and marvels.'

Someone in the ninth century composed a famous poem entitled 'Hail Brigid'. Its theme is the disappearance of the pagan world of Ireland and the triumph of Christianity. This was symbolised by the abandonment of the ancient hill-fort of Allen as the seat of the once powerful kings of Leinster, and its replacement by Brigid and her Kildare monastic network. This had become the main source of blessing and protection for the people.

In later times Brigid was imagined to be the mid-wife, or the wet-nurse, present at Christ's birth, and she was made a symbol of the Bride of Christ. She became the guardian of the poor who work the land, and the patron of those who study. Beautiful prayers have come down to us which reflect these traditions.

> May the fruits God gave Brigid lie on me.
> May the delights God gave Brigid lie on me.
> May the healings God gave Brigid lie on me.
> May the virtues God gave Brigid lie on me
> And on my loved ones.

The Spirit led Jesus to go into the desert, where he stayed for forty days, being tested by Satan.
Mark 1:12

Even the busiest Celtic Christians made time to get away for prayer vigils, especially during the weeks before Easter. Samson used to keep Lent by taking just three small loaves and withdrawing to a remote spot for the forty days. Sometimes Samson would eat nothing for six days, but refresh himself with food on Sundays, the day that celebrates Jesus's resurrection. Sometimes he would stand throughout the night in prayer, with his staff which had dropped from his hands.

What do ordinary mortals do on a vigil? Some of us may emulate these aspirations of an unknown Celtic hermit:

> A remote, hidden little cabin for forgiveness of my sins
> A conscience upright and spotless before Heaven.
> Making good the body with good habits
> Treading it boldly down
> Feeble tearful eyes for forgiveness of my passions.
> Eager wailings to cloudy Heaven
> Sincere and truly devout confession
> Fervent showers of tears . . .
> Dry bread weighed out, well we bow the head
> Water of the fair coloured hillside
> That is the draught I would drink.
> Stepping along the paths of the Gospel
> Singing psalms every hour
> An end of talking and long stories
> Constant bending of the knee.

Sorry Lord –

> for the shabbiness of my LIVING
> for the shoddiness of my WORKING
> for the shallowness of my PRAYING
> for the selfishness of my GIVING
> for the fickleness of my FEELING
> for the faithlessness of my SPEAKING
> for the dullness of my HEARING
> for the grudgingness of my SHARING
> for the slothfulness of my THINKING
> for the slowness of my SERVING
> for the coldness of my LOVING.

Jesus, Son of David, have mercy on me.
Mark 10:48

Just as failure to give a car its M.O.T. can be a matter of life or death, so can our failure to check up on faults that may have been developing, unnoticed, in ourselves. Celtic Christians had check-lists of common faults; these were incorporated in what were known as 'Penitentials'.

The following prayer of confession is a useful check-list. It may be worth while taking the time to detect examples of each type of fault in our lives, and to take these to the heavenly Mechanic who can put them right. It is also worth remembering that Celtic Christians believed that God has made us horizontal, and not just vertical; in other words, we are designed to share our secrets with another trusted human being, an 'anamchara' or companion along the way. Have you thought of doing that at this stage in your life?

> Jesus, forgive my sins.
> Forgive the sins that I can remember
>   and also the sins I have forgotten.
> Forgive the wrong actions I have committed
>   and the right actions I have omitted.
> Forgive the times I have been weak in the face of temptation
>   and those when I have been stubborn in the face of correction.
> Forgive the times I have been proud of my own achievements
>   and those when I have failed to boast of your works.
> Forgive the harsh judgments I have made of others
>   and the leniency I have shown myself.
> Forgive the lies I have told to others
>   and the truths I have avoided.
> Forgive the pain I have caused others
>   and the indulgence I have shown myself.
> Jesus have pity on me, and make me whole.
>   *From* Celtic Fire, *Robert Van der Weyer (Unattributed).*

Love your neighbour as you love yourself.
Leviticus 19:18

Teilo is celebrated in *The Welsh Triads* as one of the three blessed
'Visitors of the Isle of Britain', the other two being David and Padarn.
He was greatly used in the Christian formation of Wales and Britanny
in the 6th century, and one gets a sense of warm fellowship being
generated throughout the many Christian communities that he helped
to establish. He was born opposite Caldey Island and trained under
Paulinus, where he met another pupil who was to be greatly used,
David. When David started his main establishment at the modern St
David's, Teilo went with him; he was good at teamwork.

Teilo obtained grants of land and established many Christian
communities. Notable among these was his own , which was probably
at Great Llandeilo. Entries in the margin of the Gospels of St Chad
(written about 700) refer to him as the founder of a monastery known
as 'the Family of Teilo'. This was a prototype of the kind of
community that was led by a monk who was also a bishop of his
people. Such a monastery was the hearth, or hub, of a large extended
family of Christians.

When the plague decimated the population in 547, Teilo led a mass
exodus of Christians to Britanny, where he linked up with Samson who
had settled at Dol. The two of them were said to have planted a big
orchard of fruit trees, three miles long, reaching from Dol to Cai. He
stayed there seven years and established further communities.

It is said that the hermit Cadoc once asked Teilo, 'What is the
greatest wisdom in a person?' He answered 'To refrain from injuring
another person when one has the power to do so.' Teilo had the
power to do so, but the winning quality of saints such as himself was
that that they did not abuse power, they followed the golden rule, 'Do
to others what you would like them to do to you'.

> Teach me
> Gentle Jesus of the cradle and the cross
> To forego vengeance at all times
> And to reach out my hands in love to all.

They were stoned, they were sawn in two, they were killed by the
sword. They went round clothed in skins of sheep or goats – poor,
persecuted, ill-treated. The world was not good enough for them! They
wandered like refugees in the deserts and hills, living in caves and holes
in the ground. What a record all these have won by their faith!
Hebrews 11:37–39

Have you ever wished you could so completely lay down your life for
Christ that this would even include being put to death on account of
your witness to him? Celtic Christians were inspired by stories of
Christians who, in the early era of persecution, had been killed because
they refused to denounce Christ. The Celts' instinct for being all-out
led them not only to admire these martyrs, but, since there was no
longer physical persecution, to find non-physical ways of becoming
martyrs.

They may have read what Jerome wrote to a young woman whose
widowed mother had given away all her possessions and entered a
convent, 'Your mother has been crowned because of her long
martyrdom. It is not only the shedding of blood which is the mark of a
true witness, but the service of a dedicated heart is a daily martyrdom.
The first is wreathed with a crown of roses and violets, the second of
lilies.'

They also read in *The Life of St Martin* (who was the first official saint
not killed for his faith): 'He achieved martyrdom without blood. For of
what human sorrows did he not, for the hope of eternity, endure the
pain – in hunger, in night watchings, in nakedness, in fasting, in the
insults of the envious, in the persecutions of the wicked, in care for the
sick, in anxiety for those in peril.'

Sulpicius Severus

They called those who had shed blood 'red martyrs', and those who
gave up home and possessions 'white martyrs'. The Irish came up with
the idea of 'glas (blue – the colour of death) martyrs', linked to
extended penance, or an extended pilgrimage, going into exile from
home comforts for the love of God.

The 20th century has had more red martyrs than any other century.
Perhaps the 21st century will have more white and blue martyrs than
any previous century? For we can be a martyr by laying aside
everything that comes between us and God or by laying down our lives
for our neighbour.

Take my life
Let it be laid down.

Let them tell of God's works with songs of joy.
Psalm 107:22.

> The first of English poets he
> Who nurtured by the Whitby sea
> A poor and simple cowherd seemed.
> Yet here the gold of poetry gleamed
> Though hidden deep within his soul
> For from the company he stole
> Fearful to be found afraid
> When they their entertainment made
> The very least among the throng
> With little speech nor any song.
> Then in the stillness of one night
> His soul was filled with heavenly light
> A vision of the world being made
> Of God's creation all displayed
> As in the stable stall he lay
> Dreaming he heard an angel pray
> And speak to him of God's great world
> And how its majesty unfurled.
> Then day by day to his inspired mind
> That had seemed deaf and dumb and blind
> There came sweet words so bright and clear.
> Then Mother Hilda came to hear
> And stayed with all her Abbey folk
> While Caedmon, poet of Whitby, spoke.
> No longer now to steal away
> When came his turn the harp to play
> For in his Saxon mother tongue
> Were all his splendid verses sung
> And improvised with great delight
> In many a stormy winter's night
> When firelight filled the raftered hall
> In far off ancient Streonshalh.
> Then folk would learn the poems by heart
> Or memorise a favourite part
> Making them one with Christian praise
> In those remote, unlettered days.
>
> *Tom Stamp*

Praise you, wisdom and Founder of all.

Do not be ashamed, then, of witnessing for our Lord; nor be ashamed of me, a prisoner for Christ's sake.
2 Timothy 1:8

When we are teenagers, so many things are uncertain and yet to be made certain, that we find temporary security by going along with the crowd. It is all too easy to go along with the crowd in things such as smoking, swearing, sex, shop-lifting or drugs, or simply in making fun of someone. It takes exceptional courage to stand up to peer pressure. So we can all, whatever our age, take courage from the example of Cuthbert.

When Cuthbert was a teenager he saw a crowd gather by the river Tweed to watch an unusual sight, so he joined the crowd. Some monks who had recently built a monastery were trying to get timbers to it along the river estuary, but a contrary wind was driving their rafts out to sea. There were five rafts, looking like birds bobbing up and down on the waves. The monks inside the monastery saw what was happening, but their efforts to help came to nothing. So they gathered round a rock and started to pray for their brothers.

The crowd of peasants did not like incomers, especially people who brought in new beliefs and had done away with pagan ways of worship, like these Christians, so they started to jeer and to wish the monks, who were in danger of drowning, good riddance.

Cuthbert was not prepared to remain silent. 'Do you realise what you are doing?' he asked them. 'Would it not be more human of you to pray for their safety rather to gloat over their misfortune?' The crowd now directed their verbal abuse at Cuthbert. 'Nobody is going to pray for them,' they shouted.

So Cuthbert, having listened to them, simply knelt down on the ground and prayed. The wind at once completely changed direction, and brought the monks to a perfect landing beside the monastery. Many in the crowd began to feel ashamed and awed. They felt a genuine respect for Cuthbert and thought well of him from that time on.

> Lord, I crave the approval of others
> And I don't like standing out in a crowd
> Yet you want me to be true and honest.
> Give me grace to pray for and stand by
> People who are mocked because of their faith.

Releasing a blessing

I promise that I will give you a land which is flowing with milk and honey.
Exodus 3:8

We know that God frequently promised to bring the people of Israel to a land full of honey, which meant a land full of blessing. And we know that Celtic Christians frequently invited God to give blessings to the land, which included lots of honey. But what happened to Modomnoc, who is celebrated today, is the ultimate in generous blessing.

Modomnoc, who is said to have come from Ireland's great O'Neill family, came to study under David at his Pembrokeshire monastery. One of his duties during his many years there was bee-keeping, an essential part of the monastery's provision, which he had greatly developed. When the time came for him to return to Ireland, the whole monastery had a prayer time with him, and sent him on his way with God's blessings, but unfortunately the entire swarm of bees followed him and settled on his boat. Bee keepers know the effort required to get a swarm of bees back into their hive. Modomnoc succeeded in doing this, and a day or two later, he repeated his farewells and set out again for the boat. The same thing happened all over again and Modomnoc once again painstakingly returned the bees.

Modomnoc went back to David, and suggested that he hang around until the bees were tired and sleepy, and then he would quietly slip away. His return afforded another opportunity for all the brothers to pray over him and invite God's blessings on him and his new ministry in Ireland. This time, as David prayed, he realised that God intended the bees to be part of the blessing he was to give to Ireland. So David started to pray for the bees in the words of the blessing below. David's twelfth century biographer observed that the blessing had been fulfilled completely, that bees sent back from Ireland had dwindled to nothing in Wales, and the bees in Ireland, which had previously had no reputation for bees, had flourished beyond measure. Think about the blessings you are meant to give. Why not adapt this blessing for a person or place God is asking you to pray for? Remember, however, that in order to bless another you may need to release to them something that is precious to you.

May the land to which you are journeying
Abound with your offspring.
May you for ever leave our land and your offspring never increase
 here.
But may they never fail to increase in the land to which you go.

My whole being desires you . . . Your constant love is better than life itself, and so I will praise you . . . I will give you thanks as long as I live . . . My soul will feast and be satisfied . . . all night long I think of you . . . I cling to you.
Selected from Psalm 63:1–8

It reaches out beyond all human feelings. It is neither the sound of the voice nor the movements of the tongue nor articulated words. The soul, bathed in light from on high, no longer uses human speech, which is always inadequate. Like an overabundant spring, all feelings overflow and spring forth towards God at the same time. In this short moment, it says so many things that the soul, once it has recovered itself, could neither express nor go over them in its memory.

John Cassian

Columba went to seek a place remote from men and fitting for prayer.

Adamnan

Cuthbert dwelt (at Lindisfarne) also according to Holy Scripture, following the contemplative amid the active life, and he arranged our rule of life which we composed then and which we observe to this day along with the rule of St Benedict.

Life of Cuthbert *by an anonymous monk of Lindisfarne*

Cuthbert finally entered into the remoter solitude he had so long sought, thirsted after, and prayed for. He was delighted that after a long and spotless active life he should be thought worthy to ascend to the stillness of Divine contemplation.

Bede

There is a contemplative in all of us
almost strangled but still alive
who craves quiet enjoyment of the Now
and longs to touch the seamless garment of silence
which makes us whole.

Alan P. Torey

Lord, you are my island, in your bosom I rest
You are the calm of the sea, in that peace I lie
You are the deep waves of the ocean, in their depths I stay
You are the smooth white strand of the shore, in its swell I sing
You are the ocean of life that laps my being
In you is my eternal joy.

Attributed to Columba

Very early the next morning, long before daylight, Jesus got up and left the house. He went out of the town to a solitary place, where he prayed.
Mark 1:35

The one who abides in solitude and is quiet, is delivered from fighting three battles – those of hearing, speech and sight. Then that person will have but one battle to fight – the battle of the heart.

Antony of Egypt

Cuthbert served as prior at Melrose monastery, but 'finally fled from worldly glory and sailed away privately and secretly. . . . After some years, desiring a solitary life he went to the island called Farne, which is in the midst of the sea and surrounded on every side by water, a place where, before this, almost no one could remain alone for any amount of time on account of the many illusions caused by devils. But he fearlessly put them to flight, and, digging down almost a cubit of a man into the earth, through very hard and stony rock, he made a space to dwell in. He also built a marvellous wall another cubit above it by placing together and compacting with earth, stones of such great size as none would believe except those who knew that so much of the power of God was in him; therein he made some little dwelling places from which he could see nothing except the heavens above.'

Life of Cuthbert *by an anonymous monk of Lindisfarne*

In Wales and Ireland there are still as many as five hundred place names (for example Dysart or Disserth) that recall a place where some believer, inspired by the desert Christians, made the desert of the heart their own. In the Channel Isles there is still a place named, simply, Egypt. Today people create desert places of their own, and 'desert days' in their homes. Solitude is an essential part of the foundation of any civilisation that is to last.

> Still is the earth;
> Make still my body.
> Still is the night;
> Make still my mind.
> Still are the spheres;
> Make still my soul.

A broken and a contrite heart, O God, you will not turn away.
Psalm 51:17

The soul, harassed with sin and toil, finds repose only in humility.
Humility is its sole refreshment amid so many evils . . . Mortification is
indeed intolerable to the proud and hard of heart, but a consolation to
the one who loves only what is meek and lowly.

Rule of Columbanus

I read and write. I worship my God every day and every night.

I study the Scriptures, puzzling over their meaning, I write books for
the guidance of others.

I eat little, and sleep little. When I eat I continue praying, and when
I sleep my snores are songs of praise.

Yet I weep for my sins, because I cannot forget them. O Mary, O
Christ, have mercy on this wretched soul.

A scribe in a Celtic monastery

I asked God for strength, that I might achieve;
I was made weak, that I might learn to humbly obey.
I asked for health, that I might do great things;
I was given infirmity, that I might do better things.
I asked for power, that I might have the praise of people;
I was given weakness, that I might feel the need of God.

An unknown American soldier

Spirit of the living God
fall afresh on me
Break me, melt me
mould me, fill me
Spirit of the living God
fall afresh on me.
Daniel Iverson

Consider yourselves fortunate when all kinds of trials come your way.
James 1:2

Cuthbert, Bede tells us, began to be prepared by the fires of temporal
pain for the joys of eternal bliss. Herefrith, the abbot of Lindisfarne,
told Bede exactly what happened. He came with some monks on a care
visit to Cuthbert on Farne island, and discovered Cuthbert was
terminally ill. Cuthbert declined Herefrith's offer to leave some brothers
on the island to care for him, but advised 'Come back when God
directs you.' Five days of violent storm ensued, which prevented any
brothers from returning to Cuthbert. Herefrith reported, 'As events
proved, this was a divine dispensation. For in order that Almighty God
might, by chastisement, purify his servant from all blemish of worldly
weakness and in order that he might show his adversaries that they
could avail nothing against the strength of his faith, he wished to test
him by bodily pain and by a still fiercer contest with the ancient foe,
cutting him off from human beings for that length of time.'
    When they did return Herefrith attended to his needs, and told
Cuthbert he was amazed that he had insisted on being left unattended.
'It happened through the providence of God,' Cuthbert assured him,
'that destitute of human company and care I should suffer some trials.'
Cuthbert told him how after he had left his illness immediately became
worse, and he crawled over to the guest hut by the shore, and lay there
without moving for five days, his only food being a few nibbles of
onions. 'My adversaries have never persecuted me so frequently, during
all the time I have been living on this island, as over the last five days,'
he told his friend. After that, Cuthbert had some brothers with him
until he died, one of whom, Beda, had been a long-standing friend.

> Lord, if this day you have to correct us
>   put us right not out of anger
> but with a mother's and a father's heart.
>   So may we, your children,
> be kept free of all falseness and foolishness.
> *From Mexico*

Be angry, but do not sin. Do not let the sun go down on your anger.
Ephesians 4:6

Anger is the most fierce passion. It is a boiling and a stirring up of
wrath against one who has caused injury – or is thought to have done
so. It constantly irritates the soul and above all at the time of prayer it
seizes the mind and flashes the picture of the offensive person before
one's eyes.

Evagrius

A restless brother in a desert community frequently became angry with
his brothers. So he thought to himself: 'I'll go and live in a place of
solitude; once I won't have to speak to or listen to anyone I shall be at
peace and the anger thing will disappear'. So he went to live alone in a
cave. One day he filled a jug with water for himself, and placed it on
the floor. It suddenly overturned. He filled it a second time and the
same thing happened, as it did a third time. His anger flared up and he
smashed the jug in rage.

Later, when he came to himself, he realised he had been subverted
by the spirit of anger, and that he had no one to blame. 'Here am I
alone', he said to himself, 'and despite this the spirit of anger has
conquered me. I shall return to the community, for in every place there
is need for struggle, for patient perseverance, and above all, for the help
of God.' So he returned to his community.

Sayings of the Desert Fathers

A love that cannot find an outlet turns inward, and not being able to
reach out and touch the thing it loves, be it a place or a people in that
place, turns to anger and becomes confused.

Brian Keenan An Evil Cradling

The Desert Fathers and Mothers did not focus on who is to blame for
the passions that bind us. They knew that there are wounds within us
that destroy our own and other lives. Our task, they thought, was to
fight against the passions, and to seek healing with the help of God and
each other in order to be able to love as we were made to love.

> Help me conquer anger by gentleness
> Greed by generosity
> Apathy by fervour.

Return to the Lord with fasting, weeping and mourning for your God
is gracious and merciful.
Joel 2:12,13

When we die, we will not be criticised for having failed to work
miracles. We will not be accused of having failed to be theologians or
contemplatives. But we will certainly have some explanation to offer to
God for not having mourned unceasingly . . . When the soul grows
tearful, weeps, and is filled with tenderness, and all this without having
striven for it, then let us run, for the Lord has arrived uninvited and is
holding out to us the sponge of loving sorrow, the cool waters of
blessed sadness with which to wipe away the record of our sins. Guard
these tears like the apple of your eye until they go away, for they have
a power greater than anything that comes from our own thoughts and
our own meditation.

John Climacus Abbot of Sinai 7th century

David of Wales was 'overflowing with daily fountains of tears'. This is
how he comforted the mother of a dead boy, 'Filled with compassion
for human weakness, he approached the body of the dead boy, whose
face he watered with his tears and restored him to his mother.'

Rhigyfarch

When Cuthbert offered up the saving Victim (that is, when he
celebrated Holy Communion) as a sacrifice to God, he offered his
prayer to the Lord not by raising his voice but by shedding tears which
sprang from the depths of his heart.

Bede

Grant me tears when rising
Grant me tears when resting
Beyond your every gift altogether for love of you
Mary's Son.
Grant me tears in bed to moisten my pillow
So that his dear ones may help to cure the soul.
Grant me contrition of heart so that I may not be in disgrace
O Lord, protect me, and grant me tears.
For the dalliance I had with women, who did not reject me,
Grant me tears,
O Creator, flowing in streams from my eyes.
For my anger and my jealousy and my pride,
A foolish deed
In pools from my inmost parts bring forth tears.

Old Irish (trans. Davies)

Physical exercise has value as far as this life goes, but spiritual exercise has value for both this life and the next.
1 Timothy 4:8

Probably a majority of us enjoy taking part in or watching sport. There is:

    the enjoyment of a strong or supple body
    the thrill of pitting oneself against the odds
    the pulsing juices
    the sweat, the brawn, the skill, the brain.

Cuthbert, who was agile and acrobatic as a youth, went on to become, in Bede's words 'our athlete of God'. The Fathers and Mothers of the deserts, as well as the Celtic saints, were known by this title of 'athletes of the Spirit'. Why?

Built in to their lives was disciplined training and daily exercise of body, mind and spirit. That was part of the monastic ideal. They looked for a prize – an eternal prize. Their chosen way of life involved pitting themselves against opponents, though their opponents were spiritual forces within and without. It was a race, a race against encroaching apathy, unbelief, or arrogance; and it took all that they had.

> Wondrous the warriors who lived in Iona
> Thrice fifty in monastic rule
> With their boats along the main sea
> Three score men a-rowing.
> > *From the* Book of Lismore

> Bless to me my body
> Bless to me my brain
> Bless to me my training
> Bless to me my game.

Taming the tongue

Does anyone think they are religious? If they do not control their tongue, their religion is worthless . . . the tongue is like a forest fire.
James 1:26; 2 6

A group of desert monks travelled by boat to visit Antony. Another old monk whom they did not know was also on the boat, and it turned out that he, too was visiting Antony. Antony said to the old monk, 'Did you find good brothers to accompany you?' 'Indeed they are good', said the monk, 'but their house has no door. Whoever wishes may enter the stable door and set the ass loose.' He said this because whatever came into their minds they spoke about with their mouths.
Sayings of the Desert Fathers

The elders at Iona agreed that Aidan ' was worthy to be made a bishop and that he was the man to send to instruct those ignorant unbelievers, since he had proved himself to be pre-eminently endowed with the grace of discretion, which is the mother of all virtues.'

Bede

Three sisters of lying: perhaps, maybe, guess.

Three elegant things that are best ignored: elegant manners in someone whose heart is false; elegant words from someone who is foolish; elegant prayers from a priest wanting money.

Three signs of rudeness: a visit that lasts longer than the welcome; sharp questions that cut a person's soul; effusive gratitude when none is meant.

Celtic Triads

Could you sell your parrot to the town gossip with an easy mind?
Will Rogers

> Teach me when to be silent and when to speak
> When to listen and when to leave
> When to praise and when to refrain
> When to laugh and when to weigh
> When to tell and when to wait.

Jesus said, 'You are Peter and on this rock I will build my Church. And the gates of the underworld can never hold out against it. I will give you the keys of the kingdom of heaven: Whatever you bind on earth shall be bound in heaven; whatever you loose on earth shall be loosed in heaven.'
Matthew 16:18, 19.

In the Celtic Church appointments followed the anointings. It was the custom for Celtic Church leaders in the west of Britain to come together for a synod during the forty day period of prayer before Easter. Samson was not among them, for he had made up his mind to be free of all worldly involvements, and was on a prolonged prayer vigil in a cave. Such was the attraction of his holiness, however, that these leaders sent a letter urging him not to work for himself alone, since his ministry would be profitable to many, and to come to the synod. On the day of Samson's arrival at the synod they appointed him abbot of a monastery which Bishop Germanus had founded.

At that same synod Samson had a dream of himself surrounded by crowds of 'delightful beings' and by the apostles Peter, John and James, dressed in silk vestments with golden crowns (the garb of Eastern bishops). They went in to the church in order (as Samson thought) to pray, but in fact ordained Samson deacon. Samson did not disclose this dream.

Then on February 22, the day when bishops ordained three new priests, Bishop Dubricius had a dream that Samson was ordained. Since it was the custom to ordain three new priests, and only two candidates had been so far agreed upon, Dubricius and his fellow bishops took it that God wished Samson to become the third ordinand. When they informed Samson, he confided to them the dream God had given him. What a confirmation this was!

As Samson sat in the special chair for the ordination, those who stood by saw a dove hover over him throughout the ceremony. And when Samson celebrated Holy Communion they saw what looked like fire coming out of his mouth and nostrils. Samson confided in someone that from that day onwards, whenever he celebrated Holy Communion, he could see angels assisting him.

Celtic Christians followed the anointings. Do we?

> Lord, help me so to give up worldly ambitions
> That I may be free for you to use me this day.
> May my appointments always be divine appointments.

Do not judge others, or you, too, will be judged. For in the same way that you judge others, you will be judged.
Matthew 7:1

The camel never sees its own hump, but its neighbour's hump is ever before it.

Arab proverb

A desert Christian, coming into Scete, asked a local brother to lead him to two desert fathers he had long desired to meet. His first choice was to see Arsenius. Arsenius received him, prayed, and sat with him in silence; so the brother who acted as guide said, 'I must take my leave,' and the confused visitor did likewise. Then they went to Abba Moses, a former thief who had been converted. Moses gave them a meal and entertained them both royally. The guide asked his visiting friend, 'Which of the two is more to your liking?' 'To my mind the one who gave us a good welcome and meal', the visitor replied.

This came to the ears of one of the fathers who prayed: 'Lord, reveal to me how it is that one man serves you by withdrawing from sight and speech, and another serves you by being a good fellow with everyone.' He was shown the answer in a dream: Two ships sailed down the river. In one he saw the Holy Spirit sailing with Father Arsenius in silence and peace. In the other boat he saw Father Moses, and the angels of God were feeding him with lashings of honey.

Sayings of the Desert Fathers

Whenever I say 'they' I should hear an alarm bell.
D. Prescott

There but for the grace of God go I.
Traditional British saying

> Christ be in heart of foe and stranger
> Christ be in those who drive me to anger
> Christ be in me to welcome and 'manger'.

'Do you think you are going to be a king and rule over us?' Joseph's brothers asked him. So they hated him even more because of his dreams . . . plotted against him and decided to kill him.
Genesis 37:8, 18

Joseph's brothers thought they would not reach their own potential if their brother fulfilled his, as revealed in his dreams. This fear was the opposite of the truth. In reality, Joseph's brothers reached their own historic leadership roles through, not in spite of, Joseph.

Of all the emotions and desires within the human breast, the one that is most often misunderstood and misused is ambition. This emotion distinguishes us from all the other creatures which inhabit the world. An animal, bird, fish or insect has no ambition; it simply looks for food in order to sustain itself for another day. But the human being can look ahead, anticipating the consequences of present actions far into the future.

Ambition in itself is neither good nor bad; what matters is how it is directed. Ambition may be directed towards the accumulation of power and wealth, towards material superiority over others. Such ambition is evil, because power and wealth can only be gained at the expense of others. Or ambition may be directed towards holiness and moral perfection, towards becoming like Christ himself. The emotion which lusts after power and wealth is the same emotion which yearns for holiness and perfection; the difference lies in the way in which the emotion is directed.

Pelagius

The approach of the Celtic missionaries was essentially gentle and sensitive. They sought to live alongside the people with whom they wanted to share the good news of Christ, to understand and respect their beliefs and not to dominate or culturally condition them.

Ian Bradley

> Give me the ambition
> To use everything I have for the highest purposes
> To abuse no person
> To misuse no powers
> To harness skills to service
> And to bring great things to flower.

Lord, have mercy upon me, a sinner.
Luke 18:13

St Patrick urged his followers to make their own these words, which he had learned was the constant prayer of the universal church: 'Lord, have mercy, Christ, have mercy'.

In the story (Luke 18) Jesus contrasts the wordy triumphalism in the prayers of the religious person, with the simple heart-cry of the man who knew how sinful and needy he was: 'Lord, have mercy on me, a sinner'.

The desert Christians began this prayer with the words, 'Lord Jesus Christ', to make sure that God's own Son, and not any old lord, was being addressed. Some groups would repeat this constantly, hundreds and thousands of times, until in the end it became 'a conditioned reflex'. This custom has been continued amongst some Eastern Orthodox Christians and is now reviving also in the West. It is known as *The Jesus Prayer*.

This is not vain repetition, as some have alleged, if it comes from the heart and not just from the head. Some Christians reserve the Jesus Prayer for Saturday evenings, when they say it repeatedly as a preparation for Sunday. Others shorten the prayer to just the name 'Jesus'.

For myself, this prayer comes into its own when I am desperate, despondent, physically frail, or pressed by competing demands. In these circumstances I lack the energy to form my own prayers, I lack the purity to be sure that my prayers are not really ego demands, and I lack the wisdom to know how to sort out competing demands. So I give up trying to be in charge, or on top (like the Pharisee in the story); I carry on doing whatever I have to do, praying the Jesus Prayer in my weakness.

Isn't that all that God requires of any of us?

Lord Jesus Christ, have mercy on me, a sinner.

We seem to have nothing, but we really possess everything.
2 Corinthians 6:10

Unless a person say in their heart 'I alone and God are in this world',
they shall not find quiet.

Abba Allois

> I adore not the voice of birds
> Nor snuff, nor gambling in this world
> Nor a boy, nor gambling, nor women.
> My Druid is Christ, the Son of God
> Christ, Son of Mary, the Great Abbot
> The Father, the Son and the Holy Spirit.

Attributed to Columba

Let us be careful that no image except that of God take shape in the
soul.

Columbanus

I wears life like a loose robe.

A Negro woman

> Let nothing disturb you, nothing dismay you
> All things pass, God never changes
> Peace attains all that it strives for
> They who live in God find they lack nothing.
> God alone suffices.

St Teresa of Avila

> Said the robin to the sparrow
> 'I should really like to know
> Why these busy human people
> Seem to fret and worry so'.
> Said the sparrow to the robin
> 'Friend, I think that it must be
> That they have no heavenly Father
> Such as cares for you and me'.

Anon

> Wean me from false anxieties
> Wean me from false addictions
> Lead me to desire nothing but you
> Till my soul is at peace.

So put on God's armour now! Then when the evil day comes you will
be able to resist the enemy's attacks and after fighting to the end, you
will still hold your ground.
Ephesians 6:13

It is not for quiet or security that we have formed a community in the
monastery, but for a struggle and a conflict. We have met here for a
contest, we have embarked upon a war against our sins . . . The
struggle upon which we are engaged is full of hardships, full of dangers,
for it is the struggle of a person against themself . . .

For this purpose we have gathered together in this tranquil retreat,
this spiritual camp, that we may day after day wage an unwearying war
against our passions.

Faustus of Riez

While Cuthbert sang his psalms, he worked with his hands, and so by
toil he drove away the heaviness of sleep, or else indeed he went round
the island finding out how everything was getting on . . . he used to
blame the faintheartedness of brothers who were upset if aroused during
the night. 'No one annoys me by rousing me from sleep,' he used to
say, 'rather, the person who wakens me gladdens me . . .' In his zeal
for right living he was keen to reprove sinners, yet he was kind and
forbearing in pardoning those who were penitent, so that sometimes,
when someone was confessing their sins to him, he would burst into
tears, and so, by his own example, show the penitent what he should
do . . .

Not until he first gained victory over our invisible enemy by solitary
prayer and fasting did he take it upon himself to seek out a remote
battlefield further away from his fellows . . . (the Inner Farne Island) At
the entry of our soldier of Christ armed with, 'the helmet of salvation,
the shield of faith and the sword of the spirit which is the word of
God' the devil fled and his host of allies with him.

Bede's Life of St Cuthbert

> Teach us, good Lord
> To serve you as you deserve
> To give and not to count the cost
> To fight and not to heed the wounds
> To labour and not to ask for any reward
> Except that of knowing that we do your will.
>
> *Ignatius Loyola*

We know that the whole world lies under the power of the evil one. And we know that the Son of God has come and given us understanding so that we may know him who is true.
1 John 5:19, 20

Thirty years before David was born God spoke to his father in a dream in which he was hunting. He came upon a stag, a fish, and a hive of bees. He was told to send the hive, portions of the stag meat and of the fish to a local monastery, where they would be preserved for a son who would be born to him.

The three gifts, he was told in the dream, were symbols of three features of his future son. The honeycomb symbolised wisdom, for as the honey lies embedded in the wax so his son would perceive the spiritual meaning embedded in words of the Bible. The fish symbolised his life-style; for as fish live in water so this son would say 'no' to addictive food and drink, and live in God – eating only basics such as bread and water. The stag represented the power he would have over Satan, who is often depicted as the ancient serpent. As a stag, after it has fed itself off the snakes it has killed, longs for a water spring to re-invigorate its youth, so this future son, after overcoming humanity's ancient enemy, the Devil, would choose a spring of life with tears often flowing.

In this way, the future son, in the power of the Trinity, and in the strength obtained by his fights against physical cravings, would acquire a healing knowledge of the way to overcome evil spirits.

All this was fulfilled in David's life a generation later. We, in our turn, can gradually learn mastery of self and evil.

> Lord, as fish live in water, may I live in you.
> Grant me the strength to do without things.
> Grant me the wisdom to see the 'within' of things.
> Grant me the knowledge
> To take the measure of evil spirits
> Grant me understanding to know you
> Who alone are true.

There is a fragrance about you. No woman could help loving you.
Take me with you, and we'll run away; be my king and take me to
your room. We will be happy together, drink deep, and lose ourselves
in love.
The Song of Songs 1:3, 4

Once every four years, on February 29, girls, so it is said, take a leap
and ask a lad to marry them. However that may be, it is a day when all
of us may take a leap into the Spring that will soon be here, and into
the love that is in the air.

> I praise two who is one and two
> Who is really three
> Who made . . .
> Love in our senses
> A girl dear and tender
> And burned five cities
> Because of false union.
> > *Early Middle Welsh*

> The month of February, a feast is rare
> The spade and the wheel are hard at work
> The ox has no voice to complain.
> The evenings grow longer, the mornings earlier.
> The sun grows brighter, but the clouds are darker
> A rainbow is seen after storms.
> 'The greatest pleasure is friendship'.
> > *From* Welsh Gnomic Poems

> Lord, place these nine choice graces
> in the upturned faces
> of this day's hopeful lasses:
> the grace of form
> the grace of voice
> the grace of provision
> the grace of goodness
> the grace of wisdom
> the grace of caring
> the grace of femininity
> the grace of a lovely personality
> the grace of godly speech.
> > *Inspired by the* Carmina Gadelica

The earth shall be filled with the glory of God as the waters cover the sea.
Isaiah 11:9

> David the faithful witness of Christ's new Law
> Like a bright star from heaven shines forth in Britain
> His illustrious life and teaching adorn Wales
> Like the birth of the Forerunner, the Baptist, his birth was divinely foretold.
> The future greatness of Christ's servant is declared by heavenly signs:
> Honey, water and mystic deer.
> This is the champion of the British, the leader and teacher of the Welsh, Supporting the citizens of God.
> Single-hearted he condemns luxury
> Spurning the city, he seeks the valley as befits the lowly.
> At his birth the people name him 'Dewi ddyfryr', which means 'Aqua life David'.
> He cures the blind, he expels diseases and he drives away the devil.
> A doctor of Christ's Law, he writes a book which God completes.
> May David, our leader and strong champion, overcome by his prayers the Goliaths, the giant enemies, of our time.
> > *Adapted from the Ancient Welsh Missal Text about 1440*

David and the Christians he enlisted as monks were known as the Watermen:

> As fish live in water so these folk live in God
> As birds fly high and care-free so these folk move in God
> As deer run straight and graceful so these folk run with God
> As waters flow so clearly so these folk flow with God
> As fire burns bright and fiercely so these folk blaze for God.

> > Lord, inspired by David and the Watermen
> > Help us to live in you as fish live in water
> > Help us to move in you as birds fly in air
> > Help us to run for you as deer run
> > Help us to flow with you as water flows
> > Help us to burn brightly for you as fire burns.
> > And may the fire of faith blaze afresh in Wales
> > And may the fire of faith blaze afresh in us.

Jesus said, 'When you are invited to a celebration do not sit down in the best place. It may be that someone more important than you has been invited . . . Instead, when you are invited, go and sit in the lowest place, so that your host will come up and say, "Come on up, my friend, to a better place"'.
Luke 14:8, 10

Chad, though he was probably the youngest of four brothers who trained under Aidan at Lindisfarne, was also the brightest. This never went to his head, and he was always a model of humility. He went over to Ireland for his 'further education'. When his brother Cedd, who was Abbot of Lastingham, died, Chad was sent back to Northumbria to take his place as abbot. There he became known as an admirable teacher, though he also encouraged a recruit who arrived one day, wanting to do practical work but no book work.

The king of the Northumbrians, Oswy, had gone along with the appointment of a monk named Wilfred as Bishop of the Northumbrians. But Wilfred was so mesmerised by the practices and pomp of the Roman style of church life that he went to the continent to be 'properly' consecrated, and stayed on and on, leaving the post back home vacant. Oswy became restive and eventually asked Chad to fill the vacant post.

Chad was Bishop of the Northumbrians for three years until 669. Then the Bishop of Rome sent the powerful Theodore of Tarsus to be Archbishop of Canterbury and to bring the English Church into line with standard Roman organisation. Theodore explained to Chad that his consecration as bishop had not met these norms. Chad replied that he had never considered himself worthy to be a bishop in the first place, and that he was willing to resign, which he did in favour of Wilfred.

His genuine humility and holiness made such an impression on Theodore that he re-consecrated him as a bishop, and, when the Bishop of Mercia died, asked Chad to take his place. On one point Theodore was firm. Chad, like Aidan, loved to evangelise by walking everywhere, and he refused to ride about on a horse. Mercia, however, was a huge diocese, so Theodore not only ordered him to use a horse, but physically lifted him on to a horse with his own hands!

> Servant King –
> Be king of my hearth and king of my heart
> Be king of my hands and king of my head
> Be king of my shoes and king of my style.

The people tried to prevent Jesus from leaving, but he said to them, 'I must preach the Good News about the Kingdom of God in other towns also because this is what God sent me to do.'
Luke 4:42, 43

David's ministry in Wales started with a splash. The priest who baptised him was assisted by a blind man named Movi who immersed David under the water. Some of this water splashed over Movi's eyes and he regained his sight. It seems that God gave David a healing touch with eyes, as the following story of Paulinus illustrates.

David was ordained and trained under Paulinus, who had a reputation as 'a fosterer of righteousness', somewhere in Carmarthenshire. During those years Paulinus' eyesight deteriorated badly, and one day he invited each of his pupils to come up in turn and pray for his eyes, making the sign of the cross over them. The young David, who was shy, and who had had no eye contact with his esteemed mentor, held back, but Paulinus said to him, 'Touch my eyes, and, even without you looking at me, I shall be healed.' His sight did indeed return, and David's stature increased.

After several years there Paulinus felt God saying: 'Dewi' (the Welsh name for David) 'has used the talents I have given him as fully as he can while he is here. Now I want to send him out so that he can use different approaches to win as many people as possible, from different walks of life, to my way. He must be free to give strong food to strong people, and milk to weak people.' Paulinus commissioned David to go out and 'win bundles of souls'.

David did just that, he gathered a mission team and established monastic centres in twelve key places, some as far from Wales as Glastonbury, Bath, and Crowland. He also helped families and people in ordinary jobs to lead a Christian life. It was said that the Mission Team gave four rules to the people: 1. pray; 2. watch; 3. work; 4. abstain from strong drink. David and his team became 'all things to all people'.

> Great God, who called your servant David
> To be an apostle and father in God to the people of Wales
> Grant that, inspired by the fire of his faith
> And the flexibility of his approach
> We too may see divine fruit in our land.

The Lord rejected the descendants of Joseph, he did not select the tribe of Ephraim; instead he chose the tribe of Judah, and Mount Zion, which he dearly loves. There he built his temple like his home in heaven . . . He chose his servant David.
Psalm 78:67–70

Before David of Wales embarked on his great apostolic mission he and some close friends had waited on God in the shadow of the Black Mountains. There they built a chapel and a cell, where Llanthony Abbey now stands. They took it for granted that on their return they would establish their permanent headquarters there.

However, the mission opened David's eyes. During a conversation back at the home base with his uncle, Bishop Giuisdianus, David said: 'My angel companion told me that in this place which I intend to make my base scarcely one person in a hundred will gain their eternal reward, but there is another place not far away, where hardly any of those buried in the Christian cemetery will be cut off from God.'

That is how David and his friends were guided by God to change their plans, and to build a large, permanent centre in the valley where David was born, near the site of today's St David's Cathedral.

Are you willing to change your plans? Are you allowing God to show you larger horizons, different approaches to mission? God wants to give you a feel for the spirit of people and places, so that you move in inspired ways, to inspired places, with inspired timings, and so that you experience inspired outcomes. Why not apply the following prayer to a place that God is laying upon your heart?

> O God,
> although you do not live in man-made temples
> you choose to work through them.
> Pour down your blessing upon this place
> and all who minister here
> that it may be a strength to those who have oversight
> a joy and inspiration to all faithful Christians
> a home of prayer and devotion
> setting forth to the world a pattern of
> true holiness and worship.
> *From the Prayer of St David's Cathedral, adapted*

You will earn the trust and respect of others if you work for good; if you work for evil, you are making a mistake.
Proverbs 14:22

Buried beneath the sands near Perran-Zabulo in Cornwall lies the remains of a prayer cell built by Piran, a monk who landed here in the fifth century. A tall Celtic cross now stands beside it. Although little else is now known about Piran, his life has inspired many working people throughout the centuries in the West Country of Britain and in Britanny. The Cornish tin miners made him their patron and celebrated his festival on March 5 with great fervour.

This development can encourage us to be aware, in our everyday work, of the example of Christians who treated their work as prayer in action; also, to be aware of the presence of heavenly persons, inspiring us to link our work with the relationships we have with others on earth and in heaven.

> I will build the hearth
> As Mary would build it.
>
> Who are they on the lawn outside?
> Michael the sun-radiant of my trust.
> Who are they on the middle of the floor?
> John and Peter and Paul.
> Who are they on the front of my bed?
> Sun-bright Mary and her Son.
>
> I am smooring the fire as the Son of Mary would smoor.
> (*To smoor is to damp an overnight fire with the day's ashes.*)
>
> *Carmina Gadelica*

I see to the fridge in the presence of the angel of the loveliest delights
I see to the washer in the presence of Mary of the pure-white demeanour
I see to the garage in the presence of Joseph of the fine workmanship
I see to the office in the presence of the Creator of order
I see to the people I shall meet in the presence of the all-friendly Christ
I see to the things that will batter my mind
In the presence of the Spirit who brings calm.

Overcome evil

Do not let evil defeat you; instead, overcome evil with good.
Romans 12:21

In the reading two days ago we learned how David and his friends
were divinely directed to build their headquarters in a different place.
Having done that, they had to learn the hard lesson that being in the
place of God's choosing does not make us immune to opposition. Once
God's kingdom gets a foothold, things that are not of God in that
place, however well established, come under threat; so they react,
sometimes ferociously.

First came the honeymoon. Many Christians gathered to celebrate
the opening of David's new centre in the place which was then known
as Rosina Vallis. They lit a bonfire which seemed to encircle the whole
area with the presence of God, and even to light up Ireland as well.
Then came the reaction. The local big-wig, the pagan Baia, went
berserk when he saw the crowds and the engulfing smoke, which
seemed to symbolise the very thing that would happen to the region
under the influence of David.

Baia's wife persuaded him to retaliate. They armed their slaves with
knives who set out to kill the monks. On their way, however, they
were afflicted with sudden fever. On arrival all they had strength for
was to hurl four-letter words at the monks; they had to return with
their mission unaccomplished. Before they reached the gates, Baia's wife
rushed towards them: the cattle too, had been infected and had died.
'Go back to the servant of God,' she told them, 'and ask him to pray
God to have mercy on the cattle.' They told David 'The land where
you have settled shall be yours for ever.' 'Your cattle shall come to life
again,' he responded! And both things came true.

Baia's wife soon reverted to spite. She forced her female servants to
undress in full view of the monks every day. This torpedoed their aim
of being single-minded. They became so demoralised that a delegation
urged David to re-locate the monastery elsewhere. This was David's
reply, 'You know that the world hates Christ's followers. You know
that God's people Israel faced innumerable setbacks on their desert trek
to the Promised Land. They were beaten to their knees, but not
overthrown. Learn from them not to let evil overcome us but to
overcome evil with good.' The monks stood firm. Not long after this
Baia's jealous wife killed a step-daughter and fled, and an enemy
murdered Baia.

> Director, Saviour, Strengthener, help me to stand firm
> And to overcome evil with good.

St Paul wrote: When we were with you we used to say to you
'Anyone who is unwilling to work should not eat.'
2 Thessalonians 3:10

David's monastery became a byword for honest, hard manual work.
The monks did not hire oxen to do the ploughing, they did it
themselves. Placing the wooden beam which drew the plough on to
their own sweating shoulders; they tirelessly dug the ground with picks,
spades and hoes; and they cut wood with saws. Each person meditated
while he worked; they only spoke when they needed to.

No complaints were heard at the end of a hard day's work, when
they returned to the cloisters for a period of study, prayer and writing.
The instant the church bell rang they would leave whatever they were
doing, however absorbing, and go silently to the church to chant
psalms. Visitors noticed that both their voices and their hearts were in
tune. They spent the time before nightfall in silent prayer in the
church. After the brothers had left, David would stay alone in the
church, pouring out his prayers.

The food and drink at supper was sparing but creative. Special dishes
were cooked for the frail, and for visitors who were weary after a long
journey. Before retiring to bed the monks kept vigil in church for three
hours, avoiding the common pitfalls of sneezing, yawning and spitting!
At cock-crow they would get up and have a prayer time, and on
Saturday nights, imitating the women who went to Jesus's tomb the
night before his resurrection, they kept vigil until the early hours of
Sunday.

The monks wore simple clothes, mainly leather. They shared their
hearts and their failings openly with David, who was a real father to
them. And they accepted his authority, willingly carrying out practical
requests without question.

None of them had any personal possessions, not even a psalm book.
The 'this is mine' mentality did not mar the monastery. When someone
joined the monastery they had to dispose of their wealth before
entering, but David would not accept a penny of it for the monastery,
and he declined donations from people who wanted to control them.
Like the Taizé Community of today, the entire income of the
monastery came through the work of the monks, and they each had an
equal share.

> Teach me, good Lord, to work with all my heart
> Until it can be said of me
> 'To work is to pray'.

Friends always show their love. What are brothers for if not to share trouble?
Proverbs 17:17

I have been to a number of Christian communities where brothers or sisters seem to flow together in mutual love. They have trust in their eyes, and esteem in their hearts for one another, and they help each other in practical ways. That spirit marked David and his brothers, as the stories about Brother Aidan reveal.

Aidan was one of David's inner circle of three from the beginning whom the biographer describes as 'being alike of one mind and desire'. Once Aidan was out of doors studying one of the monastery's books, which had no doubt been painstakingly transcribed, when David asked him to go on an errand; this involved taking two oxen and a wagon to carry some timber which was some distance away. Aidan was, as always, so keen to carry out errands in a good spirit that he left immediately, leaving his precious book still open. Having harnessed the oxen, loaded the wagon with the timber, and begun his return journey, the wagon and oxen careered over a cliff. Aidan made the sign of the Cross over them, and retrieved them safely from the sea. Further on the journey there was such a downpour that the ditches overflowed, and Aidan then thought of that precious book!

Having unloaded the timber he went back for the book, no doubt thinking of the damage the downpour had done to it He found it, however, in exactly the same condition as it was when he left it. The brothers felt that the humility and faith in the way Aidan carried out the errand had provided a shield for the oxen, and that David's fatherly faith on behalf of his dear brother had provided a shield for the book.

Aidan's rapport with David at a deep spiritual level continued when he moved far away to Ireland, where he founded a monastery. One day before Easter Eve he was praying in the monastery, when he 'knew' that someone would poison David's food at their Easter Day supper. He sent one of his monks, who managed, with divine guidance, to cross the sea and reach David in time to tell him.

> May the great God be between your two shoulders
> To protect you in your going and your coming.
> May the Son of Virgin Mary be near your heart
> And the perfect Spirit be upon you pouring.
> *Carmina Gadelica*

The crowd was amazed at the way Jesus taught. He wasn't like the teachers of the Law; instead, he taught with authority.
Matthew 7:28, 29

There are two kinds of authority – outer and inner. Outer authority is often decried, but inner authority, though it is so elusive, is widely desired. It was this kind of authority that drew so many people to Jesus, and still does draw them. David had this kind of authority too.

One hundred and eighteen British church leaders, concerned lest the people no longer followed their lead, called a major synod for leaders and members of churches at a place named Brevi. David, who was not interested in church politics, stayed away. So many people came to the synod that they had to pile clothing to create a mound from which the speakers could be seen and heard. But speaker after speaker failed to get the ear of the people, and the leaders panicked, lest the the people returned disillusioned with the organised church. Then Paulinus, under whom David had studied, urged that they bring David to the synod, for he 'conversed with angels, was a man to be loved,' and had stature. Three times David refused the invitation, until his holy old friend Bishop Dubricius personally went to him. The modest David told him, 'I can't preach but I will give what little help I can with my prayers.'

As they reached the outskirts of the crowd David heard the wailing of mourners. Dubricius wanted to hurry him on to the platform, but David insisted on going to the bereaved person, a mother whose son lay dead. He comforted the mother, who begged him to restore her son. David spent more time praying over the son, who revived. She instantly dedicated him to serve God under David. David gave this young man the Gospel Book he carried, and he walked with it in front of David to the front. All eyes followed them, word spread fast, and there was a clamour for David to speak. For years afterwards people swore that that mound of clothes grew bigger as David spoke. For he spoke with authority and not as others had done. His heart was to be with the people in all their needs, not to be up front. But the people's heart went out to him, and through him to God. That is true authority. A church in Wales recently spent time meditating on 'the mound that grew'. In what areas does God want you to grow authority? True authority makes its mark through prayer and service.

> God take from me delusions of grandeur.
> Give to me the authority that belongs to me.
> May it grow through prayer and service.

God made us simple, but we have made ourselves very complicated.
Ecclesiastes 7:29

David gave the Welsh people rules to help them live simply for God. A
growing number of Christians make a Rule of Life today. Some do it
for the good of their soul, others do it for the good of the poor in
other countries who receive unjust payment for what they produce;
some do it for the good of nature, to prevent natural resources being
squandered.

William Penn the Quaker observed: 'People must follow the 10
commandments of God or they condemn themselves to the 10,000
commandments of men.' The saying of Jesus in Matthew 5:8 basically
means, 'Blessed is the person whose motives are unmixed.' Consider the
effects of being pulled in more than one direction: Stress levels, and the
vast increase in National Health requirements; dishonesty, and the vast
increase in bureaucracy; family break-down. Even in the church, it can
mean committees and meetings to satisfy every conflicting demand.
These use up the energy and time that should be directed to one
purpose only: being Jesus for others.

We wish to 'live simply that others may simply live', to avoid any sense
of judging one another; and God will make different demands of each
of us. Our common responsibility is to hold regularly before God (and,
as appropriate, to share with our Soul Friend) our income, our savings,
our possessions, conscious that we are stewards, not possessors of these
things, and making them available to him as he requires.

A simple lifestyle means setting everything in the simple beauty of
creation. Our belongings, activities and relationships are ordered in a
way that liberates the spirit; we cut out those things that overload or
clutter the spirit.

From the Way of Life of The Community of Aidan and Hilda

> Too long have I worried about so many things.
> And yet, my Lord, so few are needed.
> May I today live more simply – like the bread.
> May I today see more clearly – like the water.
> May I today be more selfless – like the Christ.
> *From Russia*

Out of the mouths of infants you have ordained strength, in order to stop anyone who opposes you.
Psalm 8:2

Sometimes small children blurt out something which communicates God's heart in a way that an adult cannot. The reason is that children pick up the spirit of a person or a place more quickly than do adults, who have protected themselves with layers of sophistication. It was an infant having a Spirit-led tantrum who caused the boy Cuthbert to think again about his life.

For the first eight years of his life Cuthbert had a mind for nothing except games, pranks, and careering around. He used to boast that he had beaten all those of his own age, as well as many older boys, at wrestling, jumping, running and many other exercises. When the others were tired out he would look around in triumph as though he was ready to start afresh.

One day a great crowd of children were playing together in a field, twisting around in all sorts of contortions. Suddenly a three year old rushed up to Cuthbert and began to scold him in the way an adult would. He told him he should not spend all his time just mucking about, but should exercise control of mind over body. Cuthbert pooh poohed the idea, at which the little boy promptly went into a tantrum. He tearfully told Cuthbert that God wanted him to be a holy priest and leader in the church, so how could he waste his life doing things that were against his nature and his calling?

Cuthbert soothed the child in a friendly way, and did, in fact, go home at once to think about what had been said. From that time people noticed that he behaved in a more mature way, and they concluded that the Spirit who spoke to him through the words of an infant, spoke to him also in the recesses of his heart.

> I pray, Lord, for the children whom I know.
> Help me to encourage them
> To listen to the thoughts and pictures
> You put into their minds.
> Help me to receive humbly what they tell me,
> And to keep at least half an ear cocked
> For your voice coming to me through them.

Temptation

Now Jesus can help those who are tempted because he himself was tempted in all ways as we are.
Hebrews 2:18

If you fall into temptation in the place where you live, do not desert that place when the temptation comes; for if you do, you will find that, wherever you go, the temptation you are running away from will be there ahead of you.

Sayings of the Desert Fathers

God's will would I do
My own will bridle.

God's due would I give
My own due yield.

God's path would I follow
My own path refuse.

Christ's death would I ponder
My own death remember.

Christ's agony would I meditate
My love to God make warmer.

Christ's cross would I carry
My own cross forget.

Repentance of sin would I make
Early repentance choose.

The love of Christ would I feel
My own love know.
Carmina Gadelica

O Christ, the Champion of the tests
When the first thought strikes, help me to resist
When the first look overwhelms, help me to resist
When the first fascination takes hold, help me to resist.
If I fall, save me.

How can a young man keep his life pure? By obeying your commands.
With all my heart I try to serve you.
Psalm 119:9, 10

I, Patrick, am a sinner, the most awkward of country bumpkins, the
least of all the faithful, and the most contemptible amongst very many.
My father was Calpornius, a deacon, son of a certain Potitus, a priest of
the village of Bannavem Taburniae, and there I was captured by slave
traders.

At the time I was about sixteen years old, and I did not know the
true God. Along with thousands of other people, I was taken in
captivity to Ireland. It was no more than we deserved, for we had
turned our backs on God and did not keep his laws. Neither did we
obey our priests who reminded us of our salvation. So the Lord
scattered us among many nations, even to the utmost part of the earth,
where my insignificance might be seen by strangers.

In Ireland the Lord opened my eyes to my unbelief, so that I might
at last face up to my wickedness and be converted with all my heart to
the Lord my God. He respected my humbling and had mercy on my
youth and ignorance. Even before I knew him, he watched over me.
Before I was able to tell good from evil, he protected me and
comforted me as a father would his son.

So I cannot keep quiet — nor should I —about the tremendous
blessings and the grace that the Lord poured out on me in the land of
my captivity.

The Confession of Patrick

I arise today in vast might,
Inviting the Trinity
Entrusting myself to the Three
Honouring the One
Meeting in the Creator.
          St Patrick's Breastplate

The Spirit comes to help us, weak as we are. For we do not know how we ought to pray, but the Spirit pleads with God for us in groans that words cannot express.
Romans 8:26

As a beardless adolescent I was captured before I knew what to look for and what to avoid. I was like a stone lying deep in the mud; but he that is mighty came and lifted me up in his mercy, and raised me to the top of the wall. That is why I ought to shout in a loud voice, and return something to the Lord for all his benefits here and in eternity, which the human mind cannot even begin to comprehend.

After coming to Ireland I was put to work tending cattle, sheep and hogs, and many times during the day I would pray. More and more the love of God and the fear of God came to me, so that my faith was strengthened and my spirit was moved. In a single day I would pray as often as a hundred times, and nearly as often at night, when I was staying in the woods and in the mountains. I would rouse myself before daylight to pray, whether in snow, frost, or rain; it made no difference, and I felt no bad effects. Because the Spirit in me was fervent, I knew no sluggishness.

The Confession of Patrick

> Christ beside me, Christ before me
> Christ behind me, Christ within me
> Christ beneath me, Christ above me
> Christ to right of me, Christ to left of me
> Christ in my lying, my sitting, my rising
> Christ in heart of all who know me
> Christ on tongue of all who meet me
> Christ in eye of all who see me
> Christ in ear of all who hear me.
> *St Patrick's Breastplate*

A voice said to him 'Elijah, what are you doing here? Return to the desert near Damascus, then enter the city.'
1 Kings 19:13, 15

One night in my sleep I heard a voice saying to me, 'Fast well, for soon you will be back to your own country.' And in a little while the same voice said to me, 'See, your ship is ready.' But it wasn't close by, it was perhaps two hundred miles away, at a place I had never been to, nor did I know a single person there. But I made up my mind to run away, and so I left the man with whom I had spent the last six years. I went in the strength of the Lord who guided me well, and I feared nothing up to the time I came to that ship.

On the day I arrived, the ship was scheduled to depart, and I told them I had the wherewithal to sail with them. But the ship's captain was displeased, and his answer was sharp and indignant, 'You are wasting your time trying to book a passage with us.' When I heard this I left them to return to the little shack where I was staying. On the way I began to pray, and before I had finished praying I heard one of the sailors shouting at me from behind. 'Come quickly,' he called out, 'the men are asking for you.' Immediately I reversed my direction and headed back. 'We are taking you on faith,' the crew explained. 'Make friends with us in any way you like.' But I did not become intimate with them through fear of God; and yet I hoped that an opportunity would open up when I could say to them, 'Come to faith in Jesus Christ,' for they were pagans. So I came aboard and we sailed immediately.

The Confession of Patrick

> This day I call to me
> God's strength to direct me
> God's power to sustain me
> God's wisdom to guide me
> God's vision to light me
> God's ear to my hearing
> God's word to my speaking
> God's hand to uphold me
> God's pathway before me
> God's shield to protect me.
> *St Patrick's Breastplate*

In your goodness you fed your people with manna and gave them
water to drink. Through forty years in the desert you provided all that
they needed.
Nehemiah 9:20, 21

After three days we reached land (probably modern France), and for the
next four weeks we travelled through a deserted countryside. We ran
out of food and became famished. One day the captain spoke to me,
'What do you say, Christian? Your God is supposed to be great and all-
powerful, why can't you pray for us? We are starving to death. It's hard
to believe we will ever see another person alive.'
　　I then said plainly to them all, 'Turn in faith and with all your hearts
to the Lord my God, for whom nothing is impossible. He will send
you food on your way until you have all that you can eat, for he has
abundance of it everywhere.' And with God's help it happened.
Suddenly a herd of pigs appeared on the road right before our eyes.
The men killed a number of them and spent two nights there until
they regained their strength. Their hounds were also fed, and from that
day they had plenty of food.

The Confession of Patrick

> I arise today
> in the might of Heaven
> brightness of sun, whiteness of snow
> splendour of fire, speed of lightning
> swiftness of wind, depth of sea
> stability of earth, firmness of rock.
> God's legions to save me
> To protect me
> from snares of the demons
> from evil enticements
> from failings of nature
> from one man or many
> that seek to destroy me
> nearby or afar.
>
> *St Patrick's Breastplate*

Happy is the people whose God is the Lord.
Psalm 32:12

After a few years I was back with my parents in Britain. They received
me as a son, and begged me never to go away from them again after all
the trials I had been through. But then I saw in a vision of the night a
man who seemed to be coming from Ireland, carrying many letters. His
name was Victoricus. He gave one of them to me and I read the
opening lines, which were, 'The voice of the Irish.' While I was
reading I thought I heard the voices of the people who live by the
wood of Voclut, which is by the western sea. They cried as with one
voice, 'We ask you, son, to come and walk once more among us.' I
was heartbroken at this, and could read no further, and so I woke up.
Years later, thanks be to God, the Lord granted them what they had
asked.

I owe an immense debt to God, who granted me so much grace that
many people in Ireland were reborn in God through me. Clergy were
ordained everywhere to look after these people, who had come to trust
the Lord who called them from the ends of the earth. It was essential
that we spread our nets so that a great multitude should be taken for
God, and that there were plenty of clergy to baptise and counsel the
people, as the Lord tells us to do in the Gospel.

So it came about that Ireland, a land filled with people who never
had the knowledge of God, but worshipped idols and other foul
objects, now has a people of the Lord who are called the children of
God. It was not my grace, but God, victorious in me, who resisted all
opposition when I came to the people of Ireland to preach the Gospel
and to suffer insults from unbelievers. If I should be worthy, I am ready
to give even my life most willingly and unhesitatingly for his Name. I
am bound by the Spirit who witnesses to me. Christ the Lord told me
to come here and stay with the people for the rest of my life, if he so
wills, and he will guard me from every evil that I might not sin before
him.

The Confession of Patrick

Christ for my policing today:
Against poison and burning, against drowning and wounding
That there may come to me a multitude of rewards.

St Patrick's Breastplate

Come with boldness

In union with Christ we have boldness to go into God's presence with every confidence.
2 Corinthians 3:12

> The month of March, great is the pride of the birds
> The wind is bitter blowing over the ploughed field
> The crops are short while the days grow longer
> Every creature knows its enemy
> Every bird knows its mate
> Every plant springs out of the earth
> 'The bold person succeeds while the reckless person fails'.
> *Welsh Gnomes*

> Around me I gather
> these forces to save
> my soul and my body
> from dark powers that assail me;
> against false prophesyings
> and false gods all around me
> against spells
> against knowledge unlawful
> that injures the body
> that injures the spirit.
> *From St Patrick's Breastplate*

> As surely as the seasons unfold
> and Spring follows Winter
> so sure is your steadfast love,
> O God.

> As burns
> released from winter's bondage
> leap joyously in the sea,
> melt our frozen hearts
> that we may worship you.

> As buds uncurl
> and flowers open their faces to the sun
> turn us
> to the light and warmth
> of your presence.
> *Kate McIlhagga*

Love the Lord your God with all your . . . strength.
Deuteronomy 6:5

Better late then never? In the light of eternity, it is best to dedicate our youth and our strength to God. For God wants the flower of our lives, and, in fact, we are unlikely to reach our full flower if we do not give the physical powers, passions and purposes of our youth to God.

We must not think that our physical powers are something to keep separate from our spiritual destination. They need to be harnessed, not hand-cuffed to God. God has a use for both physical weakness and physical strength. We can be a fragile reed for God or a body builder for God. It was said that Patrick used the strong man Mac Carton as his bodyguard. The muscular young Cuthbert, too, was strong for God.

In accordance with the example of Samson the strong, who was once a Nazirite, Cuthbert sedulously abstained from all intoxicants; but he could not submit to such abstinence in food, lest he became unfit for the work he needed to do. For he was robust of body and sound in strength, and fit for whatever labour he cared to undertake.

Bede's Life of Cuthbert

I pass over the many other great things Cuthbert did in the flower of his youth, because I am keen to describe how as a mature adult he showed peaceable qualities and the power of Christ in serving God. So I omit how Cuthbert, when based at an army camp, face to face with the enemy, and with the most meagre of food rations, yet lived in abundance throughout that time. He was strengthened by divine aid, just as Daniel and the three young men, though they refused the royal food that their religion did not allow, grew greatly in physical stature on the meagre food allowance of slaves.

Life of Cuthbert, *Anon*

God who created me
Nimble and light of limb
In three elements free
To run, to ride, to swim
Not when the sense is dim
But now from the heart of joy
I would remember Him . . .
H.C. Beeching

Listen! Wisdom is calling out. Reason is making herself heard. . . . at the crossroads she stands.
Proverbs 8:1,2

The Spring equinox, one of the two days in the year when day and night are of equal length, owing to the sun's crossing of the equator, is also St Cuthbert's Day.

> As the heralds of Spring
> golden trumpet
> the arrival of Easter,
> as the dark night of Lent passes
> and the days lengthen
> so like Cuthbert,
> bright star of the North,
> we would become
> your Easter people, O Christ,
> shepherds of your sheep,
> peace makers and hospitality givers
> open to change and partnership
> Spirit led, in solitude and costly service.
> *Kate Mdlhagga* Cuthbert's Folk

I also omit how Cuthbert saw the soul of a farm manager carried up to the sky at his death; how he wonderfully sent demons packing; or how he healed people of disturbed mind through his prayers.

Life of Cuthbert, *Anon*

> God of Spring-time
> While the sun is crossing over the equator
> May I be crossing over
> From dark to light
> From complaining to appreciation
> From dither to boldness
> From stagnation to creativity
> From coldness to love
> From me to you.

May everything that has breath Praise the Lord!
Psalm 150:6

The 8th century Celi De (Friends of God) community at Tallaght, Ireland, sang the Benedicite every day between the evening meal and vespers.

> O all you works of the Lord, O bless the Lord
> To the Lord be highest praise and glory for ever!
>
> And you angels of the Lord, O bless the Lord
> To the Lord be highest praise and glory for ever!
>
> And you, the heavens of the Lord, O bless the Lord
> And you clouds of the sky, O bless the Lord
> And you, all armies of the Lord, O bless the Lord
> To the Lord be highest glory and praise for ever.
>
> And you, sun and moon, O bless the Lord
> And you, the stars of heaven, bless the Lord
> And you, showers and rain, O bless the Lord
> To the Lord be highest glory and praise for ever.
>
> And you, all breezes and winds, O bless the Lord
> And you, cold and heat, O bless the Lord
> To the Lord be highest glory and praise for ever.
>
> And you, all that grows in the ground, O bless the Lord
> And you, all that swims in the waters, O bless the Lord
> And you, all birds that fly in the air, O bless the Lord
> To the Lord be highest glory and praise for ever.
>
> And you, all people on earth, O bless the Lord
> And you holy ones and humble in heart, O bless the Lord
> To the Lord be highest glory and praise for ever.
>> *Selected from the Septuagint version of the Book of Daniel*

> And may all that is within me
> And all things I touch
> And all people I meet
> This day
> Give highest glory and praise to you!

The Lord watches over those who obey him, those who trust in his constant love. He saves them from death; he provides for them in time of famine.
Psalm 33:18, 19

The young monk Cuthbert was travelling by horse on a Friday. On Fridays many Christians refrained from eating until afternoon because they wanted to make an act of solidarity with their Lord who was nailed to the cross on a Friday. Cuthbert stopped at a house during the morning to ask for food for the horse. The housewife there urged him to have something to eat also, because it was winter and there was a long road ahead without any stopping places for food. Cuthbert resolutely declined. As the journey wore on, however, he realised that he would not get to his destination by night. Since he and the horse were now weak through lack of food, he sought shelter in a shepherd's hut that was not used in winter, and tethered the horse. As he did so some straw fell from the roof and a folded cloth fell too. He picked this up and found to his amazement that there was half a warm loaf inside it and some meat. 'Praise God', he said, 'who has deigned to provide a supper for me who am fasting out of love for him,' and he divided the bread with the horse.

From that day Cuthbert became more ready than ever to fast, for he realised that the same God who had fed the fasting prophet Elijah in a deserted place had provided for him also, and delights to do this for those who follow the path of denial. We, too, can follow this path, which means taking up our Cross daily.

Christ's Cross over this face and thus over this ear
Christ's Cross over these eyes . . . this mouth . . . this throat . . .
the back of this head . . . this side . . .
to accompany before me . . . to accompany behind me . . .
Christ's Cross to meet every difficulty
both on hollow and on hill . . .
Christ's Cross over my community
Christ's Cross over my church
Christ's Cross in the next world
Christ's Cross in this world.

Early Irish Lyrics

The lamb that was slain from the creation of the world.
Revelation 13:8

As the flash of a volcano briefly reveals the fires at the earth's centre, so the light on Calvary was the bursting forth of the very nature of the Everlasting – the great love which like a fire burns always in God's heart.

Celtic Christians profoundly understood the truth that there was a cross in the heart of God before there was a cross on the hill outside Jerusalem.

God foresaw that evil would enter the creation and prepared for it by building into it a cross. But why did God go ahead with a universe in which evil was a possibility? Just think what kind of a world it would have been if sin was an impossibility: a world in which creatures would have been like robots and would have responded to God's commands in the way a computer responds to our touch. By creating beings with the dangerous gift of free will God brought into existence the conditions in which evil became a possibility. Evil was not God's intention, but by creating a universe in which evil could break out, higher good could be achieved for human beings and greater glory for God.

In designing the universe God made sure that the possibility of sin was met by the possibility of sinful people being redeemed. Thus the broad beams on which the universe is built are in the shape of a Cross. The Cross, the ultimate expression of the law of self-sacrifice runs like a scarlet thread through the Bible, through human experience, and through all creation. Will I sense this and know this in my life today?

> I see his blood upon the rose
> And in the stars the glory of his eyes
> His body gleams amid eternal snows
> His tears fall from the skies.
>
> I see his face in every flower
> The thunder and the singing of the birds
> Are but his voice – and carven by his power
> Rocks are his written words.
>
> All pathways by his feet are worn
> His strong heart stirs the ever beating sea
> His crown of thorns is twined with every thorn
> His cross is every tree.
>
> *Joseph Mary Plunkett Ireland,*
> *died in the 1916 rebellion.*

But the Lord made the punishment fall on him, the punishment all of
us deserved.
Isaiah 53:6

> Himself to himself offering
> The dying God becomes
> Brother to reed and thorn.
>
> The lash unmakes him,
> Bearer of the tree; he bears also
> The inner wounds of scorn.
>
> He learns death's lore.
> To unlock this dark chamber:
> Five potent wounds in the flesh,
> On hand, foot, flank.
>
> Himself, himself abandoning,
> He sings, dry as stone –
> A desolate cry, sweeter than lark-song.
>
> Last fires consume him.
> And the surge from below the oceans' floor
> Carries him, vessel of sorrow, Father-ward.
>
> *David Alston, Dean and Chapter of Durham Cathedral*

How different our lives would be if we could see that sin is not just a
collision with the divine will, but a wound in the divine heart.

Selwyn Hughes

> Nothing in my hand I bring
> Simply to your Cross I cling
> Naked, come to you for dress
> Helpless, look to you for grace
> Foul I to the fountain fly
> Wash me Saviour or I die.
>
> *A.M. Toplady*

The angel said to Mary 'God has been gracious to you. You will become pregnant and will have a son . . . The Holy Spirit will come upon you and God's power will rest upon you.'
Luke 1:30, 35

Since there was no record of the precise day of the year on which Christ was born, Jesus was given an official birthday on December 25 to coincide with the winter solstice celebrations. Once this date was fixed in the fifth century it was a natural progression to celebrate the conception of Jesus on a date exactly nine months earlier, March 25. What a day to dwell on the woman who made her womb and every fibre of her being so wholly available to the Son of God!

> Smooth her hand
> Fair her foot
> Graceful her form
> Winsome her voice
> Gentle her speech
> Stately her mien
> Warm the look of her eye
> Mild the expression of her face
> While her lovely white breast heaves on her bosom
> Like the black-headed sea-gull on the gently heaving wave.
>
> The shield of the Son of God covers her face
> The inspiration of the Son of God guides her
> The word of the Son of God is food to her
> His star is a bright revealing light to her.
>
> The darkness of night is to her as the brightness of day
> The day to her gaze is always a joy
> While the Mary of grace is in every place
> With the seven beatitudes encompassing her.
>
> *Carmina Gadelica*

> Glory be to you
> For the anointing of joy that you gave
> To Mother Mary.
> Glory be to you
> For this queen among the angels
> Causing such delight in heaven
> Such Life on earth.

Jesus went out, carrying his cross, and came to 'The Place of the
Skull' . . . There they crucified him . . . Pilate wrote a notice and had
it put on the cross. 'Jesus of Nazareth the king of the Jews' is what he
wrote.
John 19:17, 19

The large wooden cross beam on to which Christ was nailed was often
called a tree; another term for this was rood. Celtic Christians
understood that this tree, like all creation, was affected by the
crucifixion of Christ, which had cosmic significance. In the ninth
century their imagination produced deeply moving poetry that expresses
this idea. The eighteen foot high Cross that stands inside the church at
Ruthwell, Dumfriesshire, has carved on its sides words spoken by the
Cross. Some one took those few words and expanded them into one of
the great Christian poems in English literature, known as *The Dream of
the Rood*. In this first extract the poet speaks:

> Wondrous was the tree of victory
> and I was stained by sin, stricken by guilt.
> I saw this glorious tree
> joyfully gleaming, adorned with garments,
> decked in gold; the tree of the Ruler
> was rightly adorned with rich stones;
> yet through that gold I could see the agony
> once suffered by wretches, for it had bled
> down the right hand side. Then I was afflicted,
> frightened at this sight; I saw that sign often change
> its clothing and its hue, at times dewy with moisture,
> yet I lay there for a long while
> and gazed sadly at the Saviour's cross;
> until I heard it utter words;
> the finest of trees began to speak.
>   The Dream of the Rood *trans. Kevin Crossley-Holland*

> In the name of the Father it is I come to rest
> Lying on my bed in your name
> O noble King . . .
> I place the tree upon which Christ was crucified
> Between me and the heavy-lying nightmare
> Between me and each evil thing.
>   *From County Cork, collected by Douglas Hyde*

Christ himself carried our sins in his own body to the tree, so that we might be finished with sin and be alive to all that is good.
1 Peter 2:24

In the poem *The Dream of the Rood* the tree now speaks:

> I remember the morning a long time ago
> that I was felled at the edge of the forest
> and severed from my roots. Strong enemies seized me,
> bade me hold up their felons on high,
> and made me a spectacle. Men shifted me
> on their shoulders and set me on a hill.
> Many enemies fastened me there.
> I saw the Lord of humankind
> hasten with such courage to climb upon me.
> I dared not bow or break there
> against my Lord's wish, when I saw the surface
> of the earth tremble.
> I could have felled
> all my foes, yet I stood firm.
> Then the young warrior, God Almighty,
> stripped himself, firm and unflinching.
> He climbed upon the cross, brave before many, to redeem
> humankind . . .
> They drove dark nails into me; dire wounds are there to see,
> the gaping gashes of malice; I dared not injure them.
> They insulted us both together; I was drenched in the blood
> that streamed from the Man's side after he set his spirit free.
>
> The Dream of the Rood *trans. Kevin Crossley-Holland*

> I wrap my soul and my body of fears
> Under your guarding, O Christ.
> O Christ of the tears, of the wounds, of the piercings,
> May your cross this night be our eternal shield
> Your cross between us and all enemies without;
> Your cross between us and all enemies within;
> Your cross our sure way from earth to heaven.

We despised and rejected him; he endured suffering and pain. No one would even look at him – we ignored him as if he were nothing.
Isaiah 53:3

> At the cry of the first bird
> They began to crucify you
> O cheek like a swan
> It was not right ever to cease lamenting
> It was like the parting of day from night.
> Ah! though sore the suffering
> Put upon the body of Mary's Son
> Sorer to Him was the grief
> That was upon her for His sake.
> > *Early Irish Poem*

> We are guilty and polluted, O God
> In spirit, in heart, and in flesh
> In thought, in words, in act
> In your sight we are hardened in sin.
> Put forth to us the power of your love
> Come leaping over the mountains of our transgressions
> Wash us in the blood of conciliation
> Like coming down the mountainside, like the lily of the lake.
> > *Carmina Gadelica*

> Father everlasting and God of Life
> Give us your forgiveness
> In my wild thought
> In my foolish deed
> In my rough talk
> In my empty speech
> Father everlasting and God of life
> Give us your forgiveness
> In my false desire
> In my hateful acts
> In my destructive courses
> In my worthless tastes
> O Father everlasting and God of life
> Crown me with the crown of your love
> > *Carmina Gadelica*

Joseph took the body down, wrapped it in a linen sheet, and placed it in a tomb which had been dug out of solid rock . . . The women who had followed Jesus from Galilee went with Joseph and saw the tomb . . . and went back home and prepared spices and perfumes for the body.
Luke 23:53, 55, 56

There they lifted Him from his heavy torment;
they took Almighty God away.
The warriors left me standing there, stained with blood;
sorely was I wounded by the sharpness of spear-shafts.
They laid him down, limb-weary;
they stood at the corpse's head,
they beheld there the Lord of Heaven;
and there he rested for a while, worn out after battle.
And then they began to build a sepulchre;
under his slayer's eyes, they carved it from the gleaming stone,
and laid therein the Lord of Victories.
Then, sorrowful at dusk
they sang a dirge before they went away, weary
from their glorious Prince;
he rested in the grave alone.
But we still stood there, weeping blood,
long after the song of the warriors
had soared to heaven.
The corpse grew cold, the fair human house of the soul.
        The Dream of the Rood *trans. Kevin Crossley-Holland*

Lord we mourn
for a life of such goodness, cut down in its flower
for a people who forfeited the flowering of their destiny
for a city which turned away from its Saviour
for a planet which rejected its Maker
for ourselves, who languish, alone and lost.

Lord we offer you
like the women who came to your tomb
our tears
the memories of your life
the spices of our faith
the ointment of our tenderness
the flowers of our personality.

Change our sadness into joy

Mary Magdalene and Mary the mother of Jesus were watching and saw
where the body of Jesus was placed.
Mark 15:47

> Today a grave holds him
> who holds creation in the palm of his hand.
> A stone covers him
> who covers with glory the heavens.
> Life is asleep and hell trembles
> and Adam is freed from his chains.
> Glory to your saving work
> by which you have done all things!
> You have given us eternal rest,
> your holy resurrection from the dead.
>
> With a mother's sorrow Mary wept and cried
> 'What Simeon foretold in the temple
> has happened today:
> a sword pierces my soul.
> But change my sadness into joy
> by your resurrection'.
>> *From an Orthodox liturgy for Holy Saturday*

You may be a scholar, able to speak Greek and Hebrew
But in death only the language of God matters.

You may be a craftsman, able to fashion fine furniture
But in death only God's spiritual handiwork survives.

You may be a musician, able to play the harp and lyre
But in death only the Spirit's music persists.

You may be a priest, able to recite long prayers
But in death only prayers of the heart are heard.

Death is only a breath away.
So listen for God's word.
Be transformed by his hand.
Move to his rhythm, And pray to him with all your heart.
>> *Irish, from* Celtic Parables, *Robert Van der Weyer*

Change my sadness into joy by your resurrection.

New every morning, fresh as the sunrise, are the Lord's faithful mercies.
Lamentations 3:23

When last the raging spring storm had abated
And the night's dark banners from the East had fled;
He swiftly rose, and donned his simple raiment
And barefoot left behind his narrow bed.

Heedless of thorn and stone, he sought the seashore
And on a rock he sat and watched the sun
Rise in the East flooding resurrection.
A gull called out, a new day had begun.

Across the calming waters sang the sea-hounds,
Mothers calling for their snowy young
A shoal of fish swam near the rock he sat on
Spinning, spinning silver in the sun.

And one by one he watched the world renewing –
A cricket chirped, a bee sought out a flower.
He picked a shell strewn careless on the shoreline
And marvelled at the Architect's great power.

The sand, each grain, lay perfect in arrangement
To leave the imprint of his searching feet,
Refreshed and calm he retraced his journey
And Oh! the upward climb seemed hard yet sweet.

Who knows this man, what words he used in praying
Or what his soul had seen beyond the sea
Perhaps he was out fishing with his Master
Or busy storing sweetness like the bee?

L. Smith, Dean and Chapter of Durham Cathedral

Deep peace of the green-blue sea
Deep peace of the rising sun
Deep peace of the shore-side Christ
Deep peace of the Risen One
Be ours today.

RISING UP

Fire, water and the tree of life (formed in the shape of a resurrection cross)
illustrate our new life in Christ, in the power of the Holy Spirit.

You have died with Christ . . . you have been raised to life in
Christ . . . you have taken off the old self with its habits and have put
on the new self.
Colossians 2:20; 3:1, 9, 10

The people say that the sun dances on Easter day in joy for a risen
Saviour.

Alexander Carmichael

The glorious gold-bright sun was after rising on the crests of the great
hills, and it was changing colour – green, purple, red, blood-red,
intense white, and gold-white, like the glory of the God of the
elements to the children of men. It was dancing up and down in
exultation at the joyous resurrection of the beloved Saviour of victory.

Old Barbara Macphie told this to Alexander Carmichael

Risen Christ we welcome you.
You are the flowering bough of creation;
From you cascades music like a million stars,
Truth to cleanse a myriad souls.
From you flee demons, omens and all ill will; Around you
  rejoice the angels of light . . .

I rise up clothed in strength of Christ.
I shall not be imprisoned, I shall not be harmed
I shall not be down-trodden, I shall not be left alone
I shall not be tainted, I shall not be overwhelmed
I go clothed in Christ's white garments
I go freed to weave Christ's patterns
I go loved to serve Christ's weak ones
I go armed to rout out Christ's foes.

A Celtic Eucharist, Community of Aidan and Hilda

Christ of the Easter morning
Hope is one of your best gifts to us
So teach us to give it to others.

A prayer from Brazil

Jesus asked his disciples 'Why are you talking about having no bread?
Do you still not see or understand? Are your hearts hardened? . . .
Don't you remember? When I broke the five loaves for the five
thousand, how many baskets of pieces did you pick up?' 'Twelve', they
replied. 'And when I broke the seven loaves for the four thousand,
how many baskets of pieces did you pick up?' They answered, 'Seven.'
Jesus said to them, 'Do you still not understand?'
Mark 8:19–21

Once Ninian sat down for dinner with his brothers and realised that
there were no green vegetables on the table. 'Run down to the garden
and pick some of the vegetables that are springing up,' he asked
someone. The chief gardener intervened: 'There won't be any growth
yet, I was still planting seeds this morning.' 'In that case,' said Ninian,
'go in the faith of the Lord to search for vegetables, for God Almighty
can accomplish anything.' The gardener quickly made his way to the
heart of the garden, and to his surprise found all sorts of vegetables
springing up and sprouting. He returned to the brothers and was able
to share vegetables with them all.
   Ninian was given a gift of faith for a particular occasion. This was
possible because he constantly cultivated an attitude of faith. We, too,
can cultivate an attitude of faith, by frequently meditating on Scriptures
and stories like those for today. As we do this, we will be given
promptings that are in fact a gift of faith for a particular need. Look out
for such an occasion today.

   May the blessing of the five loaves and the two fishes,
   which God shared out among the five thousand, be ours.
   May the King who did the sharing bless our sharing.

   May the food we eat restore our strength,
   give new energy to tired limbs, new thoughts to weary minds.
   May our drink restore our souls
   give new vision to dry spirits,
   new warmth to cold hearts.
   And once refreshed, may we give new pleasure to you
   who gives us all.

                                                  Celtic graces

The righteous will ask 'When, Lord, did we see you hungry and feed you? . . .' The King will reply, 'I tell you, whenever you did this for one of the least important of these my brothers and sisters, you did it for me.'
Matthew 25:37, 40

The story is told that one Easter day, when King Oswald had sat down with Bishop Aidan, a silver dish was placed on the table before him full of rich foods. They had just raised their hands to ask a blessing on the bread when there came in an officer of the king, whose duty it was to relieve the needy, telling him that a very great multitude of poor people from every district were sitting in the precincts and asking alms of the king. He at once ordered the dainties which had been set in front of him to be carried to the poor, the dish to be broken up, and the pieces divided amongst them.

The bishop, who was sitting by, was delighted with this devoted action, grasped Oswald by the right hand, and said, 'May this hand never decay.' His blessing and his prayer were fulfilled in this way: when Oswald was killed in battle, his hand and arm were cut off from the rest of his body, and they have remained uncorrupt until this present time; they are in fact preserved in a silver shrine in St Peter's church, in the royal city (later named Bamburgh).

From Bede's The Ecclesiatical History of the English People

O beloved Father who has redeemed us
and who reigns serenely as sun and sea
may you forgive us our sins both past and present.
Remedy in heaven our faults
and may we today welcome with joy our Lord.

An Timire *collected by Sean O Floin.*
Mount Melleray Monastery, Ireland.

Women received back their dead, raised to life again.
Hebrews 11:35.

A number of Irish Christians gained a remarkable reputation for
bringing dead people back to life. Among these was Tighernach, who
went to heaven on 4 April 549. Eithne, the daughter of the king of
Munster had committed suicide rather than be forced to marry a British
Prince against her will. She had desired to follow a calling as a virgin
dedicated to God. Tighernach prayed over her and brought her back to
life.

It seems the Lord gave Kieran the Elder a unique ministry to the
victims of group casualties. Seven harpers of Aengus were waylaid and
killed by brigands while on a journey, and were found, apparently dead,
beside the track. Kieran prayed over them and they were all restored.

According to legend, a local ruler wanted to arrange decent funerals
for a group of his soldiers who had been killed in battle, but there were
not enough vehicles to arrange the funerals. Kieran once again came to
the rescue, prayed over the soldiers, and they, too, were restored to life.

We have accurate accounts of Cuthbert's visits to the plague-ridden
Northumbrian people. He trudged through the devastated villages to
minister to the few poor people who remained. Cuthbert was about to
leave one village when he asked the priest, 'Are you sure there is no
one left whom I have not seen?' The priest looked around, and found
one tear-stained woman standing at a distance. She had lost one son in
the plague, and now seemed about to lose her other son, whom she
was holding in her arms. Cuthbert made his way to her, blessed her,
kissed the boy, and said to his mother, 'There is no need to be sad any
more. Your infant will be healed and will live, and no one else in your
family will die from this plague.' Mother and son both lived long to
bear witness to Cuthbert's life-giving ministry.

> Lead us from death to life
> From the death of disease to the life of wholeness
> From the death of despair to the life of hope
> From the death of the body to the life of resurrection.

Eutychus fell to the ground from the third storey and was picked up dead. Paul went down, threw himself on the young man and put his arms around him. 'Don't be alarmed', he said. 'He's alive!' The people took the young man home and were greatly comforted.
Acts 20:9, 10, 12.

Thieves planned to carry off by night some bullocks that belonged to Ninian's community. That same day, however, Ninian prayed for God's blessing on his herds before staying the night with a neighbour.

This had an effect on the thieves. First they were overcome with dizziness and stumbled around in a way that unsettled a bull. The bull attacked them and gored the leader.

Next morning, as a Spirit-filled Ninian returned, he found the panic-stricken men around their leader who was now dead. 'Tell me, why did you wish to harm a person who never wished to harm or cheat you in even the smallest way?' Ninian asked them. Then he made a most magnanimous gesture. In the name of God he released them from sin and from all ill effects of what they had done.

But that is not the end of the story. Ninian knelt beside the dead man and prayed, 'O Christ, throned on high, I beg you to give life to this corpse. Impart warmth to his whole body; let the spirit enter into his frozen limbs and restore the functions of life.' The deceased man came back to life. The men, who were terror-struck, started to speak heartfelt words to the Lord.

> Raise us from greed to generosity
> Raise us from falseness to friendship
> Raise us from death to life.

You have been raised to life with Christ, so set your hearts on the
things that are of heaven.
Colossians 3:1

The resurrection of Christ turned the page of human history. It can also
bring a new page in to our tatty and tattered lives.

In the Book of Kells there is no picture of the resurrection but only
the word 'Una', in the centre of the page, to denote the first day of the
week, the day of resurrection. George Otto Sims describes the
resurrection page of that book as follows:

Angels are guarding the capital letter U, one at each of its four
corners. It looks at first like a dark, dull page, but out of the dim
gloom the feet, the hands and the faces of the four angels, painted with
white lead, shine out gleaming and bright. These angels are looking up
and out from the page . . . They are alive and alert, not asleep, nor
downcast. Their message is 'Christ is risen, he is not here. Why look
for the living among the dead?'

We also observe, in the top right-hand corner, that the fierce
monster is speeding away out of the picture. The power of this enemy
has been overcome. The beast is on his way out, defeated . . . The
capital U, with a tangle of graceful birds in the heart of the letter, and
surrounded by guardian angels, helps us to have a picture in our minds
of the empty tomb on the first Easter Day.

> *George Otto Simms in* Exploring the Book of Kells *Dublin 1988*

> Last night Christ the Sun rose from the dark.
> The mystic harvest of the fields of God
> And now the little wandering tribes of bees
> Are brawling in the scarlet flowers abroad.
> The winds are soft with bird song all night long
> Darkling the nightingale her descant told
> And now inside church doors the happy folk
> The Alleluia chant a hundredfold.
> O Father of your folk, be yours by right
> The Easter joy, the threshold of the light.
>
> *Sedulius Scottus*

As members of a sinful race all people die; as members of Christ all people shall be raised to life.
1 Corinthians 15:22

A pious and formidable woman named Canair had a vision while praying in her hermit's hut. She saw a tower of fire rise from every church in Ireland, but the tallest and straightest towards heaven of these towers arose from an island called Inis Cathaig. 'I must leave here, and go and live there,' Canair decided, 'for that will be the place of my resurrection.'

Unfortunately for her, the hermit Senan who already lived there was equally formidable as well as pious. The presence of women on the island he had made his own was not part of his vision. Canair got there by following the vision of the tower of fire which was ever before her. Senan welcomed her at the harbour, but suggested she travel on to her sister who lived some miles away. 'I have not come here in order to do that,' Canair retorted, 'I have come here to stay with you on this island.' 'Women do not enter this island,' declared Senan, but Canair was not to be outdone.

'How can you say that? Christ came to redeem women no less than men. He suffered for women just as much as he suffered for men. Women have always tended and served Christ and his apostles. Women just as much as men enter the kingdom of heaven. So why can't you receive women on your island?' 'You are stubborn,' Senan told her. 'In that case shall I get what I ask for — a place for myself on this island and to receive the Sacrament from you?'

'You will be given your place of resurrection,' said Senan, 'but it will be here on the sea's edge; and I fear the sea will carry off your remains.' 'The spot of earth on which my dead body shall lie will not be the first spot of earth that this sea will carry away,' the lady asserted.

Who had the last word? Canair had hardly noticed that while they had been debating, the sea had come up to her waist. So they had to move a little up the shore, where Senan did give her Holy Communion. And Canair went straight to heaven.

Recorded in The Lives of the Saints *from* The Book of Lismore

Thank you, Lord, that even if we are difficult or blinkered people,
You can put holy desires into our hearts
And divine intimations before our eyes
So that we come through obstacles to our eternal resurrection.

Throughout our lives we are always in danger of death for Jesus' sake, in order that his life may be seen in this mortal body of ours. This means that death is at work in us but life is at work in you . . . For we know that God who raised the Lord Jesus to life, will also raise us up with Jesus and bring us, together with you, into his presence.
2 Corinthians 4:10,11,14

Once a year at the Spring solstice the King of Tara, High King of all Ireland, gathered together the regional kings, their druids, shamans, bards and advisors to the high Hill of Tara. There, at a giant celebration, they lit a bonfire with the aim of invoking the Sun to shower beneficently upon them and their crops in the coming season. On that day, it was forbidden for any one else to light a fire.

Patrick, knowing of this celebration, but unaware of the ban on the lighting of other fires, ascended the hill of Slane, which could be seen from Tara. There, he and his fellow Christians lit a large fire to celebrate the resurrection of their Lord Jesus Christ, true God, Sun of Suns. High King Loegaire was extremely disturbed, and ordered his staff to arrest them and bring them to him. His shamans intuited immediately what this was all about. 'If the fire of this new religion is not put out this night it will not be put out until Doomsday. Moreover, the person who kindles it will supersede the kings and rulers of Ireland unless he is banned,' they told the king.

When they came with their chariots to arrest Patrick, he, according to the medieval Life of St Patrick, quoted Scriptures such as 'Some trust in chariots and some in horses but we will trust in the name of our mighty God,' (Psalm 20:7) and 'Let God arise and scatter his enemies, (Psalm 68:1). A storm ensued so violent that the horses and their riders fled. Although the king's men lay in wait to catch Patrick and his men as they left, all they saw passing them was a herd of deer. That is how the tradition grew that as these Christians prayed 'Patrick's Breastplate' God shielded them from their enemies' eyes, and it is why that prayer is known as 'The Deer's Cry'.

I arise today
Through the strength of Christ's birth and baptism.
I arise today through the strength of Christ's crucifixion and burial.
I arise today through the strength of his resurrection and ascension.
From St Patrick's Breastplate

A man from the household of Jairus, the synagogue leader, came and said : 'Your daughter has died; do not trouble the Teacher any more.'
Luke 8:49

The Travelling People have a special place in Irish life, and they can offer fresh perspectives on old truths. Travellers assume that anyone who has a house big enough to have stairs must be very important, so they call such a person 'one of them'. Although many Travellers cannot read, they can learn and tell a Bible story like no one else, as the following version illustrates:

'T'was like this. Jesus Christ was goin' along the road and the sun was blazin' an' he was all sweatin' and the crowds were all there after him; and they were shoutin' and roarin' and beltin' each other. Then all of a sudden up cums a big man, important and one of them, an' he drops down an' looks up at Jesus Christ, and says to him: 'Jesus Christ, would ye ever help me? Me daughter's back home an' she's dead or near it. Would ye ever make her better?' Say he: 'I will, of course. Cum on back and show me where ye live'. Then back he goes, the two of 'em, till they cum to the big man's house and in they go. And ye know what? T'was a house with stairs. Stairs all the way up, and didn't Jesus go up them stairs, an' he was nearly deaf 'cos there was loads of women an' they were bawlin' and shoutin' and he's never heard anything like them. An' he stops there on the stairs with his hands shuttin' off the noise from his ears, an' says he: 'Will ye shut up and get out, the lot of ye!' An' didnt they do so, an' there was just Jesus Christ there with the daddy an' the mammy an' the corpse. An' says he to the corpse: 'Get ye up out of that!' An' she, she opened her eyes an' looks at him, an' she's able to get straight up there an' look at him again. An' she wasn't sick any more. An' Jesus Christ, he looks at her too. An' he sees she's well, an' says he to the mammy, 'Give her a cut o' bread.'

> Living Christ, you can do anything, anything, anything!
> You can come to my house, to the most out-of-reach house!
> I name the person I have lost faith for . . .
> Come to their place of unbelief.
> Come today.

Christ's Body is God's property

Mary Magdalene stood crying outside the tomb of Jesus . . . Jesus came
to her and said 'Mary'. She turned towards him . . . 'Do not hold on
to me,' Jesus told her.
John 20:11, 16, 17.

How many people are put off Christianity because the members of the
church, which is Christ's Body, treat it in a possessive way? If that is
our failing, learn the lesson Mary Magdalene had to learn from the risen
Christ, and hand his Body back to God, for it is God's property.

One of Ireland's most poignant spots is the island hermitage at
Gougane Barra, founded by Finbarr. Finbarr was instructed by Bishop
MacCuirb, a fellow pupil of David of Wales. He went to live at Loch
Iree and started a school for Bible students. Five of these students, as
well as other people, established churches and offered them to the
oversight of Finbarr. Finbarr himself established a church in his home
area, but God told him that would not be his place of resurrection. So
Finbarr crossed the river to Gougane Barra and built a place of worship
there where he stayed for a considerable time.

However, two of his former pupils received a prophecy, 'Gougane
Barra will be your place of resurrection.' They dared not believe this,
since it seemed obvious that this was Finbarr's place. Finbarr welcomed
them for a visit and they talked and prayed things through. 'Don't be
depressed,' Finbarr told them, 'I give this church and all its treasures to
you and to God.'

Finbarr built a total of twelve churches, and gave them all away. God
led him further along the river and told him 'This will be your place of
resurrection'. Today that place is Cork City, and the exquisite spires of
its St Finbarr's cathedral sparkle like jewels above the city.

> Lord of the church, Servant King,
> Take from us attitudes and practices
> That put barriers between the church and the people:
> Cultural elitism in worship
> Clerical status
> Looking down on people
> Treating the church as our property.
> Make us a pilgrim people,
> A church without walls.

I trust you will know that we are not failures. We pray to God that you will do no wrong – not in order to show that we are a success, but so that you may do what is right, even though we may seem to be failures. For we cannot do a thing against the truth, only for it.
2 Corinthians 13:7, 8

The man who wrote a biography of David of Wales five hundred years after David's death was so keen to promote his own diocese that he would record any bit of folk lore, however far-fetched, that served to make his diocese seem more important.

So although we cannot take all that is written at face value, it would be foolish not to reflect upon those episodes which, when the embroidery is removed, were clearly believed to have taken place.

One such is the belief that Patrick, when he returned to his parents on the north west coast of Britain, came on a mission to Dyfed, and intended to settle at an attractive place there named Rosina Vallis. However, an angel spoke to him in a vision, 'God has not planned this place for you, but for a son of his (David) who will not be born until the next generation.' Patrick probably felt rejected and rather a failure, until God gave him the call to be the leader of a mission to Ireland, affirming him with these words, 'You will be radiant with signs and virtues, bringing the whole nation under my rule. I will be with you.' The place where this vision was given came to be known as Patrick's Seat.

Patrick made his preparations, and before he boarded the boat for Ireland, God used him to raise someone from the dead!

How often do we feel a failure? Remember Patrick's Seat. He felt a failure, but went on to raise someone from the dead and to win a nation to Christ! Find a seat where you can contemplate, not what is not to be, but what, under God, is yet to be. There is always a 'yet to be' with God. The darkest moment of night comes just before the dawn.

> You pour your grace on those in distress
> Without stop or stint.
> Son of Mary, Son of the disappointments,
> Who was, who shall be
> With ebb and flow
> Be with me wherever I go.

The Son only does what he sees his Father doing . . . I only say what
the Father has told me to say.
John 5:19; 8:28

The importance of tuning in to the deeper, unseen currents that shape
our lives and civilisation is understood by increasing numbers of people
who are in touch with the intuitive or feminine side of human nature.
They sometimes meet Christians who fear or denounce this, and this
puts them off Christianity. These Christians may have a point – for it
may be better to be deaf than to listen in to falsehood – but why
should the devil have all the best ears? The pre-Christian Celtic people,
notably the shamans, had finely developed powers of seeing into people
and the future, but this power was divorced from a relationship with
Father God as revealed by Jesus. The Celtic saints reassure us that it is
possible for Christians to develop intuitive powers, as did Jesus, in a
way that attunes them only to the Father's wavelength.

   Cuthbert was having a working lunch with a member of the
Northumbrian royal family, the Abbess Aelfflaed, when he seemed to
have a seizure, and his dinner knife fell from his hands. At first he made
light of it, but then they drew out of him what he had 'seen' – the
soul of a man from Aelfflaed's estate being suddenly snatched from this
earth. Aelfflaed only thought to enquire about the well-being of her
monks, she did not enquire about all her lay estate workers. But the
next day they discovered that, though the monks were all well, a
shepherd named Hadwald had fallen from a tree and died at that very
hour. The point of this is not obvious, but I wonder if it was God's
way of ensuring that the least should be treated as the greatest in the
kingdom of heaven? Cuthbert had many other 'seeings' which affected
the future of political powers, the course of the church's mission, and
his own future after his death, but I like to think that these 'tunings'
come for the same purpose that Christ came – to seek and to save
those who are most needy and lost.

                Make me attentive to the lap of the waves
                Make me attentive to the movements of the sky
                Make me attentive to the grasses that grow
                Make me attentive to the soul's every sigh
                Make me aware of the landscape that must pass
                Make me aware of the new scape coming in
                Make me aware of the universe within
                Make me aware of the beatings of your heart.

Be still and know that I am God.
Psalm 46:10

> In the ground of your being I have my home
> so do not seek me in the world apart.
> Within your spirit true communion lies.
> You are no homeless stranger in a land afar
> no alien in a foreign shore
> for I am with you.
> Do but be still and know that I am God.
> I look upon the world with your dark eyes
> I feel the flowing air on your cool cheek
> I hear the twittering in the moving trees
> for with your senses I perceive.
> I am with you, I am within you.
> So do not turn away but come to rest in me.
> Within you is our meeting place.
> But be still, and I will speak in silence
> to your loving, wayward heart.
>
> *Dame Paula Fairlie*

> God with me lying down
> God with me rising up
> God with me in each ray of light
> Nor I a ray of joy without him.
>
> Christ with me sleeping
> Christ with me waking
> Christ with me watching
> Every day and night.
>
> God with me protecting
> God with me directing
> The Spirit with me strengthening
> For ever and for evermore.
> Chief of Chiefs. Amen.
>
> *Carmina Gadelica*

If you have ears to hear with, then listen!
Matthew 11:15

Go to your cell; it will teach you all things.
Sayings of the Desert Fathers

Be slow to anger, quick to learn, also slow to speak, as St James says,
and equally quick to listen.

Columbanus.

By quietly listening to the description of the stages, transitions and
miraculous deeds of a saint's life, we can begin to discern and appreciate
our life patterns as well as our own kinship with Jesus.
Edward C. Sellner Wisdom of the Celtic Saints

God gave us two ears and one mouth. Why don't we listen twice as
much as we talk?

Chinese proverb

Listen . . .

to the fragile feelings, not to the clashing fury
to the quiet sounds, not to the loud clamour
to the steady heartbeat, not to the noisy confusion
to the hidden voices, not to the obvious chatter
to the deep harmonies, not to the surface discord
Anon

You be my wisdom, you my true Word,
I ever with you, and you with me Lord
You my great Father and I your true son
You in me dwelling and I with you one.
Irish 8th century

Lord, a thousand voices shout at me this day,
Sound-bites and slogans, images and screens,
Conversations and traffic, newspapers and internet . . .
Help me to filter out and turn away
All that is not of you,
And to spot and hold to
All that is of you.

Let a person dwell alone in silence, for the Lord has laid this upon them.
Lamentations 3:28

God calls most, if not all, of us to sometimes draw apart and be silent. And God calls some people to make this the main call upon their lives. Solitaries who are following such a call (as distinct from people who are running away from something) should be encouraged. In The Catalogue of the Saints of Ireland there was an entire order of such people – anchorites.

An old Celtic word for prayer meant literally 'the quiet of Christ'. The Celtic Christians learned the value of silence from the desert fathers and mothers. It was said that Abba Agatha carried a pebble in his mouth for three years until he learned to be silent.

Allow me with your peace and charity to remain in silence in these woods.

Columbanus in a Letter to the French Bishops

Silence is the element in which great things fashion themselves together.

Thomas Carlysle

Souls of prayer are souls of deep silence. That is why we must accustom ourselves to deep stillness of the soul. God is the friend of silence. See how nature, the trees, the flowers, the grass grow in deep silence. See how the stars, the moon, and the sun move in silence. The more we receive in our silent prayer, the more we can give in our active life. Silence gives us a new way of looking at everything. We need this silence in order to touch souls. Jesus is waiting for us in the silence. It is there that he speaks to our souls. Interior silence is very difficult but we must make the effort to pray. A soul of prayer can make progress without recourse to words by learning to be present to Christ. In silence we find a new energy and a real unity.

Mother Teresa of Calcutta

> In silence I become aware of you, O Lord
> In the silence I adore you, O Lord
> In the silence my sins stand out and are washed away
> In the silence my problems fall into their rightful place.
> In the silence I become a grateful person
> And in the silence, O Lord, we become one.

I will instruct you and teach you in the way that you should go.
Psalm 32:8

Towards the end of the ninth century the monks of Lindisfarne set sail
for Ireland to escape a renewed Viking invasion. They took with them
their priceless book, now known as *The Lindisfarne Gospels*. Tragically,
they hit bad weather, the boat heeled over to one side, and the copy of
the Gospels, adorned with gold figures, fell overboard and sank to the
bottom of the sea.

The monks postponed their voyage and returned to dry land. There
they were given a vision, in which God directed them to go to the
shore at Whithorn, the Christian community on the western coast of
Scotland, founded by Ninian. When they arrived there they found that,
due to an unusually low tide, the sea had receded much further out
than usual. They went a mile or two out from the shore. There, to
their amazement and joy, they found their precious volume, still with
the covers clasped together. The gold was unspoilt, and the colours had
not run. Nobody could have guessed that it had ever had contact with
water.

Recorded in Symeon's History of the Church of Durham 12th century

Men and women guided by God are the greatest forces in shaping
history.

Dutch atomic scientist

The Holy Spirit is the most intelligent source of information in the
world.

Frank Buchman

> Lord, you have a plan
> For every person
> And for every situation in the world.
> But we are so dim.
> We are so deaf.
> Help us to be become wholly God-guided instruments
> And to always be in just the place you wish us to be.

Master and Creator of heaven, earth, and sea, and all that is in
them! . . . Stretch out your hand to heal.
Acts 4:24, 30

> Come, O Creator Spirit, come
> Enter our minds and fill our hearts
> Implant in us grace from above
> May your creatures show forth your love
> Past ages called you Paraclete
> Gift to humanity of God Most High
> Well-spring of life, fire, charity
> And anointing Spirit of peace
> You bring to us your seven gifts
> You are the Power of God's right hand
> The Promise of God to the church
> Words of life upon human lips.
> Illumine our hearts anew
> And pour your love into our souls.
> Refresh our weak frame with new strength
> Fortitude and grace to endure
> Cast away our deadly foe
> Grant us your peace for evermore
> With you as our Guide on the way
> Evil shall not more harm our souls
> Teach us the Trinity to know
> In Father, Son and Spirit, One:
> The Three in One and One in Three
> Now and ever, eternally.
>
> *A Modern adaption of* Veni Creator,
> *ascribed to Rabanus Maurus,*
> *a 6th century Solitary in Gaul*

Come, O Holy Spirit, come

The wind blows wherever it wishes; you hear the sound it makes but
you do not know where it comes from or where it is going. It is like
that with everyone who is born of the Spirit.
John 2:8

Breathe in Christ with every breath.
                    Antony of Egypt

> Long years ago across the western water
> Winds brought to this our shore
> One glorious within, a king's own daughter
> To teach our land Christ's law.
> *Cornish hymn for St Buryan (who landed near St Ives with Piran)*

> Blessed be the wind
> Without wind most of the earth would be uninhabitable
> The tropics would grow so unbearably hot.
>   *Lyall Watson*

Once when Columba was at sea a great storm, with gusts of wind
blowing from all sides, arose and his boat was buffeted by great waves.
Columba tried to help the sailors bail out the water that came into the
boat, but they said to him, 'Your doing this does little to help us in this
danger. You would do better to pray for us as we perish.' Columba
stopped bailing water, and began to pour out prayers aloud to God.
Marvellous to relate, as soon as he stood up in the prow and raised his
hands to God the wind ceased and the sea stilled. The crew were
amazed and gave glory to God.

                                    Adamnan

> Wind, wind blow on me
> Blow away the cobwebs that clog the spirit
> Blow upwards the suffocating airs of unbelief
> Blow near the things that are pure and good
> Blow through me the breath of God's presence
> Blow me along the path of your choice.

'Whoever believes in me, life-giving streams of water will pour out from their heart.' Jesus said this about the Spirit, which those who believed in him were going to receive.
John 7:38, 39

The author of life is the fountain of life . . . Let us seek the fountain of life, the fountain of living water, like intelligent and most wise fish, that there we may drink the living water that springs up to eternal life.

Columbanus.

Slake your thirst from the streams of the divine fountain. The fountain of life calls to us, 'Let whoever is thirsty come to me and drink.'

Take note what you are to drink; remember what God spoke through Jeremiah, 'They have forsaken me, the fountain of living water, and drunk from leaking cisterns.' The person who thus drinks is the person who loves, who draws satisfaction from the Word of God, who adores, who yearns, who burns with the love of wisdom.

Adapted from the Gaelic

Fechin had a God-given ability to cause water to flow in dry places. St Fechin's well, in County Sligo, Ireland, marks the place where he prayed for a source of water for a parched region. At Fore, life was so hard for the monks that Fechin hewed out rock with his own hands until water burst through. At Omly, he immersed the entire pagan population in the waters of baptism. At his death in 665 a friend saw a light so bright that all Ireland's demons fled for a time.

> What would the world be
> Once bereft of wet and of wildness?
> Let them be left, O let them be left
> Wetness and wildness.
> *Gerard Manley Hopkins*

> Bathe us in your cleansing rivers.
> Soak us in your healing waters.
> Drench us in your powerful down-falls.
> Cool us in your bracing baths.
> Refresh us in your sparkling streams.
> Master us in your mighty seas.
> Calm us by your quiet pools.

Jesus said: I came to bring fire to the earth.
Luke 12:49

From the age of eight until he entered a monastery Cuthbert was
brought up by a Christian nanny named Kenswith, a widow who had
become a nun. Cuthbert always called her 'mother' and often visited
her in her old age. Once when he was lodging in his 'mother's' village
a house on the eastern edge caught fire and a fierce wind blew the
flames towards the houses, looking set to cause a conflagration.

A panic-stricken Kenswith ran to the house where Cuthbert was
staying and begged him to ask God to save their homes. Cuthbert
calmly turned to her with the words, 'Don't worry, the flames will do
no harm.' Then he lay prostrate on the earth outside the house and
prayed silently. As he was praying a strong, fresh wind arose from the
west and drove the flames away from the houses, so that no harm was
caused. The people were not ungrateful; they took the trouble to give
thanks to the Lord.

Fire is a powerful force and, as this story illustrates, can destroy; but
it is also a positive force, and is a biblical symbol of God's Spirit. The
term 'Celtic fire' is used to describe the living faith at the heart of the
Celtic peoples. This was symbolised by the fire that, in monasteries, as
in homes, was kept alight night and day. It was said that the fire at
Brigid's monastery at Kildare was kept alight for a thousand years.

> Thank you, Father, for your free gift of fire
> because it is through fire that you draw near to us every day;
> It is with fire that you constantly bless us.
> Our Father, bless this fire today.
> With your power enter into it.
> Make this fire a worthy thing.
> A thing that carries your blessing.
> Let it become a reminder of your love.
> A reminder of life without end.
> Make the life of this people be baptised like this fire.
> A thing that shines for the sake of people.
> A thing that shines for your sake.
> Father, heed this sweet smelling smoke.
> Make their life also sweet smelling.
> A holy thing.
> A thing fitting for you.

A Masai prayer.

The Lord knows what we are made of, that we are but dust. Our days are but as grass.
Psalm 103:14, 15

Earth to earth, ashes to ashes.
Funeral Service, Book of Common Prayer

> To be of the earth is to know the restlessness of being a seed
> the darkness of being planted
> the struggle towards the light
> the pain of growth into the light
> the joy of bursting and bearing fruit
> the love of being food for someone
> the scattering of your seeds
> the decay of the seasons
> the mystery of death
> and the miracle of birth.
>
> *John Soos*

Earth teach me stillness as the grasses are stilled with light
Earth teach me suffering as old stones suffer with memory
Earth teach me humility as blossoms are humble with beginning
Earth teach me caring as the mother who secures her young
Earth teach me courage as the tree which stands all alone
Earth teach me limitation as the ant which crawls on the ground
Earth teach me freedom as the eagle which soars in the sky
Earth teach me resignation as the leaves which die in the fall
Earth teach me regeneration as the seed which rises in the spring
Earth teach me to forget myself as melted snow forgets its life
Earth teach me to remember kindness as dry fields weep for rain.
Ute Prayer

> Creator, make me malleable, like your earth
> Saviour, make me humble, like your earth
> Spirit, make me receptive, like your earth.

'Give us some of your oil for our lamps.' They replied, 'We may not have enough; go and buy some for yourselves.'
Matthew 25:8, 9

The oil in this parable, as we shall see, represents God's Holy Spirit.

The Celtic tradition of hermits living close to God and nature was lost or overlaid in the West; but in the East this tradition continued and, in a country such as Russia, it flowered in the tradition of the Staretz, or holy hermit who lived alone, but in deep solidarity with the people of his neighbourhood. Seraphim was a notable Russian Staretz of the nineteenth century whom I look upon as a Soul Friend for followers of Celtic spirituality. He once had this conversation about the Holy Spirit, sitting on a stool by his cell in the forest, with young Nicholas Motovilov, whom he called Friend of God:

'When you were a child you wanted to know the purpose of the Christian life but none of the ecclesiastics told you. I will try to tell you. Prayer and good works are good, but they are only means to an end. The true end of the Christian life is to acquire the Holy Spirit.'
'What do you mean by acquisition?' Nicholas asked. 'You know what it means to earn money, don't you? Well, the Holy Spirit is also capital, but eternal capital. Our Lord compares our life to trading and says, "Buy gold from me" (Revelation 3.18). Good works, if they are done for the love of Christ, bring us the fruits of the Holy Spirit.

'In the parable of the virgins at a wedding (Matthew 25. 9–15) the foolish virgins were told to buy oil for their lamps. What they were lacking was the grace of the Holy Spirit. So you see that the one essential thing is not just to do good, but to acquire the Holy Spirit as the one eternal treasure which will never pass away . . .

'This Holy Spirit, the All-powerful, takes up his dwelling in us and prepares in our souls and bodies a dwelling place for the Father.'

Seraphim of Zarov

> Come Holy Ghost, our souls inspire
> And lighten with celestial fire.
> Thou the anointing Spirit art,
> Who dost Thy sevenfold gifts impart.
> *Veni Creator 9th century*

Be aglow with the Spirit.
Romans 12:11

If you would get the centre of your soul right, you should first of all get ready the needed materials, so that the heavenly Architect can begin to make the building. The house must be light and airy, with windows, which are the five senses, so that the light of heaven, the Sun of righteousness, can penetrate to our inner dwelling. The door of the house is Christ in person, for he said 'I am the door.'

When mind and heart are united in prayer, without any distraction, you feel that spiritual warmth which comes from Christ and fills the whole inner being with joy and peace. We have to withdraw from the visible world so that the light of Christ can come down into our heart. Closing our eyes, concentrating our attention on Christ, we must try to unite the mind with the heart, and, from the depths of our whole being, we must call on the Name of our Lord, saying, 'Lord Jesus Christ, have mercy on me a sinner.'

To the degree that love for the Lord Jesus warms the human heart, one finds in the Name of Jesus a sweetness that is the source of abiding peace.

Seraphim of Zarov

Let us recall again St Patrick's experience:

The love and fear of God increased more and more in me and my faith began to grow, and my spirit to be stirred up, so that in one day I would say as many as a hundred prayers and nearly as many at night, even when I was staying out in the woods or on the mountain. And I used to rise before dawn for prayer, in snow and frost and rain, and I used to feel no ill effect and there was no slackness in me. I now realise it was because the Spirit was glowing in me.

St Patrick

> Eternal Creator of day and night
> Cleanse us by your refining fire
> Kindle in us the Pentecostal flame
> And make our hearts burn with heavenly desires.

The fruit of the Spirit is joy.
Galations 5:22

The expression on his face seemed so extraordinary. A light shone from within, illuminating his features. His whole being seemed enfolded in the grace of the Holy Spirit and raised above the earth.

He spoke to me about the heavenly joys of those who have a share in God's glory. It was as though he himself was actually living all this at that very moment, partaking of this bliss and enabling me to live it with him. He seemed unable to find words to express what he was experiencing, so he ended: 'O my joy, such bliss, such beatitude, I cannot describe it all!'

Anne Eropkine, describing her visit to Fr Seraphim in 1830

When Cuthbert returned to the Farne Isle to lead the life of a hermit 'he spent almost two months greatly rejoicing in his new found quiet'. Once he sent some visitors on their way with the injunction to cook the goose that was hanging in the visitors's hut. They in fact left it there, having plenty of food, but then they found the weather turned against them and they could not sail for day after day. Eventually Cuthbert went over to their hut and explained 'with unruffled mien and even with joyful words' that their problems were caused by their failure to eat the goose as he had advised. They immediately cooked the goose, and the weather immediately became fair. They returned home with some feelings of shame because they had not taken Cuthbert's words seriously, but with even greater feelings of joy, because they realised God took such good care of his servant Cuthbert that he even used the elements to give a gentle rebuke to those who took his words too lightly. They rejoiced because the Creator took such good care of themselves that he corrected them by means of a miracle.

> Grant me the grace to appreciate your providence
> To contemplate your glory
> And to become part of creation's song of joy

The fruit of the Spirit is . . . peace.
Galations 5:22

Learn to be peaceful, and thousands around you will find salvation . . .
There is nothing better than peace in Christ, for it brings victory over
all the evil spirits on earth and in the air. When peace dwells in a
person's heart it enables them to contemplate the grace of the Holy
Spirit from within. The person who lives in peace collects spiritual gifts
as it were with a scoop, and sheds the light of knowledge on others. All
our thoughts, all our desires, all our efforts, and all our actions should
make us say constantly with the Church, 'O Lord, give us peace!'.
When a person lives in peace, God reveals mysteries to them.

Seraphim of Zarov

Live in peace
Columbanus

> Peace of all felicity
> Peace of shining clarity
> Peace of joys consolatory.
>
> Peace of souls in surety
> Peace of heaven's futurity
> Peace of virgin's purity.
>
> Peace of the enchanted bowers
> Peace of calm reposing hours
> Peace of everlasting, ours.

George McLean (trans) Poems of the Western Highlanders

> Deep peace of the quiet earth
> Deep peace of the still waters
> Deep peace of the setting sun
> Deep peace of the forgiving heart
> Deep peace of the true call
> Deep peace of the Son of Peace
> Be ours, today, for ever.

He will baptise you with holy spirit and with fire.
Luke 3:16

As Seraphim enthused about people in the Bible whose lives
overflowed with the Holy Spirit , his young friend Nicholas Motovilov
interjected, 'But how can I know that I myself have this grace of the
Holy Spirit?'

Seraphim gripped him firmly by the shoulders and said, 'My friend,
both of us this moment are in the Holy Spirit, you and I. Why don't
you look at me?'

'I can't look at you, because the light flashing from your eyes and
face is brighter than the sun and I am dazzled!' Nicholas replied. 'Don't
be afraid, friend of God, you yourself are shining just like I am; you,
too are now in the fullness of the Holy Spirit, otherwise you wouldn't
be able to see me as you do.'

Nicholas later wrote about what he saw, 'You can see only the
blinding light which spreads everywhere, lighting up the layers of snow
covering the glade, and igniting the flakes that are falling on us both
like white power.'

Then Seraphim drew out of him, step by step, what he was feeling.
'An amazing well-being . . . a great calm in my soul . . . a peace which
no words can express . . . a strange unknown delight . . . an amazing
happiness . . .' Seraphim related each of these to experiences recounted
in the Bible.

Seraphim of Zarov

In whom does the Holy Spirit dwell? In the one who is pure without
sin. It is then that a person is a vessel of the Holy Spirit, when the
virtues have come in place of the vices.

Colmán mac Béognae The Alphabet of Devotion

> O Thou who camest from above
> The pure, celestial fire to impart
> Kindle a flame of sacred love
> On the mean altar of my heart.
> *Charles Wesley*

Be filled with the Spirit.
Ephesians 5:18

In 1931 Seraphim asked his young God-seeker, Motovilov,
'What are you feeling, friend of God?' 'I'm amazingly warm,' his friend
replied. 'Warm? What are you saying my friend? We are in the depths
of the forest, in mid-winter, the snow lies under our feet and is settling
on our clothes. How can you be warm?' 'It's the warmth one feels in a
hot bath.' 'Does it smell like that?' 'Oh no! Nothing on earth can
compare to this. There's no scent in all the world like this one!' 'I
know,' said Father Seraphim, 'for it is the same with me. I'm only
questioning you to find out what you are discovering. It is indeed true,
friend of God, that no scent on earth can compare to this fragrance,
because it comes from the Holy Spirit . . . The warmth isn't in the air,
it is within us. This is what the Holy Spirit causes us to ask God for
when we cry to him "Kindle in us the fire of the Holy Spirit."
Warmed by it, hermits are not afraid of winter hardship, protected as
they are by the mantle of grace which the Holy Spirit has woven for
them . . . Now you know, my friend, what it is like to be in the
fullness of the Holy Spirit.'

Seraphim of Zarov

The fifteen strengths of the soul: the strength of faith, the strength of
gentleness, the strength of humility, the strength of patience, the
strength of mortification, the strength of obedience, the strength of
charity, the strength of justice, the strength of mercy, the strength of
generosity, the strength of forgiveness, the strength of serenity, the
strength of moderation, the strength of holiness, the strength of divine
love.

Colmán mac Béognae The Alphabet of Devotion

> Spirit of God
> The breath of creation is yours.
> Spirit of God
> The groans of the world are yours.
> Spirit of God
> The wonder of communion is yours.
> Spirit of God
> The fire of love is yours.
> And we are filled
> And we are filled.

I pray that you may have the power to understand how broad and long, how high and deep, is Christ's love. Yes, may you . . . be completely filled with the very nature of God.
Ephesians 3:17, 18, 19

To receive and be aware of the light of Christ within one, it is necessary to withdraw from outward things, as far as this can be done. After purifying one's soul by contrition and good works and proclaiming one's faith in Christ crucified, a person should shut their eyes and concentrate on bringing their mind down into the depths of their heart, ardently calling on the name of our Lord Jesus Christ. Then according to the ardour of their heart for the Beloved, they will find a sweetness, through inviting the Name, that evokes a longing to seek the supreme illumination. When the mind is concentrated in the heart through this exercise, then the light of Christ begins to shine, lighting up the temple of the soul with its radiance.

Lost in contemplation of the uncreated Beauty, a person forgets the things of the senses, even themself, and prefers to be buried in the earth rather than lose their unique treasure – God.

Seraphim of Zarov

Faith with action, desire with constancy, calmness with devotion, chastity with humility, fasting with moderation, poverty with generosity, silence with discussion, distribution with equality, endurance without grievance, abstinence with exposure, zeal without severity, gentleness with justice, confidence without neglect, fear without despair, poverty without pride, confession without excuse, teaching with practice, progress without slipping, lowliness towards the haughty, smoothness towards the rough, work without grumbling, simpleness with wisdom, humility without favouritism, the Christian life without pretence – all these are contained in holiness. It is then that a person is holy, when he or she is full of divine love.

Colmán mac Béognae The Alphabet of Devotion

May I be lost in wonder, love and praise.

I will put my law within them and write it on their hearts.
Jeremiah 31:33

God warms the heart and inward parts. When we feel a chill in our hearts coming from the devil (for the devil is cold) let us call on the Lord. God will come and warm us with perfect love, not only love for himself but for our neighbour as well; and at the touch of this fire Satan's chill will vanish.

Nothing so much as idle words has power to extinguish that fire brought by Christ and enkindled in our heart by the Holy Spirit.

When mind and heart are united in prayer and the soul is wholly concentrated in a single desire for God, then the heart grows warm and the light of Christ begins to shine and fills the inward being with peace and joy.

One must constantly watch over the heart. The heart cannot live unless it is full of that water which boils in the heat of the divine fire. Without that water the heart grows cold and becomes like an icicle.

Seraphim of Zarov

The person who will not have fear of God will not have love of God. The person who will not have love of God will not have fulfilment of God's commandment. The person who will not have fulfilment of God's commandment will not have eternal life in heaven. For fear underlies love. Love underlies holy work. Holy work underlies eternal life in heaven.

Love of the living God cleanses the soul. It satisfies the mind. It increases rewards. It drives out vices. It despises the world. It cleanses, it concentrates thoughts.

Colmán mac Béognae The Alphabet of Devotion

> Kindle in our hearts, O God
> the flame of that love which never ceases
> that it may burn in us, giving light to others.
> May we shine for ever in your temple,
> set on fire with your eternal light,
> even your Son Jesus Christ,
> our Saviour and our Redeemer.
>
> *Columba*

In the beginning, when God created the universe, the earth was
without form and void . . . and the spirit of God moved over the face
of the waters.
Genesis 1:1, 2

The Hebrew word for 'spirit' used in this passage also means 'power',
or 'awesome wind'. Jesus said that God's Spirit is like the wind that
blows where it wills: it may be a gale or it may be a breeze; and there
is no point in us trying to control it.

Non-religious people over the millennia have tried to ignore the
Spirit of God; religious people have tried to tame the Spirit. Some of
the Celtic Christians knew better than to do either. That is no doubt
why Celts have used the symbol of the Wild Goose for the Holy Spirit.

The Holy Spirit is not a tame bird, kept in a clean cage, to be released
for short bursts at charismatic meetings . . . The Holy Spirit makes his
habitation in some of the wildest and darkest places this world has to
offer . . . The Holy Spirit is wonderfully free, able to go to the dark
places of our own lives, for healing, to the dark unvisited places of our
churches, and to the dark and demon-infested places of our society.

Michael Mitton

> Spirit of God, be wild and free in me.
> Batter my proud and stubborn will
> Blow me where you choose
> Break me down if you must
> Re-fashion me as you will
> Move me powerfully away
> From the games I play
> In order to try and tame you.
> Lead me into the wild places
> The places of dream or scream
> The new frontiers or the total quiet
> The long dark tunnels
> Or the wide, sunny vistas
> To speak to lions
> To move mountains
> To bear tragedy
> To mirror you.

In every work that he undertook, he did it with all his heart and prospered.
2 Chronicles 31:21

May 1 marks Beltane, the season of growth. We look back and thank God for preserving the earth and its produce through winter and spring. We look forward to the cattle going out to the higher summer pastures; to people everywhere going out to experience the fullest potentialities of work and enterprise.

May Day is also a celebration for the workers of the world. The word agriculture, which means 'cultivation of the land', retains the Celtic understanding of the intimate relation between human work and earth's work. Only when that relation, in high tech industry, commerce, as well as in agriculture, is one of care and prayer, does either earth or human society experience the fullness of blessing that is inherent in them both.

In a true understanding of work the owners of capital, managers and employees work together like fingers on a hand to serve the needs of the world, all aware that the hand is an instrument of God. Curse will come upon us if our motive is to treat the world as a cake, from which we get a bigger slice for ourselves. Blessing, which selfishness denies us, is the true birthright of the world of work.

This means that our involvement in work has to go beyond mere good management into heartfelt participation, in a way that the Celtic farmers understood when they blessed the May-time shearing of the sheep:

> Go shorn and come woolly
> Bear the female Beltane lamb
> The lovely Brigid endow you
> And the fair Mary sustain you.
> *Carmina Gadelica*

Be up and doing to make progress, slack to take revenge, careful in word, eager in work.

Columbanus

> May the wealth and work of the world
> Be available to all
> And for the exploitation of none.
> May I do no work that I cannot pray over.
> May this May Day be a holy day
> When rest from work makes us blest in work.

Work as if you were serving the Lord, not human beings.
Ephesians 6:7

When Noel Dermot O'Donogue was a child in the south west of
Ireland every step in the working day had a prayer to go with it. He
writes, 'The seedsman is his own priest. The work is equally labour and
liturgy.'

The language of this chicken farmer's prayer song may be quaint, but
we need the sentiment behind it in our work today, whatever it is we
have to count up or multiply:

> I will rise early on Monday morning
> I will sing my rhyme
> I will go sunwise with my egg bowl to the nest of my hen.
> I will place my left hand to my breast, my right hand to my heart
> I will seek the loving wisdom of God
> Abundant in grace, in broods, and in flocks.
> I will close my two eyes quickly
> As in blind man's buff, moving slowly
> I will stretch my left hand over there
> To the nest of my hen on the other side.
> The first egg I shall bring near me
> I will whisk it round behind me and place it in my bowl.
> The next time I shall lift my left hand and place two eggs in the
>   bowl.
> Then I will lift my right hand, and seek the ruling of heaven's King
> And there shall be three more eggs in the bowl.
> I will raise my left hand a second time
> In the name of Christ, King of power,
> And there shall be ten eggs in the bowl.
> Thus when I have ceased
> My brood will be complete
> Beneath the breast of speckled hen.
> In the name of the most holy Trinity
> I will set the eggs on Thursday
> And the glad brood will come on Friday.

Carmina Gadelica

Lord, show me how to pray like this over my work
and teach me not to count my chickens until they are hatched.

Whatever your hand finds to do, do it with all your might.
Ecclesiastes 9:10

During the winter months the women of Highland households are up late and early at Calanas – the whole process of wool working from the raw material to the finished cloth. The industry of these women is wonderful, performed lovingly, uncomplainingly, day after day, year after year, till the sands of life run down. The life in a Highland home of the crofter class is well described in the following lines:

> In the long winter night
> All are engaged.
> Teaching the young
> Is the grey-haired sage
> The daughter at her carding
> The mother at her wheel
> While the fisher mends his net
> With his needle and his reel.
> *Alexander Carmichael*

May is the time of sap rising, business ventures, creative enterprise, new productivity targets, fresh fashions. All these things are like seeds, and we are like priests, and each of these labours can become a liturgy.

> If Jesus built a ship
> She would travel trim
> If Jesus roofed a house
> No leaks would be left by him
> If Jesus planted a garden
> He would make it like paradise
> If Jesus did my day's work
> It would delight his Father's eyes.
> *DMK*

> Lord, give me love and common sense
> And standards that are high
> Give me calm and confidence
> And – please – a twinkle in the eye.
> ***Christian workers' prayer***

Look at May in bloom

Where could I get away from your spirit? If . . . I travelled beyond the east or lived in the furthest place in the west, you would be there.
Psalm : 39: 7, 9, 10

When I do see the May in bloom I ain't afeard to ask the Almighty for Eternal Life.

An old Wiltshire countryman

Look at the animals roaming the forest: God's spirit dwells within them. Look at the birds flying across the sky: God's spirit dwells within them. Look at the tiny insects crawling upon the grass: God's spirit dwells within them. Look at the fish in the river and sea: God's spirit dwells within them. There is no creature on earth in whom God is absent. Travel across the ocean to the most distant land, and you will find God's spirit in all the creatures there. Climb up the highest mountain, and you will find God's spirit among the creatures who live at the summit. When God pronounced that his creation was good, it was not only that his hand had fashioned every creature; it was that his breath had brought every creature to life.

Look, too, at the great trees of the forest; look at the wild flowers and the grass in the field; look even at your crops. God's spirit is present within all plants as well. The presence of God's spirit in all living beings is what makes them beautiful; and if we look with God's eyes, nothing on the earth is ugly.

Pelagius To an elderly friend.

I programme my computer
with the love of God.
God be with me now
as I call words into being.
May they make real my work of love.
May they join the work of creation.
Called from nothing, uttered over chaos
bringing order.

Esther de Waal

Look how the flowers grow.
Luke 12:27

The face of nature laughs in the springtime, her breath fresh and her eyes clearest blue.

Horses gather at the river's edge to drink its fresh clean water; the sparkling waterfall cries with joy as its torrent hits the rocks.

The blackbirds's call is wild and free, rejoicing at the new abundance of food; the cuckoo, that lover of warmth, begins its happy chorus.

Sheep and cattle gobble the crisp, juicy grass; the meadows are alight with colours of flowers in bloom.

The sun glints through the fresh green leaves, the wind rustling through the branches is the harp of nature, playing a song of love.

Men are vigorous and strong, women pretty and gay; the whole world is in love with its Creator.

In Celtic Fire *Robert Van de Weyer (Unattributed)*

O Son of God, do a miracle for me and change my heart
You taking flesh to redeem me
was more difficult than to transform my wickedness.
It is you, who, to help me, went to be scourged.
You, dear child of Mary, are the refined molten metal of our forge.
It is you who makes the sun bright, together with the ice
it is you who creates the rivers and the salmon all along the river.
That the nut tree should be flowering
O Christ, it is a rare craft.
Through your skill too comes the kernel, you fair ear of our wheat.
Though the children of Eve ill deserve the bird flocks and the salmon
it was the Immortal One on the cross
who made both salmon and birds.
It is he who makes the flower of the sloes grow through the surface of the blackthorn
and the nut flower on other trees.
Besides this, what miracle is greater?

Tadhg Og O Huiginn d. 1448 trans. by K.H. Jackson (adapted)

Almighty God who blesses you with blessings of corn and flowers,
blessings of ancient mountains, delightful things from everlasting hills.
Genesis 49:25, 26

Celtic Christians never lose sight of the fact that God delights to have a
world that overflows with blessings. Since Augustine too many
Christians have looked at the world only to see what is wrong with it,
and a jaundiced outlook has set in. Yet blessing is an essential part of
our biblical and our Celtic birthright that we need to recover.

In the Old Testament blessing is life, health and fertility for the people,
their cattle, their fields . . . blessing is the basic power of life itself.
Claus Westermann

Abraham, whom we call our father in the faith, has his entire vocation
carved out for him in terms of blessing: 'All the communities of the
earth shall find blessing in you' (Genesis 12:4). When Jacob gave his
final blessings to the twelve tribes that grew out of his twelve sons he
gave each one a blessing that was appropriate to their character and
circumstances (Genesis 49). Blessings of a whole tribe were passed on
through a father and sons. Christ's final act before his ascension was to
bless his assembled apostles. Through the hands of the apostles and their
successors the Lord continues to bless his people even now.

> O, King of the Tree of Life,
> The blossoms on the branches are your people,
> The singing birds are your angels,
> The whispering breeze is your Spirit.
>
> O, King of the Tree of Life,
> May the blossoms bring forth the sweetest fruit,
> May the birds sing out the highest praise,
> May your Spirit cover all with his gentle breath.
>
> The blessing of God and the Lord be yours,
> The blessing of the perfect Spirit be yours,
> The blessing of the Three be pouring for you
> Mildly and generously,
> Mildly and generously.
>
> *Carmina Gadelica*

In the trees the birds make their nests and sing. From the sky you send rain on the hills, and the earth is filled with your blessings.
Psalm 104:12, 13

> Maytime is the fairest season
> With its loud bird song and green trees
> When the plough is in the furrow
> And the oxen under the yoke
> When the sea is green
> And the land many colours.
>
> But when cuckoos sing on the tops
> Of the lovely trees, my sadness deepens
> The smoke stings and my grief is clear
> Since my brothers have passed away.
>
> On the hill and in the valley
> On the islands of the sea
> Whichever path you take
> You shall not hide from blessed Christ.
>
> It was our wish, our Brother, our way,
> To go to the land of your exile.
> Seven saints and seven score and seven hundred
> Went to the one court with blessed Christ
> And were without fear.
>
> The gift I ask, may it not be denied me
> Is peace between myself and God.
> May I find the way to the gate of glory
> May I not be sad, O Christ, in your court.
> *Early Middle Welsh*
>
> May the road rise to meet you
> May the wind be always at your back
> May the sun shine warm upon your face
> The rain fall soft upon your fields
> And until we meet again
> May God hold you
> In the hollow of his hand.
> *Traditional Irish Blessing*

The earth is the Lord's and everything in it.
Psalm 24:1

In 1854 the USA Government offered to buy a large area of Indian
land, and promised a 'reservation' for the Indian people. Chief Seattle's
reply has been described as the most beautiful and profound statement
on the environment ever made:

We are part of the earth and it is part of us. The perfumed flowers
are our sisters; the deer, the horse, the great eagle, these are our
brothers. The rocky crests, the juices in the meadows, the body heat of
the pony, and humans beings – all belong to the same family.

The rivers are our brothers – they quench our thirst. The rivers carry
our canoes, and feed our children. If we sell you our land, you must
remember, and teach your children, that the rivers are our brothers, and
yours, and you must henceforth give the rivers the kindness you would
give any brother.

The white man treats his mother, the earth, and his brother, the sky,
as things to be bought, plundered, sold like sheep or bright beads. His
appetite will devour the earth and leave behind only a desert.

There is no quiet place in the white man's cities, no place to hear
the unfurling of leaves in the spring, or the rustle of an insect's wings.

This we know: all things are connected. Man did not weave their
web of life; he is merely a strand in it. Whatever he does to the web,
he does to himself.

You may think that you own God as you wish to own our land; but
you cannot. He is the God of all humanity, and his compassion is equal
for the red and the white people. This earth is precious to him, and to
harm the earth is to heap contempt on its Creator.

Chief Seattle

> In the name of the One who gives the growth
> may we tend the seed-bed earth.
> In dependence on the God of life
> may we cherish the precious earth,
> The earth of the God of life
> The earth of the Christ of love
> The earth of the Spirit Holy.

As they travelled down the road, they came to a place where there was some water, and the official said, 'Here is some water. What is to keep me from being baptized?' The official ordered the carriage to stop, and both Philip and the official went down into the water, and Philip baptized him.
Acts 8:36, 38

At baptisms Celtic Christians often did not collect water and pour it into a font. They went to the source of water, a spring, well or river, and were baptised there. And they frequently sprinkled or stood in water to remind them that baptism is a way of life, a way of being immersed in God. The Orthodox Christians of the east have a similar understanding:

The voice of the Lord cries out across the waters saying: Come, all of you, and receive the spirit of wisdom, the spirit of understanding, the spirit of reverence of God who is shown to us in Jesus Christ, as he wades into the waters of the river Jordan, the river which rolls back its currents as it looks upon the Lord coming to be immersed.

You came as a man, O Christ our King, to receive the immersion of a servant from the hands of the Forerunner; this was because of our sins, O you Lover of humankind.

The Forerunner, John the Baptiser, became all trembling as he looked upon you coming towards him. 'How can the candlestick illumine the light?' he cried out, 'how can a slave lay hands upon his Lord? Make me and these waters holy, O Saviour who takes away the sins of the world.'

Make this a fountain of immortality
A gift of cleansing
A remission of sins
A healing of compulsive habits
A destroying of demons
A renewing of our God-given nature.
Adapted from an Orthodox Rite of the Blessing of the Waters

Immerse us in your pure water
And your gift of a tender heart.
Immerse us in your healing water
And your gift of wisdom.
Immerse us in your renewing waters
And your gift of reverence.

You know that your bodies are parts of the body of Christ . . . so use
your bodies for God's glory.
1 Corinthians 6:15, 20

Celtic Christians use all their bodily senses, which they call 'the five
stringed harp', to express the presence of God.

Bless my hands Lord
May they be put to good use and not wasted idly.
May they work hard and honestly
Yet still grasp every opportunity to stroke and caress.
May they never be raised in violence.

Bless my feet Lord
May they always walk on hallowed ground
May they not run away in fear but plod courageously on.
May they never wander off your courageous path.

Bless my eyes Lord
May they see beyond the masks so often worn
and look deeply into the soul.
Help them to drink in the beauty of the sunrise and sunset
the shimmering sun dancing through the waves.
May they marvel at the brilliance of tiny jewel-like snow crystals
    glistening in the moonlight.
May they see into the hunger, suffering and injustices of the world.
Help me to know when to open them and when to look away.

Bless my ears Lord
That I may always hear the real message of what is being said.
Grant my ears the wisdom of knowing what to cherish and what to
    reject.
Thank you for the gift of hearing – the communication it enables –
the music which inspires my soul and the pain which moves me to
    compassion.
Thank you for the gift of silence, a calm to my soul.

Bless my mind Lord, may it always feed and grow on your holy
    word
and consider all things from your godly perspective.

                              Sue Bloomfield, Community of Aidan and Hilda

So the one who came down is the same one who went up, above and beyond the heavens, to fill the whole universe with his presence.
Ephesians 4:10

Everything spoke of a Presence, vibrated with God's love. They saw a universe ablaze with his glory, suffused with a presence that calls, nods and beckons – a creation personally united with its Creator in every atom and fibre.

David Adam

The material is shot through with the spiritual; there is a 'within-ness' of God in all life. The whole earth is sacramental: everything is truly every blessed thing.

Ron Ferguson Chasing the Wild Goose

> Earth's crammed with heaven
> And every common bush afire with God.
> *Elizabeth Barrett Browning*

> There's no plant in the ground
> But is full of his blessing
> There's no thing in the sea
> But is full of his life
> There is nought in the sky
> But proclaims his goodness
>
> Jesu! O Jesu! it's good to praise thee!
>
> There's no bird on the wing
> But is full of his blessing
> There's no star in the sky
> But is full of his life
> There is nought neath the sun
> But proclaims his goodness
>
> Jesu! O Jesu! it's good to praise thee!
> *Carmina Gadelica*

God has filled him with his spirit and given him skill, ability, and understanding of every kind of artistic work.
Exodus 35:31

The missionary company that accompanied Patrick included artists, according to the Book of Armagh. Patrick himself used to teach young people who were training for the ministry to write the alphabet in a graceful style. Before Patrick's arrival, the people of Ireland were all but destitute of a literature. In the centuries following Patrick there was a great flowering of art and calligraphy. The flower of that flowering was *The Book of Kells*.

It is thought that this book was designed at Iona in the eighth century, and taken to the monastery at Kells for safe-keeping during a Viking invasion. Many brightly coloured natural pigments were used. It abounds in spirals, knotwork and key-patterns. The ornament is profuse and varied, sometimes drawing on both Pictish and Byzantine art. Geraldus Cambrensis concluded that the *Book of Kells* was 'the work of an angel, not of a man'. Even today, Nicolete Gray in *A History of Lettering* can say that the three Greek letters that form the monogram of Christ on the Chi Rho page are 'more presences than letters'. For shining through the brilliance of the artistic skills is the splendour of spiritual understanding.

There is something of the artist in all of us and we can learn much from these Irish artists. For example, that an artist does not have to be conventional; an artist may follow angles that seem 'way out' to others but this could be a form of humility or folly for Christ. An artist must, however, attain to an inner purity, honesty, and integrity of spirit. The artist needs to understand the inner, God-given nature of each element of creation that (s)he wishes to portray, and how it reflects an aspect of the ultimate nature of the Creator.

The Irish sense of balance in imbalance, of riotous complexity moving swiftly within a basic unity, would now find its most extravagant expression in Irish Christian art – in the monumental high crosses, in miraculous liturgical vessels such as the Ardagh Chalice, and, most delicately of all, in the art of the Irish codex.

Thomas Cahill How the Irish Saved Civilisation

> God, fill your people with your Spirit
> And give us skill, ability, and understanding
> Of every kind of artistic work.

Jesus said: Whoever is faithful in little things will be faithful in large ones.
Luke 16:10

Do the little things that you have seen and heard through me.
The last words of David of Wales

Faithfulness in little things is a big thing.
St John Chrysostom

I come in the little things says the Lord.
Anon

We can do little things for God. I turn the cake that is frying on the pan, for love of God. That done, if there is nothing else to call me, I prostrate myself in worship before the One who has given me grace to work. Afterwards I rise happier than a king.

Brother Lawrence

When we read the lives of the saints, we are struck by a certain large leisure, which went hand in hand with a remarkable effectiveness. They were never hurried; they did comparatively few things, and these not necessarily striking or important; and they troubled very little about their influence. Yet they always seemed to hit the mark; every bit of their life told; their simplest actions had a distinction, an exquisiteness that suggested the artist. The reason is not far to seek. Their sainthood lay in their referring the smallest actions to God.

E. Hermon

God in my rising and lying down
God in my dressing and undressing
God in my cleaning and cooking
God in my locking and unlocking
God in my greeting and speaking
God in my counting and viewing
God in the little things
God in this thing
God in that thing
God in all things.

If your gift is practical service, give yourself to it.
Romans 12:7

How often do we think, 'How boring,' about someone we are with, or something that we do, or even about our life as a whole? We can respond to this problem in two ways. The first way is to rush into the pursuit of trifles – into anything so long as it is new and catches our fancy. Some people spend their lives doing this. It is not, of course, an answer at all; it is merely a temporary distraction. The second way to respond to the problem of boredom is to develop an attitude of 'being fully present', so that the meaning, energy, colour and adventure with which, all unseen, the present moment is crammed become available to us.

This is sometimes called 'the sacrament of the present moment'. We can 'be fully present' in all sorts of ways. Perhaps the words of someone speaking to us are like water off a duck's back. Then we decide to become fully present to that person, and we become aware of their unique history, future and present, of the wonder of a life. Or perhaps we are mindlessly reciting a familiar psalm, or Mary's Song ('The Magnificat'); then, we imagine that we are the psalmist, or Mary, and we feel as they do. Boredom flees; emotions flow; encounters, tears, healings come.

It is this ability to fuse together the unique time and place of Christ's birth in Bethlehem with our own specific present . . . which is part of the genius of Celtic spirituality; a realisation that the eternal moments of the Incarnation or the Crucifixion or the Resurrection can transcend time and space, enabling us to relocate Bethlehem or Calvary or the Garden of the Third Day in our own back yard.

Patrick Thomas

> Fill this moment, Lord.
> Open my eyes to your presence.
> Open my ears to your call.
> Open my heart to your glory
> Now, in me, in all.

I chose you and appointed you to go and bear much fruit, the kind of fruit that endures.
John 15:16

As a young man Cuthbert knew he had to give his life to God, and that God planned for his training to be at Melrose. When Boisil, the Melrose Prior, saw the way Cuthbert dismounted from his horse and treated his servant, he knew that God would one day use Cuthbert as a leader in the church. Cuthbert was a natural leader of people, yet he also had a strong inner motivation to the solitary life. How could he know which of these was God's plan? One day he was conversing on Coquet Island with Abbess Aelfledd, as to what God's plan might be for the Northumbrian kingdom and its ruler, as well as for its church . We learn that because Cuthbert heeded Boisil's prophetic words for him, he had become willing to accept a call to be a bishop for a period, yet that he also made plans to have a period as a contemplative. As we reflect upon the wisdom of friends and of our own hearts, we need to go with the flow of whatever God wills.

> I cannot invent new things like the airship
> Which sails on silver wings
> But today a wonderful thought in the dawn was given
> And the stripes on my robe,
> Shining from wear, were suddenly fair
> Bright with light falling from heaven –
> Gold and silver and bronze light from the windows of heaven.
> And the thought was this:
> That a sacred plan is hid in my hand;
> That my hand is big
> Big, because of this plan
> That God, who dwells in my hand knows this sacred plan
> Of the things God will do for the world
> Using my hand.
>
> *Toyohiko Kagawa*

There's a divinity that shapes our ends rough-hew them how we will.
William Shakespeare

> As tools come to be sharpened by the blacksmith,
> so may we come, Lord.
> As sharpened tools go back to their owner,
> so may we go back to our everyday life
> to be used by you.
>
> *A prayer from Africa*

When they pass through their sea of trouble I, the Lord, will strike the waves.
Zechariah 10:11

Shall I abandon, O King of Mysteries, the soft comforts of home? Shall I turn my back on my native land, and my face towards the sea?

Shall I put myself wholly at the mercy of God, without silver, without a horse, without fame and honour? Shall I throw myself wholly on the King of kings, without a sword and shield, without food and drink, without a bed to lie on?

Shall I say farewell to my beautiful land, placing myself under Christ's yoke? Shall I pour out my heart to him, confessing my manifold sins and begging forgiveness, tears running down my cheeks?

Shall I leave the prints of my knees on the sandy beach, a record of my final prayer in my native land? Shall I then suffer every kind of wound that the sea can inflict?

Shall I take my tiny coracle across the wide, sparkling ocean? O King of the Glorious heaven, shall I go of my own choice upon the sea?

O Christ, will you help me on the wild waves?
> *Early Irish – sometimes attributed to voyagers such as St Brendan*

> Jesus who stopped the wind and stilled the waves
> grant you calm in the storm times;
> Jesus Victor over death and destruction
> bring safety on your voyage;
> Jesus of the purest love, perfect companion
> bring guarding ones around you;
> Jesus of the miraculous catching of fish,
> and the perfect lakeside meal
> guide you finally ashore.
> > *From* The First Voyage of the Coracle,
> > *Community of Aidan and Hilda*

Some went down to the sea in ships, doing business on the great waters; they saw the deeds of the Lord, his wondrous works in the deep.
Psalm 107:23, 24

Brendan chose fourteen monks from his community, took them to the chapel, and made this proposal to them, 'My dear fellow soldiers in the spiritual war, I beg your help because my heart is set upon a single desire. If it be God's will, I want to seek out the Island of Promise of which our forefathers spoke. Will you come with me? What are your feelings?' As soon as he had finished speaking, the monks replied with one voice, 'Father, your desire is ours also . . .' When all was ready Brendan ordered his monks aboard, the sail was hoisted, and the coracle was swept out to sea. For the next two weeks the wind was fair, so that they did no more than steady the sail. But then the wind fell, and they had to row, day after day. When their strength eventually failed, Brendan comforted them: 'Have no fear, brothers, for God is our captain and our pilot; so take in the oars, and set the sail, letting him blow us where he wills.'

From The Life of Brendan the Navigator

Brothers and sisters, God is calling you to leave behind everything that stops you setting sail in the ocean of God's love. You have heard the call of the Wild Goose, the untamable Spirit of God: be ready for him to lead you into wild, windy or well-worn places in the knowledge that he will make them places of wonder and welcome.

He is giving you the vision of a spoiled creation being restored to harmony with its Creator, of a fragmented world becoming whole, of a weakened church being restored to its mission, of healed lands being lit up by the radiance of the glorious Trinity.

In stillness or storm, be always vigilant, waiting, sharing, praising, blessing, telling. Sail forth across the ocean of God's world knowing both the frailty of your craft and the infinite riches of your God.

From The First Voyage of the Coracle, *Community of Aidan and Hilda*

> Dear God, be good to us;
> Your sea is so wide,
> And our boats are so small.
> *Prayer of the Breton fishermen*

The Lord is king! Earth, be glad! Rejoice, you islands of the seas!
Psalm 97:1

Brendan and his crew at last sailed in to an island. Streams of water gushed down from the hills and there was an abundance of fish and sheep. It was Good Friday, the day of Jesus's death, so they sacrificed the finest sheep in celebration of Jesus, whom Christians know as the Lamb of God. However, the hermit who lived on the island, and who had welcomed them lovingly, felt God wanted them to go to a second island nearby to celebrate the resurrection of Jesus on Easter Day.

So off they sailed. One of the birds welcomed them, landing on Brendan's shoulders and flapping its wings with joy. Then at dusk, as they sang God's praises, the birds joined in, chirping in perfect harmony. The hermit brought over food from his island which was to last the monks forty days, for they were told to stay for the Pentecost celebration and then sail on. The day after Pentecost the hermit brought them another forty days' supplies and they again embarked on the wide sea.

From The Life of Brendan the Navigator

I am bending my knee
In the eye of my Father who made me
In the eye of the Saviour who bought me
In the eye of the Spirit who cleansed me
In friendship and affection
I am bending my knee.

O Mighty One
O Holy Three
I am bending the knee
Bestow on us fullness
In our need
The smile of God
The trust of God
In our need
That we may do on the world you made
As angels and saints do in heaven
Each day and night
In bloom and in blight
We'll be bending the knee
Carmina Gadelica (adapted)

Jesus, tired out, sat down by Jacob's well. A Samaritan woman came to
draw up some water . . . Jesus said to her, 'The water I give to a
person will be a well of everlasting life'.
John 4:6, 7, 14.

This is the traditional English day for dressing wells. Wells were a focal
point for a community's water supplies, meetings and worship both
before and after Christianity came. The Christian church met at the
sites of wells, and used water as a powerful expression of God's power
to sustain, cleanse, and renew. This parallels in Celtic lands what the
Bible records about wells.

Church Councils in Gaul and Irish church rules forbade the worship
of wells, yet we learn of Celtic Christians being divinely guided to
discover a well when a water supply was needed, using well water to
bless pilgrims, bathing in wells and being healed, using wells as
waymarks of God's deeds, and establishing churches beside wells.
Adamnan's *Life of Columba* describes a poisonous well which Picts
'worshipped as a god' and which 'was converted by the saint into a
blessed well'. David is reputed to have done something similar at
Glastonbury where he came to a well full of poison, blessed it, and
caused it to become warm; it was called the Hot Baths.

The well at Ffynnon Enddwyn in Wales became famous when St
Enddwyn was cured after bathing in it. Ffynnon Ddyfnog well in Wales
is said to owe its healing properties to the action of St Ddyfnog who
did penance there by standing under the cold water. John of
Tynemouth wrote in 1350 that the waters from the well on Ramsey
Island, 'when drunk by sick folk, convey health of body to all.' A man
suffering from a swelling in his stomach drank from it, vomited out a
frog, and was cured immediately! It was said that God caused wells to
come to light for the needs of David and Teilo, and that this well water
tasted as pleasant as wine. Celtic Christian leaders often held baptisms at
wells.

Today the advertisements of water companies emphasise truths such
as 'every drop is precious, we should never take water for granted'.
Today baptisms are held in swimming pools as well as in church fonts.
Today also prophet voices call us to 'dig up the ancient wells' – that is,
God-given sources of renewal in our heritage.

> Help me to drink deeply,
> And rediscover the ancient sources of renewal.

Whoever is not against us is for us.
Mark 9:40

A young desert Christian met a pagan priest who worshipped idols. He immediately went on to the attack, 'Demon, where are you running away to?' The other, furious, beat the Christian with a stick, left him half dead, and went on his way.

A little further on the same pagan priest met met an old desert Christian who greeted him and spoke to him warmly. Astonished, the pagan asked, 'What good do you see in me that you greet me in this way?' The old monk replied, 'It is because I saw you wearing yourself out without realising that this is all in vain.' The pagan responded, 'I was touched by the way you greeted me, and it made me realise that you come from God.'

After that the worshipper of idols joined the Christian monastic life. Moreover, he persuaded others to do the same.

The lesson of this story is that we should seek to welcome someone of another faith as a person in their own right, and to establish a relationship, before engaging in conversation about the Faith. Moreover, it is never good to put another person down, to be rude, or even to assume the worst about them.

So often Christians demonise people of another faith, and illustrate differences in beliefs only by referring to the worst aberrations of the other religion, disregarding the aberrations of Christianity. The truth is that we all have similar needs and feelings. The desert pagan had put himself down ('What good do you see in me?'); the last thing he needed was for someone else to put him down. He needed to be cherished. And look at the marvellous response to his being cherished by the old man. The pagan went on to win others to Christ, because he knew that they, also, wanted to be cherished; and they were introduced to a Saviour who cherishes.

> O Christ, you had compassion on the crowds
> You drew people to yourself
> You repelled none who knew they were needy.
> Grant us hearts like yours
> Hearts that go out in genuine greeting
> In humble welcome,
> Till, in the fellowship of sharing
> Souls are drawn to you.

When the body is buried it is mortal; when raised it will be immortal.
When buried, it is ugly and weak; when raised, it will be beautiful and
strong. When buried, it is a physical body; when raised it will be a
spiritual body.
1 Corinthians 15:42–44

Most people believe in some kind of after life; for a human life to be
snuffed out does not seem to fit with the fact of so much unfulfilled
potential, or with out of the body experiences. Many believe in
reincarnation. Its great appeal is that it keeps alive hopes of future
development. But let us look a little closer.

Some believe that we are reincarnated in either a higher or a lower
being, but this belief is often egocentric: that other people will be
reincarnated in a lower being, we ourselves will be reincarnated in a
higher being! A schoolboy whose grandfather had died was heard telling
a class-mate, 'My mum says the cat is my grandad'. I wonder if mum
found grandad difficult? To feed our own ego it is easy to claim that, in
contrast to people we don't like, we ourselves were once incarnate in,
for example, a royal personage.

These are selfish views of reincarnation. There is another, self-
negating view of reincarnation: that my essence will be absorbed into
the cosmic stream of life. I lose all individuality. I am no longer a
person in the next life.

The pre-Christian people of Britain had a third view of
reincarnation: we will be the same person in the next life, but the
environment will be immeasurably better. Thus a warrior will have
superb horses and endless victories in the Other World. The Christians
were able to say to these folk: Yes, we, too, believe that we will still be
the same persons in the next life. But we are all so selfish that our ego
as well as our body has to die first. Then, and only then, will there be
a resurrection of our true personality. If we were fighters on earth, our
fighting in the next life will be transformed. For a Christian death is not
a full stop, it is the end of the first page of our story.

> May you be as free as the wind
> As soft as sheep's wool
> As straight as an arrow
> That you may journey ever nearer to the heart of God.

The storm makes my heart beat wildly . . . at God's command wonderful things happen . . . And now the light in the sky is dazzling, too bright for us to look at; and the sky has been swept clean by the wind.
Job 37:1, 5, 21

Glowering clouds that produce sudden squalls remind me of the unpredictable outbursts of human nature. Do not assume, just because life goes smoothly now, that we shall always be immune from sudden outbreaks. If we do assume this, we will not be able to handle the squalls; we will try to run away, or cave in; panic or fear will dominate. But if we accept now that these things are part, though only part, of life's scenery, we will maintain perspective in the storm.

Clouds teach us that the threats and squalls of life soon pass; they are never permanent. They swirl in and out of clear sky.

The sun breaking out teaches us that the Lord delights to restore the goodness of life and this makes us feel good within. As God dries a wet building, so the damp evaporates from our lives. As the sun warms everything, so we learn to bask in God's rays. Yet the smoke rising from chimneys teaches us that we have a part to play: 'Lord, I will do some good for you, I will stoke the fires of the Faith'.

King, you ordained the movements of every object: the sun to cross the sky each day . . . the clouds to carry rain from the sea, and rivers to carry waters back to the sea.

The Celtic Psalter

Through his creation God encircles and strengthens us.
Hildegard of Bingen

> Lord, may the swirling storm clouds
> Remind me that I am a creature, not Creator
> That I am liable to suffer from the changes and chances
> Of this mortal life.
> May the clouds teach me to look always to you
> The Creator of both storm and sunshine.
> May they teach me to maintain joy when life is frowning
> And to maintain perspective in and out of season.

I will pour out my spirit on everyone; your sons and daughters will proclaim my message, your old folk will have dreams, and your young folk will see visions; at that time I will pour out my spirit even on servants, both men and women.
Joel 2:28, 29

The Bible records dreams through which God spoke to individuals and sometimes to nations. Yet psychologists tell us that our dreams are nearly always about ourselves.

There were several centuries in the West when most people lost touch with the world of imagination, spirit and dreams. Towards the turn of the millennium that changed. However, much of the modern glut of material on 'dream guidance' is so full of symbols of our colliding egos that it leaves enquirers more confused and self-centred than when they started. In contrast, Celtic saints, like the biblical characters, sometimes had God-given clarity in their dreams. This was because the dreams came to people whose lives and 'psyches' were pure.

We have read of dreams that accompanied the births of some of the most holy Celtic Christians. St Ita was given dreams from God throughout her life. Once she dreamed that an angel gave her three precious stones. The angel explained that these represented the Father, the Son and the Holy Spirit and said to her, 'Always in your sleep and vigils the angels of God and holy visions will come to you, for you are a temple of God, in body and soul.'

> O Christ, Son of the living God,
> May your holy angels guard our sleep.
> May they watch over us as we rest
> And hover around our beds.
> Let them reveal to us in our dreams
> Visions of your glorious truth,
> O High Prince of the universe,
> O High Priest of the mysteries.

Christ has made a unity of the conflicting elements of Jew and Gentile
by breaking down the barrier which lay between us . . . so now you
are fellow citizens with every other Christian – you belong to the one
household of God.
Ephesians 2:13, 19

The churches in Celtic Britain were part of the one catholic and
apostolic church throughout the world, yet they responded to direct
promptings of the Holy Spirit in mission. Some people maintain that in
view of later divisions it is no longer possible to be both Catholic and
Pentecostal.

These words from a famous sermon by John Wesley on *The Catholic
Spirit* suggest that it is possible:

Though we cannot think alike, may we not love alike? May we not
be of one heart, though we are not of one opinion? . . . Every wise
person will allow others the same liberty of thinking which they
desire they should allow themself . . . And how shall we choose
among so much variety? No one can choose for, or prescribe to,
another. But everyone must follow the dictates of their own
conscience, in simplicity and godly sincerity. They must be fully
persuaded in their own mind; and then act according to the best
light they have.

My only question at present is this, 'Is your heart right, as mine is
with yours?' . . . Learn the first elements of the Gospel of Christ and
then you shall learn to be of a truly catholic spirit.

While the person of a truly catholic spirit is united by the tenderest
and closest ties to one particular congregation, their heart is enlarged
towards all humanity, those they know and those they do not; they
embrace with strong and cordial affection neighbours and strangers,
friends and enemies. This is catholic or universal love.

A person of catholic spirit is one who gives their hand to all whose
hearts are right with their own . . . who is ready to 'spend and be
spent for them', yes, to lay down their life for their sake.

John Wesley

Give me a heart that is open to all
A heart that embraces every brother and sister in Christ
A heart that wills their wholeness as one family.

The chains fell off Peter's hands . . . Peter and the angel passed by the first and second guard posts . . . Peter knocked at the door where many people were praying for him. The servant girl recognised his voice and was so happy she ran back without opening the door!
Acts 12:7, 10, 12, 14

You have heard of Irish jokes, with their distinctive and delightful sense of humour. Here is an Irish faith story: Samthann, Abbess of Clonbroney, once sent a message to her local king to release a prisoner named Fallamain whom he kept in chains. The haughty king refused. So Samthann sent messengers to whom she gave these instructions: If the king will not release him, say to the prisoner, 'In the name of the Holy Trinity you will be freed from your chains and come safely to Samthann, the Servant of the Trinity'. When the king heard this he doubled the chains, put eight guards on duty at the prison and another eight at the town gate. At midnight the prisoner's chains became loose. As he passed the first guards, they said 'Who are you, going about like this?' He replied, 'I am Fallamain who was in chains'. The guards said to him, 'If you were that man you would not be appearing in public like this'. Then Fallamain, in order to avoid the second guard, climbed over the wall and escaped. The third day he reached Samthann.

Here are three ways to spell faith

1. For
    All
    I
    Trust
    Him

2. Forsaking
    All
    I
    Take
    Him

3. R
    I
    S
    K

Lord, I do believe a little bit.
Today, help me to exercise that little bit of faith
So that it grows a little bit more.

It sparks like lightning
It spreads like the plague
It burns like the fire, inside the fire, inside the fire
It radiates like the inside of the first moment of the cosmos.
Inspired by Song of Songs 8:6

What does the love of God do to a person? It kills their desires. It
purifies their heart. It protects them. It banishes vices. It incurs rewards.
It lengthens life. It cleanses the soul.

The four redemptions of the soul: fear and repentance, love and
hope. Two of them protect it on earth, the other two waft it to
heaven. Fear shuts out the sins that lie ahead. Repentance wipes out the
sins which come before. Love of the Creator and hope of the Creator's
kingdom: that is what wafts it to heaven. Any person, then, who will
fear and love, and who will fulfil God's desire and commandment, will
have respect in the sight of people in this world, and will be blessed
with God in the next.

Colmán mac Béognae The Alphabet of Devotion

Whoever loves allows themselves willingly to be corrected.
Whoever loves suffers blows willingly for their formation.
Whoever loves is willingly cast out in order to be wholly free.
Whoever loves is willing to be alone in order
to love Love and to possess her.

Hadewijch of Brabant

You keep us loving
You, the God whose name is love
Want us to be like you –
To love the loveless and the unlovely and the unlovable
To love without jealousy or design or threat
And, most difficult of all,
To love ourselves.

Evening Liturgy Iona Community

Thrice holy God
Come as the morning dew
Hold up in us your love
Which draws all lesser loves to you.

When the day of Pentecost came . . . a large crowd gathered and they exclaimed: 'Some of us are from Rome, both Jews and Gentiles converted to Judaism, and some of us are from Crete and Arabia – yet all of us hear these believers speaking in our own languages about the great things that God has done!
Acts 2:1, 7, 10, 11

Never fall into the trap of thinking that 'Celtic' means ethnic in an exclusive sense. For the essence of Celtic spirituality is a heart wide open to God in every person, in all the world. It is to do with crossing frontiers, not erecting barriers. It goes so deep that, without losing what is distinctive, it becomes universal.

Bede, the great historian of Jarrow monastery, who is honoured on this day, understood this most clearly. Despite the fact that he disliked some of the rustic habits of the Irish, he marvelled at their hospitality to foreigners:

Many in England, both nobles and commoners went to Ireland to do religious studies or to live an ascetic life. The Irish welcomed them all gladly, gave them their daily food, and also provided them with books to read and with instruction, without asking for any payment . . . The Picts now have a treaty of peace with the English and rejoice to share in the catholic peace and truth of the church universal.

Bede

Under the influence of these Irish teachers the spirit of racial bitterness was checked and a new intercourse sprang up between English, Picts, Britons and Irish . . . the peace of Columba, the fellowship of learning and piety, rested on the peoples.

Vida D. Scutta Introduction to Bede's
Ecclesiastical History of the English People
Everyman edition

Set us free, O God, to cross barriers for you,
As you crossed barriers for us.
Spirit of God, make us open to others in listening,
Generous to others in giving,
And sensitive to others in praying
Through Jesus Christ our Lord.
Brother Barnabus SSF

God said to Moses ' I am who I am. This is what you are to say to the people: "I am has sent me to you".'
Exodus 3:14

Celtic Christians have a vivid awareness of God's Presence in all creation, yet, unlike New Age devotees, they know that the creation itself is not God. The following contemporary writing makes this point in a most telling way:

I am all around you, in every single thing you experience.
I am so rich, I am everywhere at any given moment.
I am so pure, I am translucent.
Since before the dawn of all that is, I was speaking all creation into being. I am not creation. I spoke creation into being. I am not a stone, I am not the wind, I am not the earth. I am a still small voice wooing you to my way of truth.

Do not be surprised, I am more than man, I am more than woman, I speak to my creation in ways that are fitting to those who listen. I am so much more than the highest imagined sum of all humankind. But my love for each one is greater than all the thoughts of humankind.
I will meet you in the place it is hardest for you to look . . .
    In your feeling,
    In your thoughts,
    In the Truth of myself,
    I will meet you in your essence, the very stuff that makes you, you.

I will never impose myself on you. Even as I witness you in great despair or in your moments of triumph, I will not enter in to help or share without your permission. My ways are pure.

Invite me into your life moment by moment and I will be your guide, keeper, teacher, friend, counsellor, confidant. I will make you a new creature and sanctify your ways until my thoughts are your thoughts and your thoughts are mine . . .

Ted Carr

I AM, I come to you.
I bring to you everything, even my chains, spells and darkness.
Jesus of Nazareth, you always were, always are, always will be.
Spirit, may your love be my healing, my shield, and my fulfilling.

A rope made of three cords is hard to break.
Ecclesiastes 4:12

The God whom the Celtic peoples came to know and love is the God whose very essence is a loving relationship. God is one, but there are three permanent elements in God's personality, just as there are in ours, (mind, body, spirit) and it causes damage not to recognise these. In the Divine Being, these three elements are so distinctive that they are more truly called persons than elements, for each of them personally manifests love. In this understanding God is close, accessible; and something of this unity of loves is reflected in human life, which is made in God's image.

Marriage reflects the Trinity. A couple chose the above reading from the Book of Ecclesiastes which refers to 'the threefold cord' for their wedding. They understood, and they wanted all their guests to understand, that it takes three to make a true marriage: the bride, the groom, and God. In some church weddings this is symbolised by the priest, the bride and the groom joining their three hands together.

We can also see a reflection of the Trinity in:
a tender kiss
a warm embrace
sporting comradeship
an adult affirming a child
a meal shared
two people listening to each other
a group making music
hospitality
two people's love turned out to the world
young people serving the old
black and white people celebrating
people playing.

> Father, eternal Love Maker
> Saviour, eternal Love Mate
> Spirit, eternal Love Messenger
> The Three of limitless love
> I come to you
> I abandon myself to you
> I lose myself in you
> I find myself in you
> To you be all glory for ever.

As Jesus came up out of the water he saw heaven opening and the
Spirit coming down on him like a dove. And a voice came from
heaven, 'You are my dearly loved Son, I am so pleased with you.'
Mark 1:10, 11

> The Father in the form of a voice.
> The Son in the form of Jesus.
> The Spirit in the form of a dove.

When Irenaeus was asked to explain the Trinity he pointed to a
person's hands. There is more than one hand, but only one person. On
a hand there are several fingers, but only the one hand.
  The Celtic Christians could see pointers to the nature of God as
three Persons in the creation around them, too, as the legend of Patrick
picking up a three-leafed shamrock to explain the Trinity illustrates.

> Three joints in the finger, but only one finger fair
> Three leaves of the shamrock yet only one shamrock to wear
> Frost, snowflakes and ice, yet all in water their origin share
> Three Persons in God; to one God alone we make prayer.
> *Traditional Irish*

Sometimes the sun has been used as an illustration of the Trinity. There
is the sun itself, which the human eye cannot directly look at; there is a
single ray that we can see at a particular time and place; and there is the
sun's warmth which radiates.

God is at once infinite solitude (one nature) and perfect society (three
persons); one infinite love in three subsistent relations.
Thomas Merton

> The Three who are over my head
> The Three who are under my tread
> The Three who are over me here
> The Three who are over me there
> The Three who in heaven do dwell
> The Three in the great ocean swell
> Pervading Three, O be with me
> Pervading Three, O be with me.
> *Carmina Gadelica*

God said: Let us make human beings in our own image.
Genesis 1:26

> May we sense God's playfulness in the children playing in the streets
> May we feel God's intimacy in the nestling in the breasts
> May we surmise the risks that God takes in the chances and the
>   opportunity that is ours
> May we savour the flow of God's friendship when we see the
>   embraces of friends or lovers.

Deep within all of us dwells the Blessed Trinity. At the depth of our
being the Father continually loves the Son, while the Son responds to
the Father in love and prayer through the Holy Spirit. In our prayer of
meditation we desire to be part of the love and prayer of Jesus to the
Father. Rather than think up words or aspirations or images of our
own, we wish to unite ourselves with the loving prayer going on
continually within us. In this prayer we also seek to open ourselves
completely to the Holy Spirit, that the Holy Spirit may bring about in
us conversion, repentance and faith in the Good News of Jesus Christ.
  Mgr Tom Feheily, The Christian Meditation Centre, Dunlaoguire, Ireland

> O Father who sought me
> O Son who bought me
> O Holy Spirit who taught me
> > *Irish, Collected by Douglas Hyde*

> May the love of the Three
> Give birth to a new community
> May the yielding of the Three
> Give birth to a new humanity
> May the life of the Three
> Give birth to a new creativity
> May the togetherness of the Three
> Give birth to a new unity
> May the glory of the Three
> Give birth to a new society.

Little trinities

May the grace of the Lord Jesus Christ, the love of God and the fellowship of the Holy Spirit be with you all.
2 Corinthians 13:14

The Celtic peoples with their love of significant numbers have always given special significance to the Triad, an arrangement of three statements which summed up a person, a thing or a situation, often with a blend of light humour, deep meaning and paradox.

Three sisters of lying: perhaps, maybe, guess.
Three sources of new life: a woman's belly, a hen's egg, a wrong
  forgiven.

Welsh Triads

Three things are pleasant in a home:
Good food upon the table;
A man who lovingly kisses his wife;
Children who refrain from quarrelling.

Three attitudes are godly in the Church:
True love of the Lord himself;
Kindness amongst the pews;
A fair dealing with self.

Three ideas enlarge a person's mind:
A humble heart;
A generous soul;
Honesty in business.

Three things I wish for myself:
True spiritual beauty;
A heart of giving;
Eyes with pools of meaning.
Janet Donaldson A Pocket Book of Celtic Prayers

A mother whispers this prayer into the ear of her infant:

The blessing of the Holy Three little love
be the gift to you
Wisdom, peace and purity.
Carmina Gadelica

Immerse peoples everywhere in the Father, the Son and the Holy
Spirit.
Matthew 28:19

> By the singing of hymns eagerly ringing out
> By thousands of angels rejoicing in holy dances
> And by the four living creatures full of eyes
> With the twenty four joyful elders
> Casting their crowns under the feet of the Lamb of God
> The Trinity is praised in eternal threefold exchanges.
> *Altus Prosator attributed to Columba*

> Clear and high in the perfect assembly
> Let us praise above the nine grades of angels
> The sublime and blessed Trinity.

> Purely, humbly, in skilful verse
> I should love to give praise to the Trinity
> According to the greatness of his power.

> God has required of the host in this world
> Who are his, that they should at all times
> All together, fear the Trinity.
> *Early Welsh*

> Power of all powers we worship you
> Light of all lights we worship you
> Life of all lives we worship you

> Maker of all creatures we honour you
> Friend of all creatures we honour you
> Force of all creatures we honour you

> Love before time we adore you
> Love in dark time we adore you
> Love in present time we adore you.

Deepest strength

Jesus went away to a hill to pray. When evening came the boat with the disciples in it was in the middle of the lake, while Jesus was alone on the land.
Mark 6:46, 47

Glendalough, in the shadows of the Wicklow mountains, became a place of grace through the obedience to God of one man – Kevin. He lived as a hermit beside the lower lake for seven years, clad only in animal skins, with stone for his bed. He spent long hours up to his waist in the lake praising God. His great strength and endurance sprang from his extraordinary faith and his commitment to monastic celibacy and the teachings of the Desert spiritual tradition. As well as being a hermit and a founder of monasteries, he wrote poetry and prose, and a Rule for monks in Irish verse. He was attractive, gentle, loving, with an unusual affinity with animals and birds.

He was deeply attracted to the poetic experience of the hermit life; courageous in his desire to draw out to the edge to test his strength and endurance. He chose hardship quite deliberately; his cell was on the dark side of the lake which remained in shadow for six months of the year. Why was this so? Perhaps it was a desire to feel very exposed; to test himself to the limit, and through that test to find his own deepest strength, but perhaps most of all it was through an ascetic way of life that he found the poetry of his own soul.

Michael Rodgers of Glendalough

The 10th century *Life of Kevin* suggests that 'the branches and leaves of the trees sometimes sang sweet songs to him, and heavenly music alleviated the severity of his life.' Eventually many people joined Kevin, and he established a community beside the lower lake.

> Let me not spoil one leaf, nor break one branch
> Let me not plunder, blunder, pollute, exploit
> But rather see and hear and touch and taste and smell
> And in my sensing, know you well.
> *Marie Connolly, a Glendalough pilgrim*

No god is like your God, riding in splendour across the sky, riding through the clouds to come to your aid.
Deuteronomy 33:26

Petroc sailed from Ireland, where he had trained in a monastery, to Cornwall where he founded his own monastery at Padstow (Petroc's Stowe). A Celtic wheel cross may still be seen outside the door of the church, and in the churchyard are faint markings said to be of the cross that once stood at Petroc's monastic gateway.

In his old age Petroc set out with twelve companions to live as a hermit on Bodmin Moor, settling himself in a beehive hut by the river. Dom Julian Stonor locates this as the stone beehive hut by the stream that runs out of Rough Tor marsh, and claims 'it is one of the oldest Christian holy places in England'. So perhaps it was here that Petroc enjoyed that close affinity with nature that shows in many of the stories about him, such as his rescuing a stag from a hunter, and perhaps it was here that he looked out and meditated on the changing sounds and sights.

> Though I am silent there is singing around me
> Though I am dark there is vision around me
> Though I am heavy there is flight around me.
> *Wendell Berry*

God has put variety in the creation. Sometimes the sky is filled with pink streaks instead of a golden glow. That is as well. The marvellous could otherwise become mundane. This variety is reflected in the flowers, and in the range of human temperament. It is reflected in the very nature of God.

> Thank you
> Creator of the world
> For the music and medicine of flowers
> Which give us a scent of heaven upon earth
> And for their vases which enable them to give their best.
> May those who look at them see your glory.

This is My Body

The Lord Jesus on the night that he was betrayed took bread, gave thanks, broke it, and said, 'This is my Body which is given for you. Do this in remembrance of me.'
1 Corinthians 11:24

Draw near, and take the body of the Lord.
The Antiphonary of Bangor,
the Irish monastery founded by Comgall

When Cuthbert offered up the Saving Victim as a sacrifice to God, he offered his prayer to the Lord not by raising his voice but by shedding tears which sprang from the depth of his heart.

Bede

> The table of bread and wine is now to be made ready.
> It is the table of company with Jesus
> And with all those who love him.
> It is the table of sharing with the poor of the world,
> With whom Jesus identified himself.
> It is the table of communion with the earth
> In which Christ became incarnate.
> So, come to this table,
> You who have much faith
> And you who would like to have more;
> You who have been to this sacrament often,
> And you who have not been for a long time;
> You who have tried to follow Jesus,
> And you who have failed.
> Come. It is Christ who invites us to meet him here.
> An invitation to Communion, *The Iona Community*

> You are very welcome, O body of Christ.
> It was by your death on the cross
> you who were born of the fair and gentle virgin
> that the human race was redeemed
> that evil was conquered.
> Please do not hide your faithfulness from me
> a poor sinner who approaches you.
> Though I have deserved your anger
> please return and help me, Lord Jesus.
> *Collected in Inis Mean, Aran, by An tAth. Eoghan O Gramhraigh.*
> *From Mount Melleray Monastery, Ireland*

The blind can see, the lame can walk, and the Good News is preached.
Matthew 11:5

> He who so calmly rode
> The little ass fair of form
> Who healed each hurt and bloody wound
> That clave to the people of every age:
>
> He made glad the sad and the outcast
> He gave the rest to the restless and the tired
> He made free the bond and the unruly
> Each old and young in the land.
>
> He stemmed the fierce-rushing blood
> He took the keen prickle from the eyes
> He drank the draught that was bitter
> Trusting to the High Father of heaven.
>
> He gave strength to Peter and Paul
> He gave strength to the Mother of tears
> He gave strength to Brigid of the flocks
> Each joint and bone and sinew.
>
> *Carmina Gadelica*

O Lord, charity without limit and mercy without measure
of your love you have today come to me
and on my part it was hope which enabled me to receive you.
I give you my body as a temple
my heart as your altar, and my soul as your chalice.
O Lord, holy sinless lamb, O merciful redeemer
O gentle infant Jesus, cover me with your cloak
Grant me sanctuary with your heart
Draw me into your kingdom
Heal me by your sweetness and charity
Revive me by your death
Hide me within your wounds
Wash me with your blood
Fill me with your love
And make me in every way agreeable to your heart, O Lord.

An Timire 1911, collected by Sean P Floin
Mount Melleray Monastery, Ireland

While Peter was still speaking, the Holy Spirit came down on all those who were listening to his message. The Jewish believers who had come from Joppa with Peter were amazed that God had poured out the gift of the Holy Spirit on foreigners also.
Acts 10:44, 45

Once some founders of Christian communities came to visit Columba when he was on the island of Hinba. As they shared Holy Communion one of them saw a tongue of fire, flaming and very bright, all ablaze from Columba's head as he stood before the altar. It rose up all the time like a pillar until the end of worship.

On another occasion when Columba was staying on the island of Hinba the Holy Spirit was poured upon him in matchless abundance for a period of three days and nights. He remained alone inside a bolted house throughout this time, neither eating nor drinking. Yet rays of light of immeasurable brilliance could be seen flooding out by night through the chinks of the doors and the key holes. Columba was heard to sing spiritual songs that had never been heard before. Afterwards he confided in a few people that many mysteries which had been hidden from the beginning of the world had been revealed to him, and obscure, difficult passages in the Bible had been made more plain to him than the light of day.

Your son Christ, it is clear, is one of the three persons of the deity
and all things have indeed been created by him.
He is in union with the Father, with the Holy Spirit,
He is their peer, it is from Them, with the permission of all,
that the Holy Spirit proceeds.

Blathmac 6th century

O Christ, our dearest Saviour,
kindle our lamps
that they may evermore shine in your temple
and receive unquenchable light from you
that will lighten our darkness
and lessen the darkness of the world.

Attributed to St Columba

Let us not become tired of doing good; for if we do not give up, the time will come when we will reap the harvest. So then, as often as we have the chance, we should do good to everyone, and especially to those who belong to our family in the faith.
Galations 6:9, 10

These my children are my last words to you. That you have heartfelt love amongst yourselves. If you thus follow the example of the holy fathers, God, the comforter of the good, will be your helper. And I, abiding with Him, will intercede for you, and He will not only give you sufficient to supply the needs of this present life, but will also give you the good and eternal rewards which are laid up for those who keep his commandments.

Columba

It is possible to detect a restless, insensitive spirit from a person's voice. This is likely to result in clumsy actions. One day Columba was working in his study at Iona when he heard a man shouting the other side of the ferry crossing at Mull. Columba spoke these words aloud, which his servant Diarmait overheard, 'The man who is shouting is too careless to watch what he is doing. Today he will tip over my ink.' Sure enough, the ink was spilt later that day!

One night one of Columba's monks came to the door of the church when everyone was asleep and stood there in prayer for a time. Suddenly he saw the entire church filled with light. He was unaware that Columba was praying inside. The sudden flash of light frightened him and he returned to his cell. Next day Columba rebuked him for 'trying to see surreptitiously a light from heaven that is not given to you'. We must each learn to accept grace from God in the measure he wishes to give it to us, and not to grasp after what is given to others.

> Inspire us with your love, O Lord,
> that our loving quest for you may ocupy our thoughts;
> that your love may take
> complete possession of our being.

Columba

They that seek the Lord shall not lack any good thing.
Psalm 134:10

Delightful it is to stand on the peak of a rock, in the bosom of the isle, gazing on the face of the sea.

I hear the heaving waves chanting a tune to God in heaven; I see their glittering surf.

I see the golden beaches, their sands sparkling; I hear the joyous shrieks of the swooping gulls.

I hear the waves breaking, crashing on rocks, like thunder in heaven. I see the mighty whales.

I watch the ebb and flow of the ocean tide; it holds my secret, my mournful flight from Eire.

Contrition fills my heart as I hear the sea; it chants my sins, sins too numerous to confess.

Let me bless almighty God, whose power extends over sea and land, whose angels watch over all.

Let me study sacred books to calm my soul; I pray for peace, kneeling at heaven's gates.

Let me do my daily work, gathering seaweed, catching fish, giving food to the poor.

Let me say my daily prayers, sometimes chanting, sometimes quiet, always thanking God.

Delightful it is to live on a peaceful isle, in a quiet cell, serving the King of kings.

Attributed to Columba

Thank you for sleep
Thank you for heating
Thank you for your rest in my soul
Thank you for your feel within me.

The eye is the lamp of the body. If your eye is sound your whole body will be full of light.
Matthew 6:22

Since boyhood Columba had devoted himself to training in the Christian life, and to the study of wisdom; with God's help, he had kept his body chaste and his mind pure and shown himself, though placed on earth, fit for the life of heaven . . . He was brilliant in intellect and great in counsel. He spent thirty four years as an island soldier, and could not let even an hour pass without giving himself to praying or reading or writing or some other task. Fasts and vigils he performed day and night with tireless labour and no rest. At the same time he was loving to all people, and his face showed a holy gladness because his heart was full of the joy of the Holy Spirit.

Adamnan

Purity, wisdom and prophecy,
These are the gifts I would ask of Thee,
O High King of Heaven, grant them to me.

The lamp of the body is purity,
And those that have it their God shall see,
For the pure in heart know how to love,
And I have longed my love to prove.

This is the gift I would ask of Thee,
O Lord of my manhood, bestow it on me,
Your wisdom I pray for, a light for the mind,
And those that seek it shall surely find
The way in which to serve and lead;
My people are lost and a shepherd need.

The gift of the soul is prophecy;
Enlarge my vision that I may see
The past and the present and future as one
That here on this earth Thy will be done.

Purity, wisdom and prophecy,
These are the gifts I would ask of Thee;
O High King of Heaven, grant them to me
Columba's Prayer
from the play with music Columba.

A grasping person can become generous

My dear friends, do not believe all who claim to have the Spirit, but
test them to find out if the spirit they have comes from God.
1 John 4:1

During Columba's journey back from a meeting of rulers near
Limavady, Ireland, the bishop of Coleraine arranged for him to lodge at
the local monastery, and prepared a huge collection of offerings from
local believers, which were laid out in front of the monastic buildings.
As Columba looked at them and blessed them, he pointed to one gift
and said, 'The man who gave this enjoys the mercy of God on account
of his generosity and his mercies to the poor.' However, he pointed to
another gift of food with these words, 'This is the gift of a man who is
both wise and greedy. I cannot so much as taste it unless he first makes
penance for his greed.'

This word soon got around the crowd. When Columb mac Aedo
heard it he walked forward and knelt in front of Columba, confessed,
and promised to renounce greed, mend his ways, and practise
generosity. Columba told him to stand up, and announced that he was
a changed man, and was no longer grasping. Columb walked away tall
though chastened, generous, free and affirmed.

In Iona Columba once saw a threatening rain cloud moving towards
Ireland, and he knew that it would bring a life-threatening sickness to a
particular district there. So he sent one of his monks to sail over to
Ireland saying, 'Take this bread I have blessed in the name of God, dip
it in water and then sprinkle that water over both the people and their
livestock in that place, and they will soon recover their health.' The
monk, Silnan, landed and found six men in one house who were
already near to death. When he sprinkled them as Columba had said
they were all restored to health. News of this spread and many people
came to Silnan with their livestock. These were all sprinkled and were
saved from disease.

> Give me a desire to see others reach their greatness
> Give me a word to help another grow.
> May petty ways drop from us like scales.
> Step by step you lead us.
> Feed and remake us
> Till we are glad to be givers
> Till we joy in being brothers
> Till we delight in being sisters
> Till heaven laughs in delight
> At our pleasure in each other.

Whoever does not take up their cross and follow in my steps is not fit
to be my disciple.
Matthew 10:38

The restoration of Iona and the founding of the Iona Community this
century seem to be a fulfilment of Columba's prophecy, 'Iona of my
love, instead of monks' voices shall be lowing of cattle; but ere the
world shall come to an end Iona shall be as it was.' The founder of the
modern Iona Community, Lord MacLeod, wrote about the three
ancient crosses on Iona:

St John's Cross is the first to get you back to the Truth. The opening
chapter of his Gospel reads 'The world was made by Christ and
without him was not anything made that was made.' This means that
Christ is CREATOR and not just Redeemer. Jesus, here and now, is as
much involved in politics as he is in prayer. He is to be obeyed in
material problems.

St Martin's Cross. Martin was horrified that all the monks in Gaul were
interested in was their salvation. He persuaded them to get back to
comforting people in the towns, in the matters of their housing, their
education and their employment. One of his fellow monks was an
uncle of Columba, and he went to Iona and showed Columba the kind
of 'all-in' Christianity that so rapidly converted the West of Scotland.

St Matthew's Cross. Matthew was a tax collector. The love of money
was the curse of Gospel times, as it is of ours today.

George MacLeod

> Lord God, in the dawn of creation
> And in the presence of your Son
> Your light shattered the force and lure of darkness.
> We ask your help today
> For those who, in public and personal life
> Are in the grip of that which is wicked
> For those who deal in rumours and perpetrate cheap gossip
> For those who are slaves to a vice they fear to name
> For those who have traded openness for secrecy
> Morality for money, love for lust.
> We ask for a light not to blind them
> But to show them the way out of their darkness.
> *Iona Community* The Wee Worship Book

Righteousness exalts a nation.
Proverbs 14:34

Fellowship replaced hostility between brothers in many a monastery,
and this spirit overflowed into the people among whom they lived, as
this story, handed down by word of mouth, illustrates: When Columba
visited the monastery on the isle of Eigg he discovered that two monks
were preaching in a spirit of rivalry. Columba asked them both to
stretch out their right hand toward the sky. 'One of you is slightly taller
than the other, but neither of you are remotely within reach of that
cloud up there,' he said. 'So to your knees. Pray for one another and
for the people of your kingdom whom you serve.' Both monks fell to
their knees and their prayers, which used to stick in the thatch, now
reached to heaven! They were now comrades, helping to forge a
comrade people.

The Celtic people in the west of Britain called themselves Cymru
which means 'the land of comrades' (this is how we have the name
Cumbria today). The invading Anglo-Saxons renamed the southern part
Wales, which means 'land of foreigners'. This is a typical example of
the suspicions, caricatures and prejudices that developed with the
emergence of the separate nations of Wales, England, Scotland and
Ireland and one cannot but help feel that the community God intended
for this group of islands was continuously damaged by the darkness of
evil and human sin. Interestingly, many are now looking to the Celtic
church as a resource for healing the hurts and divisions between our
nations.

Michael Mitton

God-control would bring into action those latent powers which we
often hide under a cover of false reserve – and call it national character.
If those latent powers were released and mobilised under God they
would generate enough power to change the thinking and living of the
world.

Frank Buchman

Lord, may our lands find their peace and their destiny in your will.
Give us that dynamic which calls out and combines
The moral and spiritual responsibility of individuals
For their immediate sphere of action.
We pray for an uprising of people who give leadership
Free from the bondage of fear, sorry for the blindness of the past,
Rising above ambition, flexible to the direction of your Holy Spirit,
Reaching out with generous hearts to neighbouring peoples.

Do not use harmful words, but only helpful words, the kind that build up and provide what is needed, so that what you say will do good to those who hear you.
Ephesians 4:29

When Columba paid a visit to the the important Clonmacnoise Monastery, in Ireland, he was surrounded by the many brothers who wanted to be near him. A boy whose negative attitudes and looks caused people to look down upon him, crept in behind Columba. He had heard read from the Bible how a miracle occurred in a woman in a crowd who was able to touch just the edge of Jesus's cloak, so his idea was to touch the edge of Columba's cloak without being noticed. Columba, like Jesus, sensed in his spirit that someone was there, turned round and taking the boy by the neck, brought him forward. Some of the brothers tried to shoo the boy away. Columba hushed them. 'Open your mouth and put out your tongue,' he asked the boy. Columba reached forward and blessed the boy's tongue. He told the brothers, 'Do not let this boy's present disposition make you despise him. From now on he will cease to displease you. Indeed, he will please you greatly, and grow, little by little, day by day, in goodness and greatness of spirit. Wisdom and discernment will increase in him and he will become an outstanding figure in your community. God will give him eloquence to teach the way of salvation.'

This boy was Ernene mac Craseni, who was to become famous throughout the churches of Ireland, and highly regarded.

Once the foster parents of Domnell mac Aedo brought their boy to Columba. Columba looked at him for a while and then gave this prophetic blessing, 'This boy will outlive all his brothers and be a famous king. He will never be handed over to his enemies but will die at home in his bed, in peaceful old age, in the friendly presence of his household.' All this came true.

> May Father, Son and Spirit replenish and renew you
> So that an island shall you be in the sea
> A hill shall you be on the land
> A well shall you be in the desert
> Health shall you be to the ailing.
> *Attributed to Columba*

Families need fathers

Children, honour your father and mother; fathers, bring up your children with Christian discipline.
Ephesians 6:2,4

Although Samson's father and mother gave him a nanny when he was small, they made sure that they gave prime time to playing with their child. They made little plays about the Christian festivals together, and they read together.

At the early age of five Samson proudly announced that he wanted to go to school – to the School for Christ made famous by Illtyd, for boys who would go on to be ordained into the Christian ministry. At first, Samson's father Amon opposed this. He wanted his son to follow a career that would bring in money and which would continue the family's links with high society. The issue became an almost daily battle with his wife. However, God spoke powerfully to Amon in a dream. This clarified for him that this plan was not just a wish of Samson or of his wife, it was the will of God. Amon and his wife, although she was again pregnant, rose up with one united purpose to introduce Samson to his new school.

When you face God in prayer, become in your thoughts like a speechless babe. Do not utter before God anything which comes from knowledge, but approach God with childlike thoughts, and so walk before God as to be granted that fatherly care which fathers give their children in their infancy.

Isaac of Nineveh 7th century

Father
Give us all fatherly care.
Help fathers to reflect you
In the way they discharge their responsibilities.
May they be priests
To their spouses and to their children.

So then stand firm and steady. Keep busy always in your work for the Lord, since you know that nothing you do in the Lord's service is ever useless.
1 Corinthians 15:58

A mind prepared for red martyrdom.
A mind fortified and steadfast for white martyrdom.
Forgiveness from the heart for everyone.
Constant prayers for those who trouble you.
Fervour in singing.
Three labours in the day – prayers, work, and reading.
From the Rule of Columba,
now in the Burgundian Library, Brussels

Iona, Iona, Iona,
The seagulls crying,
Wheeling, flying
O'er the rain-washed bay;
Iona, Iona,
The soft breeze sighing,
The waves replying
On a clear, blue day, Iona.

Iona, Iona, Iona,
The wild winds whipping,
Comfort stripping
With the gale's chill sword;
Iona, Iona,
The waters glisten,
The wild winds listen
To the voice of our Lord;
Iona.

Iona's blessing strengthens and firmly it will hold you;
Then from this rocky fortress goes forth our island soldier;
May Christ who calmed the tempest with safety now enfold you.
From the play with music, Columba

Lord, may these graces flower as never before –
The grace of authenticity and trust
The grace of forgiving love and laughter
The maturity of pity for those who manipulate.

All of us reflect the glory of the Lord; and that same glory, coming from the Lord who is the Spirit, transforms us into his very likeness, in an ever greater degree of glory.
2 Corinthians 3:18

The glory of God is seen in a human life lived to the full.

Irenaeus

Plunge yourself into humility and you will see the glory of God.

St Isaac of Syria

> He is a bird round which a trap is closed
> A leaking ship unfit for a wild sea
> An empty vessel and a withered tree –
> Who lays aside God's wishes unimposed.
> He is the sun's bright rays, pure gold and fine,
> A silver chalice overfilled with wine
> Holy and happy, beautiful in love –
> Who does the will of God in heaven above.
> *Ancient Irish Lyric translated by Molloy Carson*

People are my scenery.
  A London landlady

Holy Spirit, Enlivener:
Breathe on us, fill us with life anew.
In your new creation, already upon us, already breaking through,
groaning and travailing,
but already breaking through,
breathe on us.
Till that day when night and autumn vanish:
and lambs grown sheep are no more slaughtered:
and even the thorn shall fade and the whole earth shall cry Glory at
the marriage feast of the Lamb.
In this new creation, already upon us,
fill us with life anew.

George MacLeod

Jesus said: Learn from me because I am gentle and humble in spirit.
Matthew 11:29

Aidan, the apostle of the English, was a gentleman.
   When Oswald came to the throne of Northumbria he sent to the
Irish leaders at Iona and asked them to send him a leader, by whose
teaching his people might learn the lessons of faith in the Lord and
receive the sacraments.

He obtained his request without delay, and was sent Bishop Aidan, a
man of great gentleness.

Bede

When Paul listed gentleness as one of the nine fruits of the Spirit
(Galatians 5:23) he used the Greek word *praotes*. This word overflows
with meanings; it is far removed from some current images of
gentleness as unreasonable sweetness, powerless passivity, or timidity.
Plato considered gentleness to be 'the cement of society'. Aristotle
defined it as the mean between being too angry and never becoming
angry; the gentle person expresses anger for the right reason and
duration and in the right way. It is the characteristic needed when
exercising discipline (Galatians 6:1), facing opposition (2 Timothy 2:25),
and opening ourselves to hearing God's Word without pride (James
1:21).

> This is the most important part of the rule;
> love Christ, hate wealth;
> Devotion to the King of the sun
> and kindness to people.
>
> If anybody enters the path of repentance
> It is sufficient to advance step by step.
> Do not wish to be like a charioteer.
> *From the Rule of St Comgall*

> Gentle Christ,
> may I see you more clearly
> love you more dearly
> and follow you more nearly
> day by day.
> *After St Richard of Chichester*

Be sure that your endurance carries you all the way, without failing, so that you may be complete.
James 1:4

> The tempests howl, the storms dismay,
> But manly strength can win the day.
> Heave, lads, and let the echoes ring.
>
> For clouds and squalls will soon pass on,
> And victory lie with work well done.
> Heave, lads, and let the echoes ring.
>
> Hold fast! Survive! And all is well,
> God sent you worse, He'll calm this swell.
> Heave, lads and let the echoes ring.
>
> So Satan acts to tire the brain,
> And by temptation souls are slain.
> Think lads of Christ, and echo him.
>
> The king of virtues vowed a prize,
> For him who wins, for him who tries.
> Think lads, of Christ, and echo him.
>
> > *Attributed to Columbanus' monks*
> > *rowing up the Rhine against the tide*

In the steep common path of our calling
Whether it be easy or uneasy to our flesh
Whether it be bright or dark for us to follow
May your own perfect guidance be given us.
Be a shield to us from the ploys of the deceiver
And in each hidden thought our minds start to weave
Be our director and our canvas.
Even though dogs and thieves try to wrench us away from the fold
Be our Shepherd of glory near us.
Whatever matter, issue or problem
That threatens to bring us to grief
Hide it from our eyes
And drive it from our hearts for ever.

> > *Carmina Gadelica*

Those who depend on their wealth will fall like the leaves of the autumn, but the righteous will prosper like the leaves of summer.
Proverbs 11:28

> The beauty of summer, its days long and slow
> Beautiful too visiting the ones we love.
> The beauty of flowers on the tops of fruit trees
> Beautiful too covenant with the Creator.
> The beauty in the wilderness of doe and fawn
> Beautiful too the foam-mouthed and slender steed.
> The beauty of the garden when the leeks grow well
> Beautiful too the charlock in blossom.
> The beauty of the horse in its leather halter
> Beautiful too keeping company with a king.
> The beauty of a hero who does not shun injury
> Beautiful too is elegant Welsh.
> The beauty of the heather when it turns purple
> Beautiful too moorland for cattle.
> The beauty of the season when calves suckle
> Beautiful too riding a foam-mouthed horse.
> And for me there is no less beauty
> In the father of the horn in a feast of mead.
> The beauty of the fish in his bright lake
> Beautiful too its surface shimmering.
> The beauty of the word with which the Trinity speaks
> Beautiful too doing penance for sin.
> But the loveliest of all is covenant
> With God on the Day of Judgement.
>
> *The Loves of Taliesin*

> God of the long day
> You who are eternally awake
> I offer you my eternal 'yes' –
> The flower of my humanity
> The energy and awareness of my days
> The creativity of my life
> The beauty of form
> And the hope of future potential.
> Amen and Amen. Praise be to you. Amen.

Rising sap

I came in order that you may have life – life in all its fullness.
John 10:10

Today is the summer solstice of the northern hemisphere.

Sap rises
Lambs frolic
Buds burst
Sports blossom
Hedgerows drip
Bodies surge
Brains storm
God's days are long
Christ's athletes race
Spirit's energies are true.

Life be in my speech
Sense in what I say
The bloom of cherries on my lips
Till I come back again.

The love Jesus Christ gave
Be filling every heart for me
The love Jesus Christ gave
Filling me for everyone.

Traversing corries, traversing forests
Traversing valleys long and wild
The fair white Mary still uphold me
The Shepherd Jesus be my shield.

The fair white Mary still uphold me
The Shepherd Jesus be my shield.
                                Traditional Gaelic

God of the longest day
May my life be a long day for you
Always reflecting your light
Open, awake.

I will sing about your strength. Morning by morning I will sing of your love.
Psalm 59:16

In the morning, my Lord, I offer you praise
As I water my plants set out in their trays,
As I think of their roots, to make the plant strong
And I feed on your Word, which never is wrong,
As I look at the leaves, turned face to the sun
May I look towards you until this day is done,
As I admire the bright flowers
Giving glory to you
May I bring pleasure in the things that I do.
As I look at the fruit, tasty and sweet,
May I taste of you to the people I meet.
As I think of the seed, hidden away,
May I plant one seed for you on this day.
In the morning, my Lord, I offer you praise
As I water my plants set out in my trays.

Craig Roberts Pocket Celtic Prayers

O Son of my God, what a pride, what a pleasure
To plough the blue sea!
The waves of the fountain of deluge to measure
dear ire, to Thee.
The host of the gulls come with joyous commotion
And screaming and sport
I welcome my boat 'Dewy-Red' from the ocean
Arriving in port.

The sounds of the winds in the elms
Like the strings of a harp being played
The note of the blackbird that claps
With the wings of delight in the glade.

Attributed to Columba

God of the rising green
God of the sweeping blue
God of the long bright day
May I sweep glory to you.

You welcome those who find joy in doing what is right, those who remember how you want them to live.
Isaiah 64:5

About 580 Columba's friend Cormac-of-the-Sea, afterwards Bishop of Durrow, had dreadful experiences adrift on the sea after visiting the Orkney and Shetland isles which he evangelised. They were attacked by dangerous sea creatures. Columba became aware of these attacks while he was praying and called the Iona brothers to intercede for a change of wind. There is a long dialogue in Old Irish which is said to have passed between Columba and Cormac when they safely arrived in Iona.

> Columba:
> You are welcome, O comely Cormac
> From over the all-teeming sea.
> What sent you forth, where have you been
> Since the time we were on the same path?
> Two years and a month to this night
> Is the time you have been wandering from port to port
> From wave to wave. Resolute the energy
> To traverse the wide ocean!
> Since the sea has sent you here
> You shall have friendship and counsel.
> Were it not for Christ's sake, Lord of the fair world
> You had merited satire and reproach!
>
> You are welcome, since you have come
> From the waves of the mighty sea
> Though you travel the world over . . .
> It is in Durrow your resurrection shall be.
>
> Cormac:
> O Columcille of a hundred graces . . .
> We shall abide in the West if you desire it.
> Christ will unfold his mysterious intentions!
>
> *Old Irish*

> God, eternally awake
> may your energies flow through me
> God of the rising sap
> May I be your sap today.

Jesus began to speak about John the Baptist to the crowds . . . You saw much more than a prophet . . . John is greater than any one who has ever lived. But the person who is least in the Kingdom of God is greater than John.
Luke 7:24, 26, 28

Every generation needs people like John the Baptist who make a radical break with comfort and convention, and prepare the way for a new move of God. In some ways Columba was a John the Baptist figure for his time, as these verses suggest.

> He broke passions, brought to ruin secure prisons
> Colum Cille overcame them with bright action.

> Connacht's candle, Britain's candle, splendid ruler
> In scores of curraghs with an army of wretches
> he crossed the long haired sea.

> He crossed the wave-strewn wild region, foam-flecked, seal-filled
> savage, bounding, seething, white-tipped, pleasing, doleful.

> Wisdom's champion all round Ireland, he was exalted;
> excellent name: Britanny's nursed, Britain's sated.

> He left chariots, he loved ships, foe to falsehood;
> sun-like exile, sailing, he left fame's steel bindings.

> Triumphant plea; adoring God, nightly, daily,
> with hands outstretched, with splendid alms, with right actions.

> Fine his body, Colum Cille, heaven's cleric –
> a widowed crowd – well-spoken just-one, tongue triumphant.
> > *The last verses of Beccan*

Give us, O God
something of the spirit of your servant John the Baptist
His moral courage
His contentment with simplicity
His refusal to be fettered by this world
His faithfulness in witness to the end

From Brendan O'Malley
A Pilgrim's Manual: St David's

Elijah went up to the people and said 'How much longer will you halt
between two opinions? If the Lord is God, worship him'.
1 Kings 18:21

A poor man named Nesan once had the privilege of giving
accommodation to Columba, and he stretched his meagre means to give
generous hospitality. Before he departed Columba asked him how many
cows he had. 'Five,' Nesan informed him. 'Bring them to me that I
may bless them,' said Columba. As he raised his hand in blessing,
Columba said, 'From today your little herd of five cows will increase
until you have one hundred and five cows. Also, your seed will be
blessed in your children and grandchildren.' All these things were
fulfilled.

On another occasion, in contrast, a rich man named Vigen declined
to offer hospitality to Columba, whom he looked down upon.
Columba made quite the opposite prophecy about him. 'The riches of
this miser who has rejected Christ in the pilgrim visitors, will from this
moment diminish little by little until there is nothing left. He will end
up a beggar and his son will run from house to house with a half
empty bag. A rival will strike him with an axe and he will die in the
trench of a threshing floor.' Unfortunately all this came true, also.

> May the yoke of the Law of God be on this shoulder
> May the coming of the Holy Spirit be on this head
> May the sign of Christ be on this forehead
> May the hearing of the Holy Spirit be in these ears
> May the smelling of the Holy Spirit be in this nose
> May the vision that the People of Heaven have be in these eyes
> May the speech of the People of Heaven be in this mouth
> May the work of the Church of God be in these hands
> May the good of God and of the neighbour be in these feet
> May God be dwelling in this heart
> May this person belong entirely to God the Father
>
> *Traditional Irish*

When the rainbow appears in the clouds I will see it and remember the everlasting covenant between me and all living beings on earth. That is the sign of the promise I am making to all living beings.
Genesis 9:16,17

My heart does indeed leap up when I see a rainbow in the sky. The wonder of a rainbow lies in its ethereal beauty, the harmony of its colours, its arching providence, its hidden depths. Pagans sense a primal meaning in a rainbow; but why should they take to themselves titles that more truly belong to followers of the God of the rainbow? For Christians, a rainbow is a sign of God's blessing, a prism of unity, and a mirror of the many coloured human personality made in God's image.

Red is the colour of sacrificial love. As Christ spilt his blood for us, so we are to 'spill' what we own and share it with our sisters and brothers.

Orange is the signal of our love. It is our witness to Christ in word and action.

Yellow is the root of our love – prayer. It may seem weak or pale. Some people will overlook it or laugh at it. We must not be paralysed by this dismissive attitude, for it has a glory all its own; without it, the other colours would be nothing.

Green is the off-shoot of our love – the nurture of life in our bodies and in the eternal things we steward. When something gets out of order in any organism it loses its health. Foster and guard vitality.

Blue is the setting of love – it is the creating of a beautiful stable environment. Our dress should enhance the features of our God-given personality. Our homes should reflect the artistry of our souls, and so draw others towards the author of our soul.

Indigo is the thinking of love – it is our study, our wisdom, our spiritual discipline.

Violet is the communion of love. It is good communication. It is like the electric current that can link up the world.

Inspired by Chiara Lubich and the Focolare spirituality

Be thou my vision, O Lord of my heart.
9th century Irish

So David summoned the people of Gibeon and said to them, 'What can I do for you? I want to make up for the wrong that was done to you, so that you will bless the Lord's people.'
2 Samuel 21:3

Restitution was the hallmark of the Penitentials which Celtic church leaders popularised throughout Europe. Unlike the continental church, where confession was made to a priest, and absolution received without restitution having to be made to the wronged person, the Celts based penitence upon restitution. Sin had to be dealt with. Wrongs had to be put right. The aim was that the relationship with the wronged person was restored.

Columba's great act of penance for his part in associating Christianity with violence was to go into exile from his beloved homeland for the rest of his life, in order to take Christ's love to another people. In recent times Christians have made penance for the way the Crusades associated Christ with mindless killing of Muslims by Prayer Walks of Reconciliation along routes where innocent people were killed. One such walker told me of local Muslims coming to the walkers in tears and in love. The aim of the walkers was not to convert, it was to make penance and to ask forgiveness. If it dawns on Muslims that following Christ is about following unconditional love, a whole new set of dynamics will come into play.

During the coming years, could we identify wrongs others feel we have committed against them, and make acts of atoning service? In that way, some of the baggage of hates, hurts, fears and mistrust of the second millenium need not be carried over into the third.

> We weep for Christian buildings that speak of domination
> for Christian communities that became places of greed
> for churches that became distant from the poor.

> > Sorry Lord for the sins committed by Christians
> > During the Age of Pisces
> > For being corrupted by power
> > For not listening to you
> > Or to the cries of the people
> > For not honouring your presence in creation
> > In the simple things all around.

Be filled with thanksgiving.
Colossians 2:7

Our most deadly sickness is the national epidemic of whining. Our cry-baby culture is influencing the world and cultivates a great and overwhelming sense of self-pity. There are two causes for this. First, an over-indulgence in the electronic media; second, the inability to express gratitude.

Michael Medved, U.S. film critic and author

My dear King, my own King, without pride, without sin, you
    created the whole world, eternal, victorious King . . .
And you created men and women to be your stewards of the earth,
    always praising you for your boundless love.

The Celtic Psalter

Hilda was attacked by a fever which tortured her with its burning heat, and for six years the sickness afflicted her continually; yet during all this time she never ceased to give thanks to her Maker and to instruct the flock committed to her charge both in public and in private. Taught by her own experience she warned them all, when health of body was granted to them, to serve the Lord dutifully and, when in adversity or sickness, always to return thanks to the Lord faithfully.

Bede

Gratitude is the root of all virtue.
    A pagan saying

My speech – may it praise you without flaw
may my heart love you
King of heaven and earth.

My speech – may it praise you without flaw
make it easy for me, great Lord,
to do you all service and to adore you.

My speech – may it praise you without flaw
Father of all affection
hear my poems and my speech.

Early Irish Lyrics

There is more happiness in giving than in receiving.
Acts 20:35

Aidan neither sought nor cared for this world's possessions, and he
loved to give away to poor people whom he met all the gifts he
received from kings and rich men of the world.

Bede

There are three causes for the inordinate love of money – desire for
pleasure, vainglory and lack of trust. And the last is stronger than the
other two.

Maximus the Confessor c. 580–662

Never be greedy, always be generous, if not in money, then in spirit.

Columbanus

> Columba tells us, that
> the generous shall never go to hell.
> But those who steal and those who swear
> Shall lose their right to God.
>
> *Carmina Gadelica*

God's work done in God's way will not lack supplies.

Hudson Taylor

> I would prepare a feast and be host to the great High King,
> with all the company of heaven.
> The sustenance of pure love be in my house,
> the roots of repentance in my house.
> Baskets of love be mine to give,
> with cups of mercy for all the company.
> Sweet Jesus, be there with us, with all the company of heaven.
> May cheerfulness abound in the feast,
> the feast of the great High King,
> my host for all eternity.
>
> *Traditional – sometimes attributed to Brigid*

Abraham named that place 'The Lord Provides', and even today people
say 'On the Lord's mountain the Lord provides.'
Genesis 22:14

Cuthbert was travelling south along the river Teviot, teaching and
baptising the country folk in the hill areas. He had a boy with him,
whom he sought to train in an understanding of God's providence. 'Do
you think any one has prepared your midday meal today?' he asked the
boy. The boy said he knew of no friends or relatives on their route and
did not expect provision from anyone. 'Don't worry, but seek first the
kingdom of God and the Lord will provide for all your needs,'
Cuthbert told him. 'I have been young; now I am old, but I have
never seen God forsake those who do what is right.'
   Some time later Cuthbert saw an eagle in the sky and said, 'This is
the eagle which the Lord has instructed to provide us with food today.'
Shortly, the eagle settled on the river bank, and, at Cuthbert's bidding,
the boy walked over to it and took away a large fish which the eagle
had brought. Cuthbert said, 'Why did you not leave half of this for our
fisherman to eat?' The boy returned half the fish to the eagle, they
broiled their half of the fish in the company of some men who had a
fire going, and shared their fish with them, too. They thanked the Lord
and worshipped him, and went on their way to the hill people.
   We can learn three lessons from this incident: to expect God to meet
our daily needs, to share what we have, and to share our experience of
life with people whose company or facilities we need. In short, to let
God into everyday affairs.

There is as much in our Lord's pantry as will satisfy all his bairns, and
as much wine in his cellar as will quench all their thirst.
                                                        Samuel Rutherford

Where God guides God provides.
          Frank Buchman

          Give us this day our daily bread.

RECONCILING ALL

People and creation are woven together depicting the importance of
wholeness and community, with Christ at the centre.

Jesus spoke to them about the Kingdom of God in parables: 'Once there was a man who planted a vineyard which he let out to tenants.'
Mark 12:1

When Cuthbert first went to live on the desolate Farne Island the ground was hard, there was no water, and the birds ate the first seeds that he planted. So he set to to dig and trench the hard land. When some guests came there was not sufficient water for them to drink, so Cuthbert invited them to help dig down into the ground where he had built his cell, and he prayed over them as they dug. Soon, water flowed out: they had dug down to a well.

Friends brought wheat seeds for him to sow in Spring, but by midsummer nothing had grown. So Cuthbert concluded it was not God's will for wheat to grow on the island, and he asked his friends to bring over some barley seed instead. This was brought long after the proper time for sowing it, but Cuthbert persevered. In fact it sprang up quickly and produced an excellent crop. But then there was another set-back. The birds began to devour the barley. So Cuthbert talked to the birds, which was also his way of sorting out things with God, along these lines, 'Why do you touch my crops? If it is because you have greater need of them than I and it is God's will for you, then go ahead. But if not, be off, and no longer damage what belongs to someone else.' The birds desisted and Cuthbert was able to live off his barley.

> Be a gardener.
> Dig a ditch
> toil and sweat
> and turn the earth upside down
> and seek the deepness
> and water the plants in time.
> Continue this labour
> and make sweet floods to run
> and noble and abundant fruits to spring.
> Take this food and drink
> and carry it to God
> as your true worship.
>
> *Julian of Norwich*

Lord, I give to you the 'seeds' that you have given me
At the present time.
Help me to to do my very best with them
That a good crop may ensue.

Soldier of Christ

Take your part in suffering as a loyal soldier of Jesus Christ. A soldier on active service wants to please his commanding officer and so does not get mixed up in the affairs of civilian life.
2 Timothy 2:3, 4

Two great saints, Samson and David (the patron saint of Wales), were pupils in the famous monastery of Illtyd, who may be regarded as the founder of the Welsh church, though holy hermits prepared the way. Illtyd was a very well educated soldier who came to Wales from Britanny, and, according to one medieval record, fought in the army of 'King' Arthur. But it was while serving the King of Glamorgan that he became a Christian.

One day Illtyd took a party of knights hunting, and became separated from them. They stumbled upon the hut of the hermit Cadoc, and treated him disgracefully, shouting obscenities at him. When Illtyd arrived he was shocked by his men's behaviour, and riveted by Cadoc's, for he refused to retaliate and smiled on them. Illtyd dismissed his men, and fell on his knees asking Cadoc to forgive their behaviour. Cadoc lifted Illtyd up and warmly embraced him.

That night, as Illtyd lay awake, his heart was filled with love for the old hermit. The life of such a man, who was victorious in the battle with Satan, seemed so much finer than that of a soldier, whose only battles were with other soldiers. When he had fallen asleep he dreamed that an angel spoke to him these words, 'Until now you have been a knight serving mortal kings. From now on you are to be in the service of the King of kings.'

At dawn Illtyd crept out of the royal palace, leaving behind his sword and his armour, and set out, clothed only in a rough woollen cloak, to be a soldier of Christ. In his mind, he would spend the rest of his life as a hermit.

> Teach me my God and King
> To fight with all of my being
> For the things that are good and true and peaceable
> As a faithful servant and soldier of our Lord Jesus Christ.

The teachings of the wise are a fountain of life; they will help you
escape when your life is in danger.
Proverbs 13:14

Illtyd had been living the life of a hermit for some three months when
a stag burst in, quickly followed by pack of hounds, the King and his
hunt. When the King realised it was Illtyd he erupted in fury and
accused Illtyd of betraying him. Illtyd, like Cadoc, simply smiled and
invited them into the hut for a meal. Astonishingly, the stag which the
hounds had been pursuing lay down outside, together with the hounds!
At the end of the meal it was the King's turn to have his heart
changed, and he asked Illtyd's forgiveness. Then the King asked if he
could send his son to Illtyd to be educated. That marked the beginning
of a miracle in Christian education. Soon Illtyd's place in the valley by
the sea became the largest school in the whole of Britain, a school for
Christ, and Illtyd became known as the wisest teacher in Britain.

Illtyd believed that hard physical labour should always be combined
with intellectual study, a body-mind balance. Everyone had to spend
four hours a day working outside, and soon the whole valley had been
farmed. Illtyd invented a new plough which doubled the speed at
which land could be prepared.

After many years King Paulinus, whose son had died, was succeeded
by a malicious man who tried to destroy Illtyd's work. The King's
henchmen, who secretly honoured Illtyd, warned him that he was to be
murdered. Illtyd took this as God guiding him to go back to being an
anonymous hermit. So he secretly trekked to a cave further along the
coast, and grew a beard and long hair so no one would recognise him.
However, a year later a monk was travelling from the old monastery to
a new monastery David had founded, with a brass bell which was a gift
for David. He took a wrong turning and passed near Illtyd's cave. Illtyd
heard the bell, came out, and struck it three times. The monk did not
recognise his former leader, but strangely, the bell stopped ringing. The
monk told David about this on his arrival. 'God has told us where our
dear Illtyd is hiding,' said David, and sent the monk to invite him to
join him. Illtyd declined the invitation to go back into a large
community, but three of David's monks went to support him and care
for him until he died.

> Lord, unlock the treasures of wisdom to me
> But first give me a heart for humble learning.

Be true to yourself

Your God is faithful and true.
Deuteronomy 32:4

To thine own self be true.
    William Shakespeare

We are meant to be faithful and true, just as God is. However, since we all want and need to be affirmed, but many of us are not, we instinctively seek illicit affirmation, by tailoring our actions in order to gain the approval of others. In a subtle way, this means that we are no longer being true to ourselves. We perhaps unconsciously say to ourselves, 'If I behave in this or that way I will not get appreciation.'

Once Columba came on a visit to the brothers on Hinba Island, and felt they needed to learn to enjoy life, to loosen up and relax their strict diet for a while; and this relaxation included people who were doing penance for some past sin. One of these, Nemen, declined to relax his diet, appearing to be most pious. Columba, however, realised that he was not really being true to himself. He predicted that, because of this, the time would come when Nemen would be back with a gang of thieves in a forest and would eat a horse that had been stolen. Later Nemen was found out to be doing just that.

How can we cure this disease of the soul? Here is an original prescription from the desert:

Abba Macarios told a monk to go to a cemetery and shout his anger at the dead. This he did. Then Macarios told the monk to go there again and this time to praise the dead. He did this, too.

Neither time, of course, did they react. The point was: Why let those who are dead to God prevent you from being true to yourself?

Help me to be
True to myself
True to you
True to others
True to the call
True to all
True to heaven.

At any time I am content, whether I am full or hungry.
Philippians 4:12

Not every one could leave home or job for God's sake in Celtic times, nor is everyone called to do so now. But many people long to experience what life is like as a pilgrim who goes into exile from life's comforts. If we share this longing, we, too, can walk to holy places in the simplicity of God's creation, or undertake an inner journey of vigil, fasting and prayer.

The point of this journey is that life's excess baggage, which we cannot take with us into eternity, might be discarded, and that the inner compass by which we can be guided might be uncovered.

We often spend our lives running away from this call, in the fear that if we are stripped of worldly securities there would be nothing left, or we would not know contentment. Be assured that, if we are truly open to whatever is God's best for us, we will find deep contentment.

In this poem the warrior king asks his brother Marvan why he has given up his top job and feather quilt in order to live as a hermit. This is Marvan's answer:

Beautiful are the pines which make music for me unhindered.
Through Christ I am no worse off at any time than you.
Though you relish that which you enjoy exceeding all wealth
I am content with that which is given me by my gentle Christ.
With no moment of strife, no din of combat such as disturbs you,
thankful to the Prince who gives every good to me in my hut.

Early Irish Poem

All that I have I offer to you
All that you wish, I leave behind for you
Wherever you lead, I will follow you
So help me God.

Lead us on our journey
To places of resurrection
To dwellings of peace
To healings of wounds
To joys of discovery.

I have complete confidence in the gospel; it is God's power to save all who believe, first the Jews and also the other peoples of the world. *Romans 1:16*

I believe, O God of all gods
That you are the eternal Father of life
I believe, O God of all gods
That you are the eternal Father of love.

I believe, O God of all gods
That you are the eternal Father of the saints
I believe, O God of all gods
That you are the eternal Father of each person.

I believe, O God of all gods
That you are the eternal Father of humanity
I believe, O God of all gods
That you are the eternal Father of the world.

I believe, O God of the peoples
That you are the Creator of the high heavens
That you are the Creator of the skies above
That you are the Creator of the oceans below.

I believe, O God of the peoples
That you are the One who created my soul and set its warp
Who created my body from dust and from ashes
Who gave to my body breath, and to my soul its endowment.

Father eternal and Lord of the peoples
I believe that you have put right my soul in the Spirit of healing
That you gave your loved Son in covenant for me
That you have purchased my soul with the precious blood of your
  Son.

Father eternal and Lord of life
I believe that you poured on me the Spirit of grace at my baptism.

Praise to the Father
Praise to the Son
Praise to the Spirit
The Three in One.

Carmina Gadelica

Set your hearts on spiritual gifts, especially the gift of prophecy.
1 Corinthians 14:1

Cuthbert decided to join a monastery. He had heard of the prophetic leadership of Boisil, abbot of Melrose, so he rode to Melrose with his boy servant. As Cuthbert dismounted and gave his sword and spear to his servant to take away, Boisil was watching. Foreseeing in spirit how great the man whom he saw was going to be, he uttered this one sentence to those who were with him, 'Mark this, here is a servant of the Lord.' Bede comments that in saying this Boisil was echoing Jesus's words on first seeing Nathaniel, 'Here is a true man of the people, in whom there is nothing false.'

Years later Cuthbert returned to Melrose monastery, where he fell victim to the plague, though he was to recover. Boisil prophesied, 'You will not get the plague again, nor will you die at the present time; however, I will die of this plague; so let me use the seven days left to me to teach you.' They spent each of those days studying John's Gospel.

In fact Boisil had predicted the plague to his abbot Eata three years before it appeared, and did not hide the fact that he himself would be carried off by it; but he declared that the abbot himself would not die of this but rather of dysentery, and events proved his prophecy was true.

Cuthbert used to tell people, 'I have known many who far exceed me in their prophetic powers. Foremost amongst these is Boisil who trained me up, and foretold accurately all the things which were to happen to me. Of all these things only one remains to be fulfilled.' This was the prophecy that Cuthbert would become a bishop. It may be Cuthbert would have refused the pressures on him to become a bishop had it not been for Boisil's prophecy. After his death Boisil appeared in prophetic dreams which helped shape the future of the kingdom.

> God of the thunder
> God of the sap
> God of the future
> God of the map
> God of the silence
> God of the gap
> God of my happenings
> God in my lap.

When you pray, go to your room, shut the door, and pray to your Father, who is unseen. Your Father, who sees what you do in secret, will reward you.
Matthew 6:6

Grant me, sweet Christ, the grace to find, Son of the Living God
A small hut in a lonesome spot
To make it my abode.

A little pool but very clear, to stand beside the place
Where every sin is washed away
By sanctifying grace.

A pleasant woodland all about, to shield it from the wind
And make a home for singing birds
Before it and behind.

A southern aspect for the heat, a stream along its foot
A smooth green lawn with rich topsoil
Propitious to all fruit.

My choice of those to live with me and pray to God as well;
Quiet friends of humble mind
Their number I shall tell.

A lovely church, a home for God, bedecked with linen fine,
Where o'er the whitened Gospel page
The Gospel candles shine.

A little house where all may dwell, and body's care be sought,
Where none shows lust or arrogance,
None thinks an evil thought.

And all I ask for housekeeping
I get and pay no fees,
Leeks from the garden, poultry, game,
Salmon, fruit and bees.

My share of clothing and of food from the King of fairest face,
And I to sit at times alone
And pray in every place.

The Hermit's Prayer, Abbot Manteith,
6th century

Every day they studied the Scriptures.
Acts 17:11

In regard to the deeper meanings of the Scriptures, so acute was Samson's understanding that he wanted to dig deeper than his teacher. Once the two of them came across a doubtful point; though they had carefully studied all the books of the Old and New Testaments, they could not find a satisfactory explanation. Thereupon Samson decided to undertake fasts and vigils until God's understanding broke through. He was praying at nearly midnight when a heavenly light appeared and a voice spoke out of the light: 'Do not trouble yourself any further on this, God's chosen one, for in future whatever you ask God for in prayer and fasting you will obtain.' Then Samson returned quite happy to his cell and told Illtyd, his teacher, all he had seen and heard.

The Life of Samson of Dol

Urged by devoted Christians and my own inmost heart, I have made as penetrating a study as possible of the entire character, body and mind, of Christians who by their active and their contemplative life shine like stars of heaven to help us.

The author of the Life of Samson

Daily Bible reading is at the heart of this way of life. In addition, we study the history of the Celtic church, becoming familiar with such saints as Aidan, Brigid, Caedmon, Columba, Cuthbert, David, Hilda, Illtyd, Ninian, Oswald and Patrick. We remember their feast days and consider them as companions on our journeys of faith. We also bear in mind their strong link with the Desert Fathers and the Eastern Church, and wish to draw them too into our field of studies. It is essential that study is not understood merely as an academic exercise. All that we learn is not for the sake of study itself, but in order that what we learn should be lived. We encourage the Celtic practice of memorising scriptures, and learning through the use of creative arts.

The Way of Life of the Community of Aidan and Hilda

> O Lord, may it be your wisdom, not my folly
> Which passes through my arm and hand
> May your words take shape upon the page.
> For when I am truly faithful to your dictation
> My hand is firm and strong.

A scribe in a Celtic monastery

Lord God . . . you show your people your love when they live in wholehearted obedience to you.
2 Chronicles 6:14

Four things by which the Kingdom of heaven may be pursued: stability and detachment from the world, devotion and constancy.

Colmán mac Béognae The Alphabet of Devotion

> O God
> manage me
> because I can't manage myself.
> *A schoolboy*

Selwyn Hughes, the veteran author of Bible reading notes, was asked by a TV interviewer, 'What is the most important lesson you have learned?' 'Dependency,' Selwyn replied. 'Life works better when you throw all your weight on Christ. Not part of your weight, not even a lot of your weight. All of your weight.'

> I am giving you worship with my whole life
> I am giving you assent with my whole power
> I am giving you praise with my whole tongue
> I am giving you honour with my whole speech
>
> I am giving you reverence with my whole understanding
> I am giving you dedication with my whole thought
> I am giving you praise with my whole fervour
> I am giving you humility in the blood of the Lamb
>
> I am giving you love with my whole devotion
> I am giving you kneeling with my whole desire
> I am giving you love with my whole heart
> I am giving you affection with my whole sense
> I am giving you existence with my whole mind
> I am giving you my soul, O God of all gods.
>
> My thought, my deed
> My word, my will
> My understanding, my intellect
> My way, my state.
>
> *Carmina Gadelica*

She answered 'We will starve to death . . .' The widow went and did as Elijah told her, and all of them had enough food for many days. *1 Kings 17:12, 15*

Christians believe that prayer can change anything. But experience shows that God is not in the business of the 'quick fix'. Frequently we go away disappointed after our initial requests. The following story reminds us that prayer, like life itself, is a process. If at first we do not get through, re-evaluate and pray from a different perspective. We will find that the good God, who is full of surprises, will not fail us.

Mungo, from his base at Clathures, became a firm friend of Rhyderch, the Christian King of Strathclyde, whose headquarters was fifteen miles down river at Dunbarton. But Morcant, the local ruler and patron of the Druid altar at Craigmaddie Moor was a bitter enemy of them both. His mercenaries looted the local crops which they stored in Morcant's barn. That winter real hunger struck Mungo's people. He walked to Craigmaddie Moor and confronted Morcant, saying the people needed food. 'You Christians teach that God will provide for those who serve him. Well, I don't serve him and I have plenty; you serve him and have nothing, so your teaching must be false,' Morcant mockingly told him.

Mungo returned to Clathures empty handed, but he was not defeated. He gathered the people to pray. Their prayers were answered in this way. After they prayed the rain came down in deluge after deluge. The rivers flooded their banks, and Morcant's barn took off towards the river Clyde like an ark on a wild cruise. On the banks of the Molindar it went hard aground beside Mungo's church!

Next morning Mungo gathered his flock to thank God and eat a good breakfast. Morcant did not find it at all funny!

> Some have meat and cannot eat;
> Some cannot eat that want it:
> But we have meat and we can eat
> Sae let the Lord be thankit!
> *Robert Burns*

I am content and at peace. As a child lies quietly in its mother's arms, so my heart is quiet within me.
Psalm 131:2

Cuthbert kept throughout the same countenance, the same spirit. At all hours he was happy and joyful, neither wearing a sad expression at the remembrance of a sin nor being elated by the loud praises of those who marvelled at his manner of life . . .

After two years he resigned the bishopric and returned to the solitary way of life on the island . . . He remained alone, satisfied with the converse and ministry of angels, full of hope and putting his trust wholly in God, though his body was now infirm and afflicted with a certain sickness.

Life of Cuthbert *by an anonymous monk of Lindisfarne*

(Following the imposition of Roman regulations at the Council of Whitby) there were certain brothers at the Lindisfarne monastery who preferred to conform to their old usage rather than to the monastic rule. Nevertheless Cuthbert overcame these by his modest virtue and his patience, and by daily effort he gradually converted them into a better state of mind. In fact very often during debates in the chapter concerning the rule, when he was assailed by the bitter insults of his opponents, he would rise up suddenly and with calm mind and countenance would go out, thus dissolving the chapter, but none the less, on the following day, as if he had suffered no repulse the day before, he would give the same instruction as before to the brothers . . . For he was a man remarkable for the strength of his patience and unsurpassed in bravely bearing every burden whether of mind or body.

Bede's Life of Cuthbert

> The serenity of Christ
> The serenity of kindly Cuthbert
> The serenity of mild and loving Mary
> The serenity of Christ, King of tenderness
> Be upon each window and door
> The four corners of this place
> The four corners of my bed
> Be upon each thing my eye takes in
> Upon each thing my mouth takes in
> Upon my body that is of the earth
> Upon my spirit that came from on high.
> *Carmina Gadelica* (adapted)

Make room for us in your hearts. We have wronged no one; we have
ruined no one; nor tried to take advantage of anyone.
2 Corinthians 7:2

A group of English people went on a week's prayer walk along the
length of the river Thames. The walk began with Celtic prayers in a
church, which is dedicated to St Samson, near the Thames' source. It
ended near a statue of Neptune, a symbol of the power of the city of
London, and of the British Empire, epitomised by the song 'Rule,
Britannia!'.

The prayer walk led these Christians into repentance for the lust for
power in the English people. Ask Irish, Scots or Welsh what they most
dislike about the English, and they will tell you it is the lust for power
that neither notices nor cherishes the other person or nation.

Yet the true birthright of the English lies in their gentle apostle
Aidan who gave up his right to ride a horse, in order to be one with
the ordinary people, armed only with the defencelessness of love.

The method of church building used by most Celts was to construct
small, provisional buildings – the church was the people growing in
relationships of love. They built churches without walls.

The Celtic clerics dressed simply; without a note of triumphalism.
Many bishops were monks, which meant that they renounced
possessions, and did not try to extend the kingdom of God through
collecting possessions 'for the church'.

When Celtic bishops met with Augustine, Archbishop of Canterbury,
perhaps on the site where that Thames Prayer Walk began, they sought
advice from a holy hermit whose authority lay in his having renounced
power. The hermit's advice was, 'If Augustine is a holy man you should
take his advice. You will know if he is holy if he is humble enough to
stand up to greet you. If he does not, you need not take his advice.'
The result was a lost opportunity for co-ordinated evangelism of the
English peoples. Yet, despite 'losing out' in terms of worldly power, the
Celtic witness, which lies in the abandonment of power, is the witness
which speaks to millions today who reject a way of being Church that
is built upon worldly power or status.

> Strip from us everything except integrity
> Bring the servant heart to flower

A Broad Mind

I will pray with the spirit, but I will also pray with the understanding.
1 Corinthians 14:15

For eagerness of the truth, it is fitting that its proper nature should be reckoned: zeal without anger, humility without neglect . . .
   What is best for the mind? Breadth and humility, for every good thing finds room in a broad, humble mind. What is worst for the mind? Narrowness and closedness, and constrictedness, for nothing good finds room in a narrow, closed, restricted mind.
                    Colmán mac Béognae The Alphabet of Devotion

Pray attentively and you will soon straighten out your thoughts.
                                        Desert Sayings

> I will not cease from mental fight
> Nor shall my sword sleep in my hand.
>   *William Blake*

Always make a practice of provoking your mind to think out what it accepts easily. Our position is not ours until we make it ours by suffering. If you cannot express yourself on any subject, struggle until you can. If you do not, someone will be the poorer all the days of their life.
                                        Oswald Chambers

If you aim at nothing, you hit it.
                    Anon

> Jesus, Son of Mary
> Have mercy upon us
> Jesus, Son of Mary
> Be with us and for us where we shall longest be.
> Be at the dawning of our life
> Be at the darkening of our day.
>
> Consecrate us —
> All that we inherit, all that we acquire
> Consecrate each mind and body
> Each day to yourself
> Each night also
> King of kings
> God of all.
>   *Carmina Gadelica*

Deliver us from evil.
Matthew 6:13

A dear friend of Cuthbert's named Hildmer was responsible for the administration of law in his locality. His wife became demented. She was writhing, shrieking and salivating. Hildmer was not only deeply upset for her, he was also embarrassed that this should happen to a respected Christian couple. He came to tell Cuthbert she was ill and to ask him to send a priest from the Lindisfarne monastery to administer the prayers for the sick and dying, but he could not bring himself to tell Cuthbert the nature of the illness (Christians aren't supposed to have demons or dementia).

Cuthbert agreed to send a priest, and Hildmer was leaving, when the Holy Spirit stirred Cuthbert to call Hildmer back and tell him, 'It is my duty to come with you, not another's.' So Cuthbert, with a group from the monastery, accompanied the weeping Hildmer to his dying wife.

Cuthbert sensed the true condition of the patient, without having to be told, and during the journey he revealed to Hildmer the things Hildmer had hidden from him. Cuthbert reassured him, 'It is not only the wicked who are tormented like this, but sometimes God also allows the innocent to be taken over not only in body, but also in the mind. But don't worry, for when we come to your house, your wife whom you think is dead will come to meet me. When she takes these reins of the horse which I have in my hand she will be restored to full health, and will look after our needs, and the demon will be driven away.'

That is exactly what happened.

> Lord, save us from making judgments about people who are ill
> Make us eager to encircle them with the prayer of loving friends
> Help us discern what you wish to do in each situation
> That a step towards wholeness may always be taken
> Not in our way, but in yours.

The apostles performed many signs and wonders among the people.
Acts 5:12

Let him who will, laugh and insult, I will not be silent, nor will I hide
the signs and wonders which were ministered to me by the Lord, many
years before they came to pass, as he who knew all things before the
world began.

Patrick of Ireland

God who judges the heart showed by signs and wonders what Aidan's
merits were.

Bede

Cuthbert became famous for his miracles. Through his persistent prayers
he restored to health many who were sick, he cured some that were
afflicted by unclean spirits, not only when present . . . praying,
touching, commanding and exorcising, but also when absent either by
prayer alone or even indeed by predicting their cure . . . Signs and
wonders whereby he shone outwardly gave witness to the inward
virtues of his mind.

Bede's Life of Cuthbert

And after raising of dead men, healing lepers, blind, deaf, lame and all
kinds of sick folk . . . after expelling demons and vices . . . after
performance of mighty works and miracles too numerous to mention,
St Brendan drew near to the day of his death.

The medieval Life of St Brendan

> Great Father of the blood-red moon
> And of the falling stars;
> Great Saviour of the miraculous birth
> And of the rising from death;
> Great Spirit of the creators and the seers;
> Come in sovereign power
> Into our dreams
> Into our thoughts
> Into our mouths
> Into our bodies
> Into our actions
> Till we become your sign, and presence, and wonder.

Now remember what you were when God called you. From the human point of view few of you were wise or powerful or of high social standing. God purposely chose . . . what the world considers weak in order to shame the powerful.
1 Corinthians 1:26, 27

The Lord prefers common looking people. That is why he made so many of them.

Abraham Lincoln

We should never forget that, although only the words and deeds of the most notable Christians get handed down, Christianity was first spread by slaves, working soldiers and traders. In Celtic times Christianity was the religion of the people, it took root in ordinary hearts and homes. This fact is reflected in the prayers of the Scottish highlanders and islanders recorded by Alexander Carmichael so many centuries later. Here we have a glimpse of an army of ordinary people who invited God to be in the warp and weft of their everyday lives. These arrow prayers for ordinary days are inspired by the *Carmina Gadelica:*

As I wash, the love of Christ be in my breast.

God protect the household
God consecrate the children
God encompass our assets.

May I do my rounds under the shield of Michael chief of angels.

May the ingredients for the meal be mixed together
In the name of God's Son who gives growth.

Circle all my business dealings,
Keep out what is false, keep within what is good.

In everything my hands do today I will keep my fingers as a cross.

In my exercise may thankfulness pulse through my body.

As I sleep may your right hand be under my head.

My dear children, just like a mother in childbirth, I feel the same kind of pain for you until Christ's nature is formed in you . . . the heavenly Jerusalem is free and she is our mother.
Galatians 4:19, 26

One Sunday the ailing Mungo felt a keen desire for a hot bath. With loving care his Christian family lowered him in to the warm soothing water. After a time he rallied and gave these, his final words, to his friends, 'My children . . . love one another . . . be hospitable . . . beware of heresy . . . keep the laws of the Church . . . she is the Mother of us all'. His jaw dropped and this dear soul, known as the Beloved by so many, was dead.

'She is the Mother of us all.' The Church is divine, though its members are all too human. Wheat and weeds grow together. Those who take their cue from the weeds become cynical about the Church. Those who take their cue from the wheat become part of its divine work of fostering and mothering. According to David's biographer, Rhigyfarch, before Illtyd and Samson brought a renewal to the church in Wales most clergy were drunk. By the end of David's life, 'everywhere are heard evidences of churches, everywhere voices are raised to heaven in prayers; everywhere the virtues are unweariedly brought back to the bosom of the Church; everywhere charitable offerings are distributed to the needy with open arms.'

> Nurture us in the tender mercies of our mother the Church
> May we grow in her wisdom
> May we be enriched in her heritage
> May we be cherished by her mothers
> May we be stretched by her teachers
> May we be corrected by her shepherds
> May we be illumined by her seers
> May we be inspired by her saints
> May we be spurred by her innovators
> May we be made to feel at ease by her little ones
> May we be mortified by her holy ones
> May we be uplifted by her musicians
> May we be warned by her erring ones
> May we be blessed by her givers
> May we be warmed by her welcomers.

To the pure all things are pure.
Titus 1:15

Some years after the death of Kevin at Glendalough a very pious monk there named Moling used to miss meals in order to pray in the place of worship. Not only did he despise food, he never allowed himself the pleasure of listening to music. Until God sent someone to cheer him up.

One day a young man arrived and asked if he could play his harp to the brothers while they were in the refectory. They welcomed this. Since Moling, who was praying in church, missed this, the young man then went to the church to play. Moling, who was kneeling, did not lift his head, but took from his pocket two balls of wax and stuffed them in his ears.

The young man smiled and continued playing. To Moling's amazement the wax in his ears began to melt. Try as he might to push it back into his ears, it just trickled down under his habit.

At that moment the young man took a stone and started to scrape the harp. Moling found this excruciating sound unbearable. Then the young man threw the stone away and played music so sweet that Moling was filled with a joy greater than he had ever known.

When the harpist had finished playing Moling asked him, 'Are you a devil sent to tempt me or an angel sent to bless me?' 'You must make your own judgement,' the young man replied. 'When I scraped the harp it made the noise of the devil, and when I played it with my fingers it made the sound of an angel. Music, like food and drink, can be an agent of evil or a source of goodness.'

The young man then left. From that day Moling welcomed all musicians to play at the monastery, and he gave up undue fasting, abstaining from food only on those days when everybody fasted. His brothers could not help noticing that from that day onwards he became more gentle and kind, and even acquired a sense of humour.

O Son of God, change my heart.
Your spirit composes the songs of the birds and the buzz of the bees.
Your creation is a million wondrous miracles, beautiful to look
    upon.
I ask of you just one more miracle:
beautify my soul.

From a traditional Celtic prayer

Avoid extremes. If you have reverence for God things will work out anyway.
Ecclesiastes 7:18

Some people wear out their bodies by denying them food or rest; but because they have no discretion they are far from God.

Antony Sayings of the Desert Fathers

And so for several years he continued to live a solitary life cut off from the sight of people; and alone in all conditions he bore himself with unshaken balance . . . His conversation, seasoned with salt, consoled the sad, instructed the ignorant, appeased the angry, for he persuaded them all to put nothing before the love of Christ. And he placed before the eyes of all the greatness of future benefits and the mercy of God, and revealed the favours already bestowed, namely that God spared not his own Son but delivered him up for the salvation of us all.

Life of Cuthbert *by an anonymous monk of Lindisfarne*

In accordance with the example of Samson the strong, who was once a Nazarite, Cuthbert carefully abstained from all intoxicants; but he could not submit to this kind of abstinence in food, lest he became unfit for necessary hard labour.

Cuthbert wore ordinary garments and, keeping the middle path, he was not noteworthy either for their elegance or for their slovenliness. Hence his example is followed in the same monastery (Lindisfarne) even to this day, but they are fully satisfied with that kind of garment which the natural wool of the sheep provides.

Bede's Life of Cuthbert

Lord, today
May the needs of my body and the needs of my mind,
The practical needs of work, and the social needs
Each be given their rightful place and kept in balance.
May the needs for rest and fun, study and sleep,
Household order and justifiable work
All be completed.

We are often troubled, but not crushed; sometimes in doubt, but never in despair; there are many enemies, but we are never without a friend; and though badly hurt at times, we are not destroyed.
2 Corinthians 4:8, 9

Did Jesus's mother Mary feel she had lost everything as she saw her son die on the Cross? Mary had become 'willing to lose' even to the utmost extremity.

Did Aidan feel he had lost everything as his dear friend in Christ Oswine, the King who opened the door to the Christian mission, was killed? Aidan died eleven days afterwards, and some think he died of a broken heart.

'I'm broken,' confessed Columbanus, but God used him to the end.

Mungo's great mission partners Cadoc, Asaph and Deiniol died. Then his royal Christian friends Aidan, King of the Scots, and Rhyderch, King of Strathclyde, died under the shadow of failure. The Britons were routed and would never act as a united force again. Now, in 603, it was Mungo's time to depart, also under the shadow of failure. What Mungo did not know was that his story had only just begun, and the greatest period of evangelisation of his people would soon be under way.

Never forget that before the brightest dawn comes the darkest night.

Never forget that our extremity is God's opportunity.

I know perfectly well that poverty and misfortune suit me better than riches and pleasure. Christ the Lord, himself, was poor for our sakes.

Patrick

> God of heaven
> do not leave me in the path where there is screaming
> from the weight of oppression.
> Great God, protect me
> from the fiery wall,
> the long trench of tears.
>
> *Dallan mac Forgaill* The Elegy of Columcille

Discipline

Everything must be done in a proper and orderly way.
1 Corinthians 14:40

Do not give room to a person who is full of idle chatter and tittle
tattle; just give them your blessing and send them on their way.

Go along with any rule that evokes devotion.

Divide your work into three parts: first, your personal needs; second,
the needs of your community; third, work that meets needs of
your neighbours, either discipling or practical work.

Give to people in need.

Do not eat until you are hungry. Do not sleep until you are ready
for it.

Do not converse with people except for a good cause.

Every time you receive something, give something away to a friend
or a poor person.

Love God with all your heart and strength.

Love your neighbour as yourself.

Make the Old and New Testaments your home at all times.

Work at your devotion until tears come, or at least until perspiration
comes.

Selected from Columba's rule

Lord temper with tranquillity
our manifold activity
That we may do our work for thee
with very great simplicity.
A 16th century prayer

I will make a covenant with the wild animals, the birds of the air and the creeping things on the ground.
Hosea 2:18

When Jesus commands us to love our neighbours, he does not only mean our human neighbours; he means all the animals and birds, insects and plants, amongst whom we live. Just as we should not be cruel to other human beings, so we should not be cruel to any species of creature. Just as we should love and cherish other human beings, so we should love and cherish all God's creation.

We learn to love other human beings by discerning their pleasure and pain, their joy and sorrow, and by sympathising with them. We need only poke a horse with a sharp stick to discern the pain it can suffer; and when we stroke and slap that same horse on the neck, we can feel its pleasure. Thus we can love a horse in the same way we can love another human being. Of course, our love for other species is less full and less intense than our love for humans, because the range and depth of their feelings are less than our own. Yet we should remember that all love comes from God, so when our love is directed towards an animal or even a tree, we are participating in the fullness of God's love.

Pelagius To an elderly friend

Encompass each goat, sheep and lamb,
Each cow and horse and store
Surround the flocks and herds
And look after them in a kindly fold
Carmina Gadelica

Father, bless the pet
Also bless the vet.
Saviour, bless the flock
Also bless the cock.
Spirit, bless the horse
Also bless my course.

Hail to you, glorious Lord

Let them all praise the name of the Lord, whose name is greater than all others. The Lord's glory is above heaven and earth. The Lord made the nation strong so that all the people should give the Lord praise. *Psalm 148:13, 14*

Hail to you, glorious Lord.

May chancel and church praise you
May plain and hillside praise you

May the three springs praise you
Two higher than the wind and one above the earth
May darkness and light praise you
May the cedar and sweet fruit tree praise you
Abraham praised you, the founder of faith
May life everlasting praise you
May the birds and the bees praise you
May the stubble and the grass praise you
Aaron and Moses praised you
May male and female praise you
May the seven days and the stars praise you
May the lower and the upper air praise you
May books and letters praise you
May the fish in the river praise you
May thought and action praise you
May the sand and the earth praise you
May all the good things created praise you
And I, too, shall praise you, Lord of glory
Hail to you, glorious Lord!

Early Middle Welsh

O Being of life! O Being of peace!
O Being of time, and time without cease!
O Being, infinite eternity!
O Being, infinite eternity!

Carmina Gadelica

Do not be proud or irritate one another or be jealous of one another.
Galations 5:29

> Whoever made you to envy
> Swarthy man or fair woman
> I will send three to overcome it
> Holy Spirit, Father, Son.
> *Carmina Gadelica*

Jealousy can cripple, whether it is in oneself, or whether one is the victim of others' jealousy. We need to guard against it in ourselves. The Worship Book of the Celtic Monastery at Cerne, Ireland contained this petition, 'Guard my eyes for me, Jesus, Son of Mary, lest seeing another's wealth make me covetous.'

What can you do if fellow Christians who work with you become jealous of you? Stand back, quietly do the essential things that have to be done, but do not aggravate the situation by pushing the boundaries. Place the situation into the hands of God and ask God to deal with it as and when God chooses. Only time will tell whether there has to be a break or whether love can replace jealousy. For jealousy feeds on a deficit of affirming love, so pray in the cure. The Three who can overcome jealousy are the affirming Father, Spirit, Son.

> I will start this day
> In the presence of the holy angels of heaven
> Without malice, without jealousy, without envy
> Without fear of any one under the sun
> The holy Son of God to shield me.
>
> God, kindle in my heart within
> A flame of love to my neighbour
> And to my foe, to my friend, to all
> To the winner, to the loser
> O Son of the loveliest Mary
>
> Without malice, without jealousy, without envy
> Without fear of anyone under the sun
> The holy Son of God to shield me.
> *Carmina Gadelica (adapted)*

Stand ready with truth as a belt, righteousness as a breastplate . . . faith as a shield . . . salvation as a helmet, the word of God as a sword which the Spirit gives.
Ephesians 6:14 – 17

When Cuthbert arrived in Farne Island, 'our soldier of Christ entered, armed with "the helmet of salvation, the shield of faith, and the sword of the spirit which is the word of God", all the fiery darts of the wicked one were quenched, and the wicked foe was driven far away together with the whole crowd of his assistants. This soldier of Christ, as soon as he had become monarch of the land he had entered and had overcome the many usurpers, built a city fitted for his rule, and in it houses equally suited to the city . . .

Moreover not only the creatures of the air but also of the sea, yes, and even the sea itself, as well as air and fire did honour to the honoured man. For if a person faithfully and wholeheartedly serves the Maker of all created things, it is no wonder that all creation should minister to their directions. For the most part, we lose dominion over the creation because we neglect to serve the Creator of all things . . .

Many came to the man of God . . . No one went away without enjoying his consolation . . . He had learned how to lay bare before those who were tempted the many tricks of the ancient foe, by which the person who lacks human or divine love may easily be trapped. But whoever goes strengthened by unwavering faith passes, with God's help, through the enemy snares as if they were spiders' webs. "How many times," Cuthbert said, "have they tried to kill me. But though they tried to frighten me away by one phantasmal temptation after another, they were unable to mar my body or my mind by fear." '

Bede

As I put on the belt of truth, may I be open to your word which is truth however it may come to me today.

As I put on the helmet of salvation, may your law be my guide and delight this day.

As I take up the shield of faith, may I hold on to your promises and know them in my life.

As I put on the sword of the Spirit may I be open to the promptings of your Spirit this day.

Michael Halliwell

In Christ there is no difference between Jews and foreigners, between citizens and alien workers.
Galatians 3:28

Brian Keenan, the Belfast journalist who became a hostage in Beirut, wrote that in his home city there was an unseen and uncontrollable malevolence: 'Out of a sense of frustration, of fear, of a raging thirst for identity and purpose. It seemed that people were drinking in this poison. Some unconsciously, and some by choice until they became intoxicated with rage and despair and helplessness.'

Keenan himself made 'the mythic leap and crossed the Jordan . . . There are those who cross the Jordan and seek out truth through a different experience from the one they are born to, and theirs is the greatest struggle. To move from one cultural ethos into another, as I did, and emerge embracing them both demands more of a man than any armed struggle. For here is the real conflict by which we move into manhood and maturity. For unless we know how to embrace the other we are not men and our nationhood is wilful and adolescent.'

Brian Keenan of Belfast An Evil Cradling

Wales's national saint David has been pictured by a modern Welsh poet as God's Gypsy who, 'brought the church to our homes, and took bread from the pantry and bad wine from the cellar, and stood behind the table like a tramp so as not to hide the wonder of the Sacrifice from us. After the Communion we chatted by the fireside, and he talked to us about God's natural order, the person, the family, the nation and the society of nations, and the Cross keeping us from turning any one of them into a god.'

David Gwenallt Jones

God of all peoples
Help us to find our deepest identity in you.
Christ incarnate in my people
Help us to forgive what has been done to us.
Spirit between peoples
Help us to be like you, by giving and receiving from others.

The woman gave birth to a son and named him Samson. The child
grew and the Lord blessed him. And the Lord's power began to
strengthen him.
Judges 13:24, 25.

Samson of Dol was born about 486 in South Wales. When he was five
his parents took him to Illtyd's famous school at Llanilltud Fawr, near
Cowbridge, and while still there, in his twenties, he was ordained
deacon and priest. God directed him to join the monastery of Piro.
From there, somewhat reluctantly, he visited his sick father, who
recovered through his prayers. As a result the entire family (with the
exception of his youngest sister) devoted themselves to God's service
and planted churches. Samson succeeded Piro as abbot. He went on a
mission to Ireland, and on his return sent his brother Umbraphel to be
abbot of a monastery given to him in Ireland. While in retreat with his
parents near the river Severn he was summoned to a synod and
ordained a bishop. This (unlike present ecclesiastical practice) freed him
to evangelise and travel widely. He longed to go over to Britanny, but
a British Christian prophesied that he was first to evangelise Cornwall.
This he did. Once he was in Britanny an amazing number became
Christians, and formed Christian communities. For a time Samson was
on a mission in Romania. He returned to Britanny, where he died on
July 28, and his remains were kept at the great monastery at Dol which
he founded.

In truth his humility, courtesy and gentleness, and above all his
wonderful love, beyond human measure, so to speak, was such that he
was regarded by all the brothers with wonderful affection.

The Life of Samson

> We bless you Lord
> That Samson's birth, schooling and calling
> Were the fruit of prophecy.
> We thank you Lord
> That his prayer, his heroic acts of witness
> His courtesy and wonderful love towards all
> Won pagans to the Faith
> And patterned a new way of being the church.
> As we contemplate his life
> Give us a holy renewal.

No one can deny how great is the secret of our religion: Christ appeared in human form; was shown to be right by the Spirit; was seen by angels. He was preached among the nations, was believed in throughout the world, and was taken up to heaven.
1 Timothy 3:16

> Any one who rejects God's will
> Is like a leaking ship on a stormy sea
> Is like an eagle caught in a trap
> Is like an apple tree which never blossoms.
>
> Any one who obeys God's will
> Is like the golden rays of the summer sun
> Is like a silver chalice overflowing with wine
> Is like a beautiful bride ready for love.
>
> *Traditional Celtic saying*

> I believe that God is One
> I believe that God is eternal
> I believe that God is Love
>
> Therefore I believe that God is relationship
> Therefore I believe that God is community
> Therefore I believe that God is Three
>
> Each of the Three Persons is God
> Without this God could not be the Highest
> Without this God could not be Eternally Love.

Loving Saviour, show yourself to us
that knowing you we may love you as warmly in return
may love you alone, desire you alone
contemplate you alone by day and night
and keep you always in our thoughts.
May affection for you pervade our hearts.
May attachment to you take possession of us all.
May love of you fill all our senses.
May we know no other love except you who are eternal.
A love so great
that the many waters of land and sea will fail to quench it.
Columbanus

I can do all things through Christ who gives me strength.
Philippians 4:13

Sometimes, perhaps especially during holiday periods when familiar helps are not to hand, we slide into the 'anything goes' mentality when faced with a catalogue of difficulties. Learn from a convert of Patrick's named Attracta how to overcome a catalogue of woes. She wanted to establish a Christian community in one place, but Patrick insisted she establish it somewhere else. This proved to be a place where one disaster after another faced her. She could easily have left in a sulk, telling him, 'I told you so', but Attracta was made of sterner stuff than to do that.

Everyone in the area was terrified of a wild animal which attacked people at whim; eventually Attracta killed it herself, using her metal cross to do so. Then a local bard drowned in the nearby lake; Attracta nursed and prayed over him and brought him back to life. They needed to cut and transport trees with which to build the monastery, but there were no horses to pull the timber; Attracta used deer instead. Then they realised that they had no ropes with which to tie the timber to the wagons; so she used everything that was to hand, including strands of her own hair, to create strong cords.

Nothing ventured, nothing gained.
        Traditional British saying

> May the cross of Christ be over this face and this ear
> May the cross of Christ be over this mouth and this throat
> May the cross of Christ be over my arms
> From my shoulders to my hands.
>
> May the cross of Christ be with me, before me
> May the cross of Christ be above me, behind me.
>
> With the cross of Christ may I meet every
> Difficulty in the heights and in the depths.
> From the top of my head to the nail of my foot
> I trust in the protection of your cross, O Christ.
>   *Attributed to Mugron, Abbot of Iona from 965*

Pray for the peace of Jerusalem.
Psalm 122:6

The exact details of how Christianity first came to the Britons are
shrouded in legend, for example that of the coming of Joseph of
Arimathea, but scholars think that Glastonbury, which became known
as 'England's Jerusalem' probably had the earliest church.

> After Jerusalem's Christians were scattered the entomber of Christ,
> the noble commander Joseph, the enlightener of Britain
> planted here the Tree of salvation.
> Gildas the Wise, first writer of the Britons, recounted for us
> in Tiberius' last year, the coming of the Light.
> In these islands, stiff with pagan coldness, the Sun's rays shone.
> With Aristobulos, first Bishop of Britain, fanning the bright flame of
>   Joseph's kindling,
> Fagan and Dyfan, for King Lucius the Glorious,
> Restored here the church built by Christ's apostles' hands.
> Set in the jewel of Avalon, a church of wattles was made by holy
>   hands
> Dedicated by command of Christ to the dearest Mother of God
> That in these northern lands this first of churches should honour her
>   who brought humanity's fullness to birth.
> We give thanks for this cradle place of faith,
> Which drew to it, so 'tis said,
> holy Irish hermits
> David and his fiery zeal
> Which draws still a multitude – saints, sinners, strangers, seekers all.

Neo–Druids, Goddess–worshippers and others are not all to be dismissed
as cranks. As I know, wise and well–disposed spirits are among them.
Yet their outlook is surely partial . . . Better any number of quests,
even if some are illusory, than the arid pretence that there is no quest at
all.

Geoffrey Ashe Avalonian Quest

> As we enter a new millennium
> we pray for the withering of gods that fail us.
> May the Christ of the cosmos be to those who quest
> also the Christ of the womb, the workshop and the wounds.
> May the Christ of the resurrection live in our bodies now and for
>   ever.

All things were created by God and all things exist through God and
for God. To God be the glory for ever!
Romans 11:36

The season of Lammas begins on August 1. In the Celtic year this
marks the first of several harvests. By Samhain, November 1, all the the
fruits and berries too had to be gathered in.

Giraldus Cambrensis, Archdeacon of Brecon, described how the
people of a locality would come together at harvest to do a circle dance
around the churchyard. With mime and movements they re-enacted the
occupations connected with the fields – the spinning, weaving,
ploughing and reaping. They knew that all life is inter-connected, and
that all life depends upon God.

Few readers will engage in harvesting in the way the following poem
depicts from 19th century western Scotland. Yet as we read these
words, God may speak to us of the encompassing of the manifold
activities of our daily lives – our shops, our office, home and locality;
and the encompassing of the people who make up the chain that brings
food to our door.

> God bless Thou Thyself my reaping
> Each ridge, each plain, each field
> Each sickle curved, shapely, hard,
> Each ear and handful in the sheaf.
>
> Bless each maiden and youth
> Each woman and tender youngling
> Safeguard them beneath Thy shield of strength
> And guard them in the house of the saints
> Guard them in the house of the saints.
>
> Encompass each goat, sheep and lamb
> Each cow and horse and store
> Surround Thou the flocks and herds
> And tend them to a kindly fold
> Tend them to a kindly fold.
>
> *Carmina Gadelica*

I will be quiet and listen to you.
Job 6:24

Our ideal should be to give our utmost attention to the words of whoever is speaking to us, or leading a meeting or worship. However, some of us suffer from wandering thoughts. This may be because we are too busy, and as we sit back, unattended business comes crowding in to our minds. This tells us that we need to do less and make our life style more simple. Or our thoughts may wander because we have repressed 'primal inner material' that has not been attended to; when we sit back this pops up to the surface. Take hold of something that pops up, and get to know that thing that has been repressed or unacknowledged and let Jesus pray with you for it. Our wandering thoughts may be because we are flowing with creativity, and these energies need to be taken at the flood. If so, write down the thoughts and the inspirations that are coming to you, so that you can do something with them as soon as you have opportunity. Your wandering thoughts may be because the brain is made like that, in which case there is nothing you can do about it. Bless whatever thought has wandered into your mind, and bless it as it wanders on its way, and then bless God for the words being spoken to you in the present moment. Return to being fully attentive!

God help my thoughts!
They stray from me, setting off on the wildest journeys.

When I am in church, they run off like naughty children,
    quarrelling, making trouble.

When I read the Bible, they fly to a distant city, filled with beautiful
    women.

They slip from my grasp like tails of eels;
They swoop hither and thither like swallows in flight.

Dear, chaste Christ,
Who can see into every heart and read every mind
Take hold of my thoughts.
Bring my thoughts back to me
And clasp me to yourself.

Prayer of a Celtic monk

Jesus said: You will find an untamed colt. Untie it and bring it here. If someone asks you why you are untying it, tell him that the Master needs it.
Luke 19:30,31

> Tame pigs and goats and baby pigs
> at home all round it
> And wild pigs also
> tall deer and their does
> badgers and their brood.
>
> In peaceful parties
> crowds from the country visit my home.
> *From a poem of Marban the hermit*

Kevin's desire for solitude was realised when he made his home in the cave near the two lakes of Glendalough. There he developed close relationships with even the wildest animals.

It was said that when he prayed for one hour every night in the cold waters a monster used to distract and annoy him by curling itself around his body, biting and stinging him. In another story we learn of a monster in the Lower Lake which brought terror to the people who lived there. Kevin did not banish this creature as an enemy; it was said he took it with him to the Upper Lake. There his prayers, his patience and the warmth of God's love in him made the monster feel that there was nothing to be hostile about.

This story can also be understood as a picture of our inner life. We all have dark or wild monsters lurking within us, things we dare not face. Kevin teaches us to embrace the shadow side of our lives, without fear, so that there is nothing in our lives that we have not made peace with.

> Lord, help me to understand my own story
> To fear nothing except fear itself
> And to live at peace
> With myself, the creatures and the world

A gentle answer turns away wrath, but a harsh word stirs up anger.
Proverbs 15:1.

St Molua who died in Ireland on 4 August in the 7th century, was
noted for using gentle persuasion rather than strictly imposed rules, as
this story illustrates.

A bard named Conan, who was quite unused to manual labour,
joined Molua's monastery in the Slieve mountains. On the first day
Molua personally accompanied him to a thicket of thistles that had to
be cut down. On that day they cut down just one. On the second day
they cut down two, and so it went on.

Molua was not afraid to reprove a person when necessary, but he
always tried to do it with gentleness, and in God's way, knowing that
God always has the last word. Once the king of Leinster arrived with
four hundred of his men and demanded that they be instantly fed.
Molua patiently explained why that would be difficult. The king,
however, insisted, and food was brought as quickly as was possible, no
doubt causing considerable disruption to the life of the community. The
very first morsel the king tasted stuck in his gullet for twenty four
hours, preventing him from either eating or sleeping. The king learned
his lesson without anything more having to be said. From that time on
he became thoughtful and generous towards the community.

> Lord, help me
> To take the time to sit in the shoes of the other person
> To start from where they are
> To listen to what they feel
> To refrain from the too hasty judgment or the too ready answer
> To smile and be gentle
> And yet not to collude with the slipshod
> But to prayerfully see a thing through.

The Lord has sought out a man after the Lord's own heart to be the leader of God's people.
1 Samuel 13:14

The ambitious king Cadwallon slew the two kings of Northumbria. Oswald, the brother of one of them, and a man beloved of God, arrived with a small army to oppose the invader. He placed a large cross in the ground, and as he held the cross he addressed the whole army, 'Let us all kneel, and together pray the true and ever living God to defend us from a proud and cruel enemy. For God knows that this is a just war which we fight in order to liberate our people.' They won the victory against huge odds. The place of battle is called Heavenfield to this day, to indicate that Heaven's standard was set up there, Heaven's victory won, and Heaven's miracles continued. Many people were healed when splinters from this cross mingled with water were brought to them.

Oswald initiated a mission to his kingdom from Iona, and cared for the poor. He was deeply devout and rose early each day to pray. Under his rule the previously warring kingdoms of Bernicia and Deira became one people, although ethnic cleansing was normal in those days. Oswald died, still young, on the battlefield; his dying prayer was for the souls of his soldiers, not for himself.

In succeeding centuries peoples throughout Europe longed for examples of Christian kingship, and Oswald became a model far and wide. Many churches in the European Union are dedicated to St Oswald.

King Baudouin of the Belgians once told a friend that his purpose in being king was: to love his country; to pray for his country; to suffer for his country. At his funeral in 1993 Cardinal Suenens said, 'We were in the presence of one who was more than a king; one who was a shepherd of his people.'

> High King of heaven and earth
> From whom all authority flows
> May the diverse authorities of our times
> Acknowledge you as the Source of life
> Emulate you as the Servant King
> And fear you as the Judge of truth.

Jesus was transfigured before them, and his face shone like the sun, and his clothes became white as light.
Matthew 17:2

The Feast of the Transfiguration is August 6. That is the day we happened to drop the bomb on Hiroshima. We took His Body and we took His Blood and we enacted a Cosmic Golgotha. We took the key to love and we used it for bloody hell.

Suppose the material order is indeed the garment of Christ, the temple of the Holy Spirit? Suppose the bread and wine, symbols of all creation, are indeed capable of redemption awaiting its Christification? Then what is the atom but the emergent body of Christ?

George MacCleod

On the Feast of the Transfiguration may we be able to pray together for the redemption of the whole creation and a speedy end to the suffering of animals through human exploitation.

Marjorie Milne of Glastonbury

The poet Waldo Williams treasured the moment which like a shooting star makes us wonderfully conscious of the mystery and vastness and glory of the universe, the moment which suddenly reveals a presence and suddenly enchants the heart, the second which makes true acquaintance shine.

Pennar Davies

When the Saviour of this globe was stretched out on the Tree of
    death,
the elements erupted and the earth gave up its dead.
His blood, spilled on the soil, transfigured earth and heaven.
May his body and blood change us and transfigure this earth
Transfigure this earth: may your kingdom come on it
Transfigure this earth: may flowers bloom on it
Transfigure this earth: may people and animals be friends on it.
Transfigure this earth: may the scarred places be healed on it
Transfigure this earth: may peace reign on it
Transfigure this earth: may our bodies be changed into bodies of
    resurrection.

From a Celtic Eucharist, Community of Aidan and Hilda

God commanded 'Let the earth produce all kinds of plants . . .. Let the earth produce all kinds of animals . . .' God took of the earth and created a man.
Genesis 1:11,24; 2:7

The earth where King Oswald died seems to have soaked in his sanctity and to have become a seed-bed. A sick horse and a sick girl were cured by touching the soil upon which Oswald met his death; the soil from that spot seemed to have power to make the grass grow greener, to resist fire and to heal all sorts of people who were touched by it.

> The earth is at the same time mother
> She is the mother of all that is natural
> mother of all that is human
> she is the mother of all
> for contained in her are the seeds of all.
>
> In me be the truth of stream-lover willow, soil-giving alder
> hazel of sweet nuts, wisdom-branching oak.
> In me be the joy of crabapple, great maple, vine maple,
> cleansing cascara and lovely dogwood.
> And the gracious truth of the copper branched arbutus
> bright with colour and fragrance
> be with me on the Earth.
>
> *Chinook Psalter*

> The earth of humankind contains all moistness
> all verdancy
> all germinating power
> It is in so many ways fruitful
> All creation comes from it
> Yet it forms not only the basic raw materials for humankind
> but also the substance of the incarnation of God's son.
>
> *Hildegaard of Bingen*

God of the earth
Forgive us for becoming proud and disconnected
From your seed-bed of wisdom, nurture and life.
Help us always to know and feel that we are of the earth
May we live this day as your humus.

Then the Lord God took some soil from the ground and formed a man out of it; he breathed life-giving breath into his nostrils and the man began to live.
Genesis 2:7

Teach your children what we have taught our children
That the earth is our mother
Whatever befalls the earth befalls the sons and daughters of the earth
If men spit upon the ground they spit upon themselves
This we know.
The earth does not belong to us; we belong to the earth
This we know.
All things are connected like the blood which unites one family.
All things are connected
We did not weave the web of life
We are merely a strand in it.
Whatever we do to the web we do to ourselves.

Chief Seattle

Holy persons draw to themselves all that is earthly.
Hildegaard of Bingen

May all I say and all I think
be in harmony with you
God within me, God beyond me
maker of the trees.
Chinook Psalter

The food which we are to eat
Is earth, water and sun
Coming to us through pleasing plants.
The food which we are to eat
Is the fruit of the labour of many creatures.
We are thankful for it.
May it give us health, strength, joy
And may it increase our love.
A Unitarian prayer before a meal

They who wait on the Lord shall soar like eagles.
Isaiah 40:31

Understand, if you want to know the Creator, created things.
Columbanus

> The beauty of the trees
> The softness of the air
> The fragrance of the grass
> Speak to me.
>
> The summit of the mountain
> The thunder of the sky
> The rhythm of the sea
> Speak to me.
>
> The faintness of the stars
> The freshness of the morning
> The dewdrops on the flower
> Speak to me.
>
> The strength of fire
> The taste of salmon
> The trail of the sun
> And the life that never goes away
> They speak to me.
>
> And my heart soars.
> *Chief Dan George*

My dear King, my own King, without pride, without sin
You created the whole world, eternal, victorious King.

King above the elements, King above the sun, King beneath the
   ocean
King of the north and south, the east and west
against you no enemy can prevail.

And you created us to be your stewards of the earth
and we praise you for your boundless love.
The Celtic Psalter

No one helped God spread out the heavens or trample the sea monster's back . . . We cannot understand the great things God does; there is no end to the miracles God can do.
Job 9:8,10

Berach, who was planning to sail the always risky journey from Iona to Tiree, asked Columba to bless this journey. Columba looked at him long and hard, 'Take special care not to cross the open sea today in a straight course, otherwise you will meet an enormous monster who will terrify and well nigh overwhelm you. Go in a zig zag around the smaller islands.'

Berach set off, but, since everything looked fine, and it seemed so much easier to go direct, he disregarded Columba's advice. Some time after this an immense whale rose up like a mountain in front of the crew, opened its jaws, gaping, full of teeth. They let down the sail in terror and rowed back for their lives. In future, they weighed God's prophetic words more carefully.

Baithene had to make a similar journey, but unlike Berach, his impulses were in harmony with God. On the morning of their departure Columba told Baithene and his crew about the whale, but gave no advice. 'That beast and I are both under God's power,' said Baithene. 'Go in peace,' said Columba, 'your faith in Christ will defend you from this peril.' They did see the whale and the crew was terrified, but Baithene himself was without fear. He raised both his hands and blessed the sea and the whale. At that precise moment the whale plunged under the waves and they did not see it again.

> God aid me
> God succour me
> When near the reefs
>
> The Son of God shield me from harm
> The Son of God shield me from ill
> The Son of God shield me from mishap
> The Son of God shield me with power
> The Son of God shield me with might.
> *Carmina Gadelica*

Not a single one of these sparrows has been forgotten by God . . . yet you are worth much more than many sparrows.
Luke 12:6,7

And then there was St Kevin and the blackbird.
The saint is kneeling, arms stretched out, inside
His cell, but the cell is so narrow, so

One turned–up palm is out the window, stiff
As a cross beam, when a blackbird lands
And lays in it and settles down to rest.

Kevin feels the warm eggs, the small breast, the tucked
Neat head and claws and, finding himself linked
Into the network of eternal life,

Is moved to pity: Now he must hold his hand
Like a branch out in the sun and rain for weeks
Until the young are hatched and fledged and flown.

Seamus Heaney

O, King of the Tree of Life
The blossoms on the branches are your people
The singing birds are your angels
The whispering breeze is your Spirit.

O, King of the Tree of Life
May the blossoms bring forth the sweetest fruit
May the birds sing out the highest praise
May your Spirit cover all with gentle breath.

Traditional Celtic Prayer

Cows and bears will eat together, and their calves and cubs will lie down in peace. Lions will eat straw as cattle do.
Isaiah 11:7

Jerome was saying evening prayer with his brothers in the monastery at Bethlehem when a large lion limped in to the cloisters with an injured paw. Jerome took the injured paw in his hand and found that wounds from a cut had festered. The brothers bathed and tended these.

So much so that the lion made himself at home! This caused considerable discussion among the brothers. Jerome's conclusion was, 'God has sent us this lion to show that He wants to look after us. So instead of worrying about having a lion here, let us give it something useful to do.' They came up with a good idea: each day their donkey would take the lion with him to pasture, and the lion would guard the donkey from any who might steal or harm it.

This arrangement worked well until one day the lion fell asleep and some travelling merchants stole the donkey. After this the lion took to roaring up and down, and at nights would hang around disconsolately, staying outside the monastery. Some brothers assumed the lion had eaten the donkey, and that he should be banished. Jerome, however, thought that Christians should not judge others, even lions, without evidence. So they continued to give the lion care and food, and they gave him a new job: to go every day with a harness to fetch branches from the wood. The lion did this faithfully, but he still longed for the donkey, and instinctively looked out for him. One day, miles away, he saw the traders returning with the donkey leading the way. With roars and bounds he raced to them; the men fled in terror, and the lion brought the donkey and drove the laden camels back to the monastery.

Soon the shamefaced traders arrived to ask for their goods and camels, begged forgiveness, and offered the brothers expensive gifts. Jerome refused the gifts, and gently explained that the best way they could show their appreciation was always to thank God for His provisions, and never to take what belongs to others. This they promised to do.

> Lord, give me gentleness towards all creatures
> Integrity in my dealings
> And wisdom to handle unsettling situations.

Swear by the swift deer and the gazelles that you will not interrupt our love.
Song of Songs 3:5

Brynach was a hermit in 6th century Pembrokeshire, who every so often felt God leading him to move on and make another little hermitage which he would furnish with his meagre belongings. But how would he move his furniture, books and kitchenware?

This man who had no human or worldly support, had developed such a harmony with creation, that he felt even wild animals were part of a support network. So when the time came for a move, he would 'invite' two of the most friendly stags from the nearby herd, and tie his furniture to them. They went ahead of Brynach, with all his belongings, to his new abode. When Brynach took the yoke off them, they returned to the rest of the herd.

Brynach also selected an especially productive cow, and introduced her to a wolf. Each day the wolf would lead this one cow to a particularly lush patch of pasture, and bring it back at evening. In this way Brynach always had ample milk, and a good security system.

This Pembrokeshire hermit emerges from the mists of legend as a person at peace with both the natural and the supernatural world. It was said that he frequently met and talked with angels on the mountain between Nevern and Newport, which, as a result, became known as The Mount of Angels ('Carn Ingli').

> Almighty Creator, you have made all creatures.
> The world cannot express
> Even though the grasses and trees should sing,
> All your glories, provisions and riches.
> O Lord, how glorious you are.

The Lord said to Moses 'Choose six cities of refuge for Israelites and
for foreigners.'
Numbers 35:13,15

Melangell was the daughter of an Irish King who, in order to escape a
forced marriage, fled to Wales and settled as a hermit for Christ at
Pennant in Powys.

In 604 the Prince of Powys went hunting at Pennant. His hounds
chased a hare into the thicket of thorns where Melangell had built her
hermit's hut. There he discovered the pure and beautiful Melangell,
sheltering the hare under the folds of her cloak as she prayed. The
prince shouted to his hounds to catch the hare, but they must have
sensed a presence more powerful than their urge to catch the hare, for
they gradually went further and further away, despite all their owner's
shouting.

The Prince was astonished. He asked the young woman who she was
and Melangell told him her story. This made a deep impression on him.
Eventually he said to her, 'Because Almighty God was pleased to
protect this little hare through you, I will give you land which you may
use for the service of God, and also as an animal sanctuary.'

This, according to tradition, is the reason why Pennant Melangell
became a place of sanctuary for humans as well as for animals.
Melangell remained a hermit there for another thirty seven years. Her
biographer states, 'And the hares, wild little animals, just the same as
tame animals, were in a state of familiarity with her every day
throughout her whole life.'

> Lord
> You look after even the smallest of your creatures
> And even the least of your children.
> You are our refuge.
> With you we are safe.
> I pray for all people suffering abuse in their homes
> For all animals who are mistreated
> And for myself;
> Protect me from all that would harm either body or soul today.

Wolves and sheep will live together in peace, and leopards will lie
down with young goats.
Isaiah 11:6

When Piran arrived in Cornwall he lay down to sleep under a tree
which a wild boar used to frequent. At first the wild boar kept away
out of fright, but soon it sensed the child-like love in Piran, and they
became friends. Piran thought of him as his first monk, and the boar
did, indeed, become a servant of the community. It tore branches and
grass with its teeth with which to make a simple cell. Soon, other forest
animals came along to join Piran and the boar; these included a fox, a
badger, a wolf and a doe. Piran regarded them all as his monks.

However, as you might expect, the fox was more crafty than the
others. He stole Piran's shoes, abandoned the 'monastery', and chewed
the shoes back at his old lair. Piran talked to the badger about this. The
badger went to the fox, bit him, and with his fur in his mouth, pulled
him back to the 'monastery'.

'Why have you done this, my brother, which is something a monk
should never do?' Piran asked the fox. 'We all share the same water and
the same food; and if you were hungry, God would have turned the
bark of this tree into food for you.' The fox became penitent, and
showed this by refraining from eating until Piran gave permission.

From then on, all the animals lived at peace with Piran as their
'abbot'.

> Deep harmony of the forest be mine
> Child-like love for God's creatures be mine
> Growing trust in God's providence be mine.

Noah and his wife went into the boat with their three sons . . . With them went every kind of animal, domestic and wild, large and small. *Genesis 7:13, 14*

I and my white Pangur
Have each his special art:
His mind is set on hunting mice,
Mine is upon my special craft.

When in our house we two are all alone –
A tale without tedium!
We have – sport never-ending!
Something to exercise our wit.

At times by feats of derring-do
A mouse sticks in his net,
While into my net there drops
A difficult problem of hard meaning.

He points his full shining eye
Against the fence of the wall:
I point my clear though feeble eye
Against the keenness of science.

He rejoices with quick leaps
When in his sharp claw sticks a mouse:
I too rejoice when I have grasped
A problem difficult and dearly loved.

Though we are thus at all times,
Neither hinders the other,
Each of us pleased with his own art
Amuses himself alone.

He is a master of the work
Which every day he does:
While I am at my own work
To bring difficulty to clearness.

Thesaurus Palaeohibernus *translation by Kuno Meyer*

Creator God with sense of fun, may I share today's fun with you.

Believers will be given the power to perform miracles . . . if they pick up snakes or drink poison they will not be harmed.
Mark 16:17,18

After Samson's father had been healed of a serious illness, he, his wife, his brother and his brother's three sons all turned to the Lord, and began a mission journey to win converts and plant churches.

One day while on a journey they came to a point in their track which bore all the signs of burning and destruction from a notorious serpent, of a type which then existed, which the whole region feared. The family, full of apprehension, discussed what to do. Samson reminded them of Jesus's promise, 'If you have faith even as small as a mustard seed you can tell this mountain to move and it will.' 'Wait here, calmly,' he told them, 'while I go off and try to hear from God on this matter.' Samson's uncle tried to go with him, fearing for his safety, but Samson told him 'stay with the others until I return in triumph.'

Samson saw and heard the fire-spitting serpent in a far-off valley. He went towards it, reciting scriptures such as, 'The Lord is my light and my salvation.' With huge swishing and hissing the serpent twisted and grabbed its tail in its teeth; and then tossed a lump of earth almost in Samson's face. Samson made the Caim Circle Prayer around the creature for protection, and placed a cross in the ground. The serpent reared up with a ghastly hissing, as if it had been pierced with a sword, and gathered itself into a ball, savagely biting its tail with its teeth. Samson continued quietly to sing psalms, holding his staff firmly in the ground. The others arrived nearby. 'Come nearer', Samson said, 'so that you may develop faith in Faith.' They witnessed an uncanny sight: the serpent slowly uncoiled and slithered along the ground until it came to Samson's staff. Over and over again it did the same thing, but never could it raise its head or go beyond the staff. This went on all through the day, and Samson used the time to instruct and build up their faith with advice such as 'Those who believe in the Creator ought not to fear the creature.' Eventually, as twilight came, Samson spoke to the serpent, 'We have a long journey, but you have no longer to live. In Jesus's name I command you to die now!' At once the serpent raised its head, as if making a final bow, cast forth all its venom, and lay down dead.

Lord, may I grow more valiant, day by day, starting today.

Give to others, and God will give to you . . . Indeed, you will receive
a full measure, a generous helping, poured into your hands – all that
you can hold.
Luke 6:38

Malo's travels through Britanny to spread the Word of God to humans
kept him busy, but he had time for birds and animals too. Far from
detracting from his mission, this helped it along.

Malo earned his keep by doing seasonal work in the vineyards. Once
when he came to pick up his coat after he had finished work he found
a wren had laid an egg in it. He decided to leave the coat just where it
was until this egg, and subsequent eggs, hatched. For once it did not
rain during the whole time the coat was in the open. The vineyard
workers were touched both by Malo's care for the wrens and by
heaven's care of his coat.

On another occasion during his travels he came across a farm
labourer writhing and crying in grief in a meadow, surrounded by
piglets, and fearful to return to his boss. The mother of these piglets
had run amock, trampling down the corn in a neighbouring farmer's
field. The well-meaning swineherd tried to chase it out of the field by
throwing a large stone at it. Unfortunately, the stone hit it in just the
wrong place, and it was wounded and died.

Now the piglets were running amock, trying in vain to find milk
from their dead mother. Malo's heart went out to the swineherd, and
his prayer went up to God. Malo stretched out his staff, and laid it on
the ear of the dead sow. The sow was restored to life and got up on its
four legs.

The emotions of the swineherd went from one extreme to the other.
Now he was almost delirious with joy, and hurried to tell his employer
and everyone he possibly could all about Malo and what had happened.
The farmer personally came to thank Malo and offered him one of his
farms as a base for a new Christian community.

> Lord, take away all penny-pinching from me.
> Give me a generous heart and a helping hand
> For every person and every creature I meet.
> And thank you that this will bring blessing.

Do not store up riches for yourselves here on earth, where moths and rust destroy, and robbers break in and steal. Instead, store up riches for yourselves in heaven, where moths and rust cannot destroy, and robbers cannot break in and steal. For where your treasure is, there will your heart be also.
Matthew 6:19–21

A friend of Columba's, Mo Chua, had a hermitage in the wilderness. Although he was on his own, he aimed to say the divine prayers at set times throughout the day and night. He had no worldly wealth, but he did have a cock, a mouse and a fly, each of whom performed a most useful work for him.

The cock woke him in time to say early morning prayer. The mouse would not let him sleep for more than five hours. Mo Chua might well have slept on after his tiring vigils, but the mouse would always nibble his ear after five hours, which made sure his master got up! Then the fly, not to be outdone, would walk along every line in the psalm book as Mo Chua read it, so he would not lose his place. And when Mo had a pause, the fly rested in the same place until Mo began to sing the psalm again.

The time came when these three treasures died. When Mo wrote a letter to his friend Columba he shared these little bereavements with him. Columba did not brush these off as trifling or ridiculous. He replied in this vein, 'Brother, you must not be too taken aback by the death of this flock that has been taken from you, for misfortune only comes where there are riches.'

Thank you, Lord, for the little messengers of blessing that you send
(If only I have eyes to see)
From all around me.
When I lose these little comforts and familiar supports
Help me to turn my eyes to you,
Who are the Source of all true blessings
And my true and lasting Treasure.

My sisters and brothers, as believers in our glorious Lord Jesus Christ, don't show favouritism.
James 2:1

Oswin, who was king of Deira for seven years of great prosperity, was tall, handsome, courteous; a man of pleasant conversation who treated people of all backgrounds in an open manner. As a result he was loved by everyone. He was especially graced with virtues that spring from self-denial, and in particular, with humility, as the following episode illustrates.

The king had given a highly bred horse to Bishop Aidan so that, although it was Aidan's custom to walk, he could ride it across rivers or for urgent missions. Not long afterwards Aidan met a poor beggar, and gave him the horse with all its expensive trappings, for Aidan was like a father to those in need.

When the king was told of this before dinner that night, he angrily asked Aidan, 'Why did you give the royal horse to a beggar? We have other things and less valuable horses which can be given to the poor without giving away the horse that I specially chose for your own use.' 'What are you saying?' Aidan instantly replied. 'Surely that son of a mare is not more precious to you than that son of God?' As the king warmed himself by the fire Aidan's words smote him; he threw down his sword, fell at Aidan's feet and asked his forgiveness. 'Never again', he said, 'will I speak of this or pass judgment on what wealth of mine you should give to God's children.' Aidan was moved to tears by these words. A priest asked him why he was weeping. 'I know that the king has not long to live,' Aidan told him. 'I have never seen a humble king before, and I therefore expect he will soon be taken from this life. This nation does not deserve to have such a ruler'. This grim prophecy was, indeed, shortly fulfilled, on August 20, and eleven days later Aidan himself died, perhaps in part out of a broken heart.

Lord, help me to look upon each person I meet as a child of God
To treat each person as a royal soul
And to share with each person in the way you desire.

Human beings have been able to tame wild animals and birds, reptiles
and fish, but no human being can tame the tongue.
James 3:7,8

Ebba, who was King Oswy's sister, kept inviting Cuthbert to stay at her
monastery at Coldingham. Eventually he came for a few days, but he
continued his lifestyle exactly as usual. This included going out alone at
night to pray while the other members of the community slept,
returning just before the Community's early morning prayer.

One night one of the brothers saw him slip out, and curiosity got
the better of him. He wanted to know where Cuthbert was going and
what he was going to do, so he secretly followed him. This benevolent
spy saw Cuthbert walk to the shore below the monastery and wade
into the sea until the waves were up to his neck and outstretched arms.
He spent all the hours of dark like this in silent vigil or in singing
God's praises, accompanied by the sound of the waves.

When dawn approached the brother spied Cuthbert go on to the
beach and kneel in prayer as he was drying out. Two sea otters came
out of the sea at the same time. They stretched themselves out on the
sand in front of Cuthbert, then they began to warm his feet with their
breath, and even tried to dry him with their fur. Having performed
these services, Cuthbert blessed the otters and they slid back into the
sea. Cuthbert soon returned to the monastery and sang the Morning
Prayer on time with everyone else.

However, the brother who had watched all this from the cliff top,
was stricken with panic that he had behaved with such deceit towards
such a holy man, and got himself into a complete state. Knowing that
God's word teaches Christians to walk in the light with one another,
next morning he flung himself before Cuthbert and asked him to
forgive him for what he had done, without saying what that was.
Cuthbert guessed, and assured this brother that he would forgive him
on one condition, that he told no one what he had seen until after
Cuthbert's death. The brother kept his promise not to tell anyone while
Cuthbert was alive, but once Cuthbert died, he told absolutely
everybody!

Holy are you, O Lord
When we are one with you, your creatures become one with us.
Help me to be so truly at one with you
that even my most unruly member, the tongue, becomes at one too.

My servant will set free those who sit in dark prisons.
Isaiah 42:7

A local Irish king loved to show off a tame fox whenever he had a special occasion. It was a favourite court mascot which had learned all sorts of tricks.

One day a simple, uneducated man who knew nothing of this, saw the fox and killed it. He neither realised whose was the fox, nor why such a large crowd gathered round to watch him kill it.

Some of the crowd, of course, immediately reported him to the king, who was furious beyond measure. The king ordered the man's wife and children to be sold as slaves, their home to be taken, and the man to be executed – unless the king received a replacement fox just as skilled – which seemed an impossible condition.

When Brigid heard of this her heart bled for the man and his family. She took her carriage and did a 'prayer ride' along the road to the king's court, pouring forth prayers for the poor family and for God to turn the situation round. As she was praying, a fox appeared, and, what is so extraordinary, jumped on to her carriage, and sat quietly beside Brigid under her cloak.

Brigid arrived at the king's castle, and implored him repeatedly to revoke his sentence and release the whole family. The king was adamant that he would only release them if he got a fox that was as clever and tame as the one he had lost. That was Brigid's cue; to the amazement of everyone she brought her fox to the centre of the court. The fox entertained everyone with just the same sort of tricks as had the other fox. The king was so pleased with the reaction of the large audience that had gathered that he ordered the man and his family to be released.

But who had the last word? It is reported that once the object of Brigid's prayers had been achieved, the wily fox slunk away, never to be seen again!

Father, so many people walk through life with their feet in fetters
Clobbered with unjust burdens
Captives in prisons of body or spirit.
Pour out your compassion through us
That we may be instruments to set others free.

Beautiful words fill my mind, as I compose this song for the king. Like the pen of a good writer my tongue is ready with a poem.
Psalm 45:1

> He is my king, in my heart he's hid
> He is my joy all joys amid
> I am a drop in his ocean lost
> His coracle I, on his wide sea tossed
> A leaf in his storm.
>
> The book of his praise in my wallet slung
> The cloak of his friendship round me flung
> Hither and thither about I'm blown
> My way an eddy, my rest a stone
> And he my fire.
>
> My meat his work and my drink his will
> He is my song, my strength, my skill
> And all folk my lovers in good and ill
> Through him my desire.
>
> In the track of the wind I trace his feet
> And none of his coming was e'er so fleet
> So sweet
>
> Often my heart is a heavy stone
> Mocked, trodden under and spat upon
> My way a mirk, and I alone, alone
>
> Then in my heart flames a climbing star
> As his pilgrim feet come flashing far
> To bring me where the blessed are
> He is the cleft in the dark sky riven
> Whereby I may leap to the bending heaven
> Through the storm.

Marjorie Milne Rhymes from a
Lindisfarne Monk

King, you created heaven according to your delight
a place that is safe and pure
its air filled with the songs of angels.

The Celtic Psalter

Praise the Lord, you servants of the Lord, from the rising of the sun to
its going down.
Psalm 113:1, 3

Celtic Christians were in touch with the rhythms of each day, of the
week (Saturday was a sabbath rest and Sunday a day of resurrection and
renewal) and of the seasons, both of creation and of the church. They
also knew about the rhythm of advance in mission and retreat in
contemplation. There was a sense of rhythm in their poetry and their
worship, which was not too centralised or wooden.

The focus of the following poem is Lindisfarne, the tidal island which
reflects the ebb and flow of the sea, but God can inspire each of us to
discover such a rhythm wherever we are today.

Ebb tide, full tide, praise the Lord of land and sea.
Barren rocks, darting birds, praise his holy name!
Poor folk, ruling folk, praise the Lord of land and sea.
Pilgrimed sands, sea-shelled strands, praise his holy name!
Fierce lions, gentle lambs, praise the Lord of land and sea.
Noble women, mission priests, praise his holy name!
Chanting boys, slaves set free, praise the Lord of land and sea.
Old and young and all the land, praise his holy name!

Ebb tide, full tide
Let life's rhythms flow
Full tide, ebb tide
How life's beat must go.

David Adam

Here be the peace of those who do your will;
Here be the peace of brother serving other;
Here be the peace of holy ones obeying;
Here be the peace of praise by dark and day.
St Aidan's Prayer for Holy Island (trad.).

Ever since God created the world, God's invisible qualities, divine nature and eternal power have been clearly seen; they are perceived in the things God has made.
Romans 1:20

Question: What is best in this world?
Answer: To do the will of our Maker.
Question: What is his will?
Answer: That we should live according to the laws of his creation.
Question: How do we know those laws?
Answer: By study – studying the Scriptures with devotion.
Question: What tool has our Maker provided for this study?
Answer: The intellect which can probe everything.
Question: And what is the fruit of study?
Answer: To perceive the eternal Word of God reflected in every plant and insect, every bird and animal, and every man and woman.

This has been named as Ninian's Catechism

Apprehend God in all things
For God is in all things
Every single creature is full of God and is a book about God.
Every creature is a word of God.
If I spent enough time with the tiniest creature – even a caterpillar -
I would never have to prepare a sermon.
So full of God is every creature.

Meister Eckhart

Teach me my God and King
In all things thee to see
That what I do, in anything
I'll do it unto thee.
Charles Kingsley

Those who lead many to righteousness will shine like the stars for ever.
Daniel 12:3

God omnipotent, who had scattered shining lights upon the world,
gave many bright stars to his people in Britain. Brilliant among these
was Ninian. He was outstanding in strength derived from heaven, in
miracles, eloquence and reliance on the gift of God. People came
together in vast crowds and opened their hearts to believe in Christ and
to follow his teachings.

On his way back to his native Galloway in 398, after training and
ordination in Rome, Ninian stayed at the 'fellowship of service'
established by St Martin of Tours, and this became his abiding
inspiration.

He became a revered teacher and won multitudes of Picts to Christ.
They worshipped graven images in the shadow of death until he
converted them through his holy living. They all vied with each other
to be bathed in the baptismal water and to be cleansed from the stain of
their sin in the everlasting fountain.

Ninian established many new churches and monasteries, and
instructed these 'kingdoms at the ends of the earth' with his teaching.

After a time he left the Pictish nations and came to his own people,
the Britons. To them he was a good shepherd, tending his sheepfold
with mind and hand, eager to protect from the enemy the flocks
entrusted to his care. He built 'the Shining House', with its foundation
of burnt bricks and lofty walls, in the midst of which he sparkled and
shone forth like a star. This is the house which many are eager to visit,
for many who have long been afflicted with disease hurry there, eager
to accept the ready gifts of health-giving healing.

From the 8th century Miracles of Bishop Ninian
*by an anonymous monk of
Whithorn*

I pray for modern Ninians who will establish
communities of light in slum places;
sanctuaries of prayer in unvisited places;
links of faith and love with the Continent, our spiritual home.
And, Lord, begin with me.

A blind man named Bartimaeus shouted, 'Jesus, Son of David, have mercy upon me!' Jesus stopped and said, 'Call him.' . . . The blind man said 'Rabbi, I want to see.' 'Go,' said Jesus, 'your faith has healed you.' Immediately he received his sight and followed Jesus along the road. *Mark 10:46, 47, 49, 51, 52*

There was a local king named Tudvael under whom Ninian cared for his flock, who was as cruel as he was ungodly. One day he expelled Ninian, who was a threat, from his territories. At once God's judgment came upon him in the form of sudden blindness. The king repented and sent his servant to Ninian to ask him to suggest some penances. The servant flung himself at Ninian's feet with loud lamentations and begged, 'Dispel the black night, you who are the glory and chief part of our fame. The offence is great, but one that is open to pardon.' Ninian told him to tell the king his sins were forgiven, 'and he sent the king gifts to express his friendship. Later he himself arrived to lay healing hands upon the king's face. Tudvael's eyesight was restored, he gave praise to God, and from that time onwards he supported Ninian's ministry.

> Lord of my heart
> Give me vision to inspire me
> That, working or resting,
> I may always think of you.
>
> Lord of my heart
> Give me light to guide me
> That, at home or abroad
> I may always walk in your way.
>
> Lord of my heart
> Give me wisdom to direct me
> That, thinking or acting,
> I may always discern right from wrong.
>
> Heart of my own heart
> Whatever befall me
> Rule over my thoughts and feelings
> My words and actions.
>
> *Ancient Irish*

Then Peter said, 'Ananias, how is it that Satan has so filled your heart
that you have lied to the Holy Spirit . . . ? You have not lied to
human beings, but to God.'
Acts 5:3,4

Ninian was refreshing ever increasing numbers of believers with Christ's
teachings, but there were pitfalls to overcome within the church. Once
he was in a crowded church when a lone mother with emotional and
guilt problems was bringing her newborn baby to be baptised by one of
Ninian's ministers. She loudly accused him of being the father. Ninian
knew this priest was a holy man, but he needed to clear this matter up
in the minds of everybody in a way which had the stamp of Christ's
authority.

He was given a bold inspiration and called for silence. 'I believe this
man is innocent, but now I ask you my child' (he pointed to the baby)
'to point out to us who is the man who committed this sin and who is
your father. I command you to do this in the name of the Thunderer.'

To the amazement of everyone this day-old child pointed its finger
at a man in the congregation, and started to make sounds, breaking the
laws of nature, so that everyone understood it was saying, 'That man is
my father and the priest is innocent.' The people were convinced this
came from God, and they moved into a time of praise.

Pray for ministers who are under attack from people who are
challenged by their holy lives or their teachings. Are there situations
over which we need to take authority in the name of the Lord?
Remember, God can show us what to do in any situation.

In Ninian there was nothing of fear, all was love.
Forgive us for the places in our lives where fear has driven out love.
In Ninian truth and holiness shone out.
Forgive us for the places in our lives which are false or frozen.
Help us to take authority in your name over every confused or
    unsavoury situation.

Jesus said: Whoever believes in me will do the works that I do also.
John 14:12

Many leading people sent their sons to be educated at Ninian's Centre
at the place now known as Whithorn. It was a Centre that educated
them for a whole life, and everything was used to help build character,
as the following story illustrates.

One youth committed such a serious offence that the 'last resort'
discipline of the cane was to be used. To escape this he ran away,
taking with him the pastoral staff that Ninian used. He stumbled upon a
curragh by the shore, not realising that it was not properly covered
with waterproof leather, and he was carried out to sea. The boat began
to leak, and the young man was in terror of his life.

However, our extremity is God's opportunity: he admitted and
confessed before God his wrongful rebellion and truly repented of it.
Then he started to talk to Ninian, as if he were present. He asked
Ninian to save him. The young man took Ninian's staff and stuck it in
the largest leaking hole, and the boat stayed afloat. An easterly wind
arose, and took the boat back to the shore.

A crowd of people had gathered. The young man, now filled with
faith and with a desire to witness to Christ, told them what had
happened, and planted Ninian's staff in the ground, as a sign that a
miracle-working God will come to the aid of all who truly believe. It
was said that the staff took root and sprouted into a tree that became a
constant reminder of God's answer to prayer.

Lord, I have rebelled, forgive my proud heart.
Lord, I reach out to you, I believe for whatever you want to do
    today.

Happy are those whose greatest desire is to do what God requires; God will satisfy them fully!
Matthew 5:6

Ninian was happy beyond measure, and the glory of our land. He respected all people and was secure in his holiness. He used to go to a cave to study and meditate on heavenly wisdom; he could understand books in different languages, and he was a powerful teacher and preacher. By his eloquence the hearts of the faithful grew strong as he spoke of the true joys of eternal life.

Ninian offered to all ethnic groups the consolations of life and generously invited them to share food. He gave beautiful clothes to those who had none. He visited people in prison. He personally took food and drink to those who were hungry and thirsty during times of famine. He was like a father to the orphan and a protective judge to the widow. He exercised an authority to be feared by wrongdoers but he was loved by all who did good.

Ninian was a humble and wise man and he closed his journey in joy.

Many people walk from Whithorn to Ninian's cave. There, innumerable prayers of today's pilgrims are scratched on the rocks.

Lord, give us happiness, true happiness
The happiness of knowing we are called by you
The happiness of knowing we are cleansed people
The happiness of knowing we are Christ's instruments
The happiness of knowing we are set free from addiction to created things
The happiness of cherishing others and being cherished by them
The happiness of being on a journey towards joy overflowing.

I heard the voice of the Lord say, 'Whom shall I send? And who will go for us?' Then I said, 'Here am I, send me'.
Isaiah 6:8

When the Christian King Oswald came to Northumbria's throne he asked the leaders of the Iona Community, where he had been brought up in the Faith, to send a mission team to his kingdom, so that the English people might be taught the blessings of the Faith and receive the sacraments. The first team leader to come was Corman, a man of stern temperament. He stayed for some time, but the people were unwilling to listen to him, and he returned to Iona.

At a post mortem meeting of the Iona community Corman laid the blame on the Northumbrian people who, he said, were stubborn and uncivilised. The leaders discussed this matter for a long time, for they were keen to evangelise new peoples.

Then Aidan, who was present, said directly to Corman, 'It seems to me, brother, that you have been unduly severe with your ignorant hearers. You should have followed the guidance of the apostle Paul and offered them the milk of simpler teaching until, as they gradually grew strong in God's Word, they were able to take in a fuller statement of doctrine and carry out the higher commands.' As Aidan spoke, everyone turned and looked at him, and they carefully considered his words. The meeting finally resolved that Aidan should be made a bishop and sent to lead a second mission, because he had shown the gift of discretion, which is the mother of all virtues.

So they consecrated him and sent him to preach. Time was to prove that Aidan was not only endowed with discretion and good sense, but with the other Christian virtues also. Above all he was a willing missionary.

Here am I Lord
I have heard you calling in the night
I will go Lord
Where you lead me.
I will hold your people in my heart
Dan Schutte S.J.

My teaching will fall like gentle rain on tender grass.
Deuteronomy 32:2

Gentleness has soothing qualities such as politeness, kindness and
courtesy; yet it is also a firestorm of indignation, kindled by the wrongs
and sufferings of others. In no one does this quality shine forth more
clearly than in Aidan.

Among the lessons that Aidan gave the clergy about their lifestyle,
none was more salutary than his own example of fasting and self-
discipline. His teaching won the hearts of everyone because he taught
what he and his followers lived out. He neither sought nor cared for
the possessions of this world, and he loved to give away to the poor
the gifts he received from the rich.

In those days poor people would travel by foot, and the influential
by horse. Aidan, however, insisted on travelling by foot in country as
well as town, unless some urgent necessity forced him to do otherwise.
So wherever he walked he was able to catch sight of people, rich or
poor, and talk to them straight away. If they were not Christians he
would invite them to accept the mystery of the Faith; if they already
believed he would strengthen their faith and encourage them by his
words and example in the practice of Christian giving and words of
mercy.

I have described . . . his love of peace and charity, temperance and
humility; his soul which triumphed over anger and greed, and at the
same time despised pride and vainglory . . . and his tenderness in
comforting the weak, in relieving and protecting the poor.

Bede

> May the raindrops fall lightly on your brow
> May the soft winds freshen your spirit
> May the sunshine brighten your heart
> May the burdens of the day rest lightly upon you
> And may God enfold you in love.
>
> *An old Irish prayer*

Jesus said: How terrible for you teachers of God's Law! You put loads on people's backs which are hard to carry, but you yourselves will not stretch out a finger to help them carry those loads.
Luke 11:46

Aidan's way of life was in great contrast to the slothfulness of later times, so much so that all who travelled with him, monks or others, were required to use the time to study the Scriptures and memorise the psalms. This was the daily task of Aidan and his disciples wherever they went. If, as occasionally happened, he had to dine with the king, he attended with one or two of his team and after eating lightly they would leave the table in order to read the Bible or pray.

Inspired by his example, many men and women undertook to fast on Wednesdays and Fridays until evening, except for the periods of celebration after Easter and Pentecost.

If wealthy people did wrong Aidan did not keep silence out of fear or favour, but would sternly correct them. He never gave money to influential people, only the hospitality of his table. He used money rich people gave him to buy the freedom of people who had been unjustly sold as slaves. Many of these later became disciples; after training and instructing them he ordained them.

Based on Bede

Celtic monks lived in conspicuous poverty; Roman monks lived well.
Celtic monks were unworldly; Roman monks were worldly.
Celtic bishops practised humility; Roman bishops paraded pomp.
Celtic bishops were shepherds of their flocks; Roman bishops were monarchs of their dioceses.
Celtic clergymen said 'Do as I do' and hoped to be followed;
Roman clergyman said 'Do as I say' and expected to be obeyed.

Magnus Magnusson

Father, whose gentle apostle Aidan
Befriended everyone he met
With Jesus Christ
Give me his humble, Spirit-filled zeal
That I may inspire others to learn your ways
And to pass on the torch of faith.

The wind died down and there was a great calm.
Mark 4:39

We know nothing of Aidan's childhood, but we may assume that his
faith was built up with stories of fellow Irish people who had wrought
great things by prayer. One of these was Mac Nissi of Connor, who
passed into heaven on September 3 about 510. As a result of his
intercessions a woman who had been infertile for fifteen years was able
to give birth to a child. Aidan certainly learned to have faith for all sorts
of situations.

A delegation from Lindisfarne had to travel far south by boat, and
bring back Princess Eanflaed who was to become Queen to
Northumbria's King. Its leader, Utta, begged Aidan to pray for their
safe keeping during this hazardous and significant journey. As he was
praying for them God revealed things to Aidan. He gave them a jar of
blessed oil to take with them, and told them that they would encounter
storms, but that the winds would drop as soon as they poured the oil
on the troubled waters.

The crew forgot about this. A storm did blow up, so fierce that the
boat began to sink and they thought they would perish. Only then did
someone remember Aidan's words and the oil. They poured the oil
over the surrounding waves, and the wind immediately receded.

This is an example of prophetic prayer, whereby a person foresees
trouble for others, and is guided by God to give them direction. It is
also the origin of the well-known phrase 'pouring oil on troubled
waters'. Why not pray for people you know who seem about to be
engulfed in a sea of troubles? You never know, God may give you a
word to pass on to them that proves to be as calming as Aidan's oil.

> Protecting Father, stalwart Steersman, guiding Spirit
> I pray for friends in a sea of troubles
> I pray for households in a sea of troubles
> I pray for work places in a sea of troubles
> I pray for communities in a sea of troubles.
> May your inspiration flow to them
> And come to them like oil on troubled waters.

There are different ways of serving, but the same Lord is served . . . All
of you are Christ's body, and each one is a part of it.
Romans 12:5, 27

Ultari, a friend of Brigid, is said to have fed with his own hands every
child in Erin who had no support, and he provided particular care for
the children whose mothers had died of the plague.

King Oswald used to pray with his hands open, easier to receive good
things from God. He would then raise his hands to bless people with
good things, and his prayers were put into practice.

For evil to triumph it is only necessary for good people to do nothing.
Edmund Burke

    Christ has no body on earth but yours
    No hands but yours
    No feet but yours
    Yours are the eyes through which Christ's compassion is to look out
        for the world
    Yours are the feet with which he is to go about doing good
    Yours are the hands with which he is to bless us now.
                                                Teresa of Avila

    Forgive us for the good we ought to have done which we have left
        undone
    And for the things we have left undone which we ought to have
        done.

                            Book of Common Prayer *(adapted)*

    With these hands I bless the lonely, the forgotten
    And the lost;
    With these hands I shield your messengers
    From attacks within, without;
    With these hands I dispel darkness and rebuke
    The evil forces;
    With these hands I pray your victory for those who fight for right.

Jesus said: If you believe you will be able to say to this hill, "Get up and throw yourself in the sea," and it will. If you believe, you will receive whatever you ask in prayer.
Matthew 21:21,22

Do you sometimes feel that something is unsatisfactory about the path you are on, but since everyone assumes there is nothing anyone can do about it, faith is pigeon-holed and you 'make the best of a bad job' with a resigned spirit? The following story of a little known Irish saint reminds us that there is nothing about which we cannot pray.

A wandering Irish monk named Molaise was on a difficult mission journey in a remote part of Ireland. It was easy to get lost and it was dangerous. Then he met a group of monks who had a rare possession — a good map. Molaise would have given his right arm to make a copy of this, but no one had the necessary instruments with them with which to do this. It would have been easy for Molaise to have shrugged his shoulders and continued his unsatisfactory journey, but he decided to go aside and make this a matter of prayer. Before long a loose feather from a goose that was flying overhead fluttered down. Molaise caught it and was able to use his new quill as a pen with which to copy the valuable map!

> May the hills lie low
> May the sloughs fill up
> In your way.
>
> May all evil sleep
> May all good awake
> In your way.
> *Collected by Kenneth Macleod*

Dear Jesus, you guide your straying sheep along lush and fragrant valleys, where the grass is rich and deep.

You guard them from the attacks of wolves, and from the bites of snakes.

You heal their diseases, and teach them always to walk in the ways of God.

When we stray, lead us back; when temptation besets us, give us strength; when our souls are sick, pour upon us your love.
Ancient Celtic song

Live by the Spirit and you will not give in to the desires of the sinful nature. For the sinful nature and the Spirit are in conflict with each other, so that you do not do what you want. The acts of the sinful nature are obvious: sexual immorality, impurity and debauchery.
Galatians 5:16, 17, 19

Most of us have times when a wave of sexual desire threatens to overwhelm us. Everything else in our life, however fruitful and of God it may be, seems as nothing compared with this. And we justify the idea of indulging our lust on the grounds that we will never have lived if we do not experience what we desire. This is a delusion, and the experience is always that of let-down, barriers, disappointment, guilt.

Is there anything we can do to avoid such a defeat? Celtic Christians offer us one drastic remedy: They stood in a cold bath or river in order to cool their passions! And from the Desert Christians comes this intriguing example of a remedy:

A young disciple was so constantly tempted that he eventually announced to his soul friend, 'I cannot go on unless I actually commit the deed.' The wise old abba replied, 'I want to do it too, so let me come with you to the prostitute's house and then we'll return together to our cell.' The abba took the money with which to pay the prostitute. When they got to her house, he asked that he should have the first session, while the younger man stayed outside. He won the trust of the prostitute, explained that his friend was at heart a holy monk, and that what he needed was not a one night stand, but for his fantasy to dissolve. She agreed to co-operate.

When the young man came in for sexual intercourse she told him, 'I too have a Rule. It requires my clients to make repeated obscene oaths with me before we lie together.' The young man started to do this, but became so sickened by all the filth, that he realised he wanted to live a life of prayer more than anything else, and left the room. The two men returned, chaste in body and heart, to continue their desert calling.

> Lord, when waves of lust roll over me,
> Remind me that my true destiny lies
> In being clean in body and mind.
> Cool me, calm me, and protect me I pray.

Jesus got up from the meal, took off his top garments, and wrapped a towel around his waist. He poured water into a basin and began to wash his disciples' feet, drying them with the towel that was wrapped around him.
John 13:4, 5

One of the desert fathers used to say: There are three things we honour – the fellowship of holy communion, the hospitality of meals, and the washing of one another's feet.

The example of Jesus in washing others' feet was not only followed in hot and dusty lands, for this practice was followed in Celtic lands too.

It was said that when Cuthbert was put in charge of guests at Melrose monastery, God sent him a visitor to test how Christ-like was Cuthbert's hospitality. One day he found a youth waiting in the guest room and gave him his usual kindly welcome. He fetched water so his guest could wash his hands; then Cuthbert washed his feet himself, tenderly dried them, and held them against his chest while he gave them a warm massage.

The reason people wondered whether this youth had been an angel in disguise is that, just before a warm evening meal was brought to him, he vanished into thin air. There was snow outside, but not a footprint could be seen.

In a society which has heated bathrooms washing feet may be an artificial way to reflect Jesus's example, but there are other ways to do this. Can you think of any? Remember, the next person you meet may be a test case!

> Lord, take my hands.
> May your compassion always flow though them.
> May they offer tender touch
> To people who are deprived of touch or tenderness.
> May they offer human warmth
> To people who are cold or dispirited.
> May they offer practical care
> To people who are weary and overworked.

After Moses had led the escaping people across the sea they journeyed three days through the desert without finding water. When they did come to water at Marah it was too bitter to drink (that is why it was named Marah, which means 'bitter'). When the people complained Moses pleaded with the Lord, who directed him to a piece of wood. Moses threw this in the water, and the water became sweet.
Exodus 15:22–25

For the one who has left behind the pleasures of Egypt, which he served before crossing the sea, life removed from these pleasures seems at first difficult and disagreeable. But if the wood be thrown into the water, that is, if one receives the mystery of the resurrection which had its beginning with the wood (you of course understand 'the cross' when you hear 'wood') then the virtuous life, being sweetened by the hope of things to come, becomes sweeter and more pleasant than all the sweetness that tickles the senses with pleasure.

Gregory of Nyssa in The Life of Moses Book 2

In the grounds of the monastery at Durrow there was a tree that provided local people with a prolific supply of apples; however, these tasted so bitter that the people complained. One autumn day, Columba went up to it, and seeing it laden with fruit that was going to give more displeasure than pleasure to the people, he raised his hand and spoke to the tree, 'In the name of almighty God, bitter tree, may all your bitterness depart from you, and from now on may your apples be really sweet.' Columba's biographer commented, 'Wonderful to tell, more swiftly than words all the apples on that tree lost their bitterness and became wonderfully sweet.'

> Sweet Jesus, I lay before you now
> Things that are needlessly bitter –
> Relationships, circumstances.
> May your sweetness turn
> Food into pleasure
> Tragedy into triumph
> And ugliness into beauty.

What wisdom is this that has been given to him? How does he perform
miracles? Isn't he the carpenter, the son of Mary, and the brother of
James, Joseph, Judas and Simon? Aren't his sisters living here?
Mark 6:2,3

Ciaran, unlike most leaders of the early Irish churches who came from
ruling families, was the son of a carpenter. Yet he became such an
influential leader that he was known as one of the Twelve Apostles of
Ireland.

How was this possible? Like David, whom we read about in the
Bible, Ciaran was brought up the hard way, looking after the cattle, yet
in the fields he had God-guided encounters which built up his
character. His tutor would say divine service some distance away;
Ciaran always knew when these began, and would join in wherever he
was. A fox befriended him and fetched his tutor's lesson notes to him
each day. So he grew in wisdom and stature, and in favour of God and
beast.

The time came for Ciaran to study under the famous Abbot Finnian
at Clonard monastery. Overcoming his mother's negative attitude,
Ciaran took a cow with him which proved so fertile it provided milk
for many more students than himself. Ciaran was so attractive, both
physically and spiritually, that many people gave him land and treasures
which he used for God's glory. He concluded that, having received the
best training in scholarship at Clonard, he now needed to receive the
best training in prayer, so he decided to go to Aran and be discipled by
Enda.

There God gave the two of them a vision of a great and fruitful tree
growing beside a stream in the middle of Ireland. This tree protected
the entire island, its fruit crossed the sea, and birds of the world came
to carry off some of the fruit. Enda told Ciaran that he was the tree,
and that God was calling him to establish a church in the centre of
Ireland by the banks of a stream. So step by step, Ciaran was led to
establish the community at Clonmacnoise. He died of the plague only
seven months after arriving there. Yet Clonmacnoise remained a great
community for a thousand years, which indicates how significant was
the foundation work Ciaran did.

> Jesus, Master Carpenter of Nazareth,
> Wield well your tools in this your workshop
> That we who come to you rough hewn
> May here be fashioned to a truer beauty by your hand.
> *Traditional*

Blest are the pure in heart; for they shall see God.
Matthew 5:8

It is not only that these (Celtic) scribes and anchorites lived by the
destiny of their dedication in an environment of wood and sea; it was
because they brought into that environment an eye washed
miraculously clear by continuous spiritual exercise that they, the first in
Europe, had that strange vision of natural things in an almost unnatural
purity.

> *Robin Flower in* Irish Tradition

As the eye is a sense faculty of the body, so is the healthy imagination a
sense organ of the spiritual mind. It can receive spiritual truths from the
material world But purity of heart is required for such a healthy
functioning of the imagination. Without this purity, the ever active
mind and imagination construct disjointed thoughts and representations
that bear little resemblance to reality. Such images debase rather than
dignify.

> *Brother Aidan, an Orthodox monk and iconographer*

Alas that no stream reaching every part flows over my breast to be a
cleansing tonight for my heart and body.

> Early Irish Lyrics

> Mary beloved! Mother of the White Lamb
> pure virgin of nobleness.
> > *Carmina Gadelica*

My strength is as the strength of ten because my heart is pure.
> *Alfred Lord Tennyson*

Make and keep me pure within.
> *Charles Wesley*

> From the unreal, lead me to the real
> From the impure lead me to the pure
> From darkness, lead me to light
> And from what passes away
> Lead me to what is eternal.

It is all too plain that it was refusal to trust God that prevented these people from entering into God's Rest.
Hebrews 3:19

Those who followed the rule of Columba would keep the Jewish sabbath and rest from work on Saturday as well as on Sunday. The emphasis of Sunday would be renewal and resurrection.

The hours of rest and recreation are as valuable as the hours of prayer and work. The Lord Jesus reminds us that 'the Sabbath was made for humankind, and not humankind for the Sabbath' (Mark 2:27). In the Scriptures, even the land was given a sabbath in the seventh year (Leviticus 15:3–5). The need for rest was built into creation (Genesis 2: 1–3). A provision for this kind of rest, which is both holy and creative, should be part of each member's personal Way of Life.

The Way of Life of the Community of Aidan and Hilda

Use the Rest.
 Notice in a billiards room

We who have lost our sense and our senses – our touch, our smell, our vision of who we are; we who frantically force and press all things, without rest for body or spirit, hurting our earth and injuring ourselves: we call a halt.

We want to rest. We need to rest and allow the earth to rest. We need to reflect and to rediscover the mystery that lives in us, that is the ground of every unique expression of life, the source of the fascination that calls all things to communion.

We declare a sabbath, a space of quiet: for simply being and letting be; for recovering the great, forgotten truths; for learning how to live again.

UN Environmental Sabbath Programme

God is the one quiet unhurried Worker in the universe. He has eternity in which to do things.

J. Paterson Smyth

I cast off the works that spring from a restless spirit.
I rest in you, my Maker and Redeemer.
Help me to order my life according to your rhythms.

Being cheerful keeps you healthy. It is slow death to be gloomy all the time.
Proverbs 17:22

A frail old desert Christian had reached about ninety years of age, and he acutely felt the devils tempting him to fall into despair. So he used the weapon of humour to get rid of them. 'What will you do, old man, for you might live like this for another fifty years?' the tempters asked him one day. In reply he said to them, 'You have distressed me greatly, for I had been prepared to live for two hundred years!' That did it. With great cries the devils left him.

At all hours Cuthbert was happy and joyful, neither wearing a sad expression at the memory of a sin nor being elated by the loud acclaim of those who were impressed by his way of life.

Life of Cuthbert *by an anonymous monk of Lindisfarne*

Caedmon, who lived at Whitby monastery, moved into the house for those who were dying. He and his nurse talked and joked in good spirits with each of the other occupants in turn until after midnight. Caedmon asked if they had the Sacrament in the house. 'Why do you need Holy Communion now?' they asked. 'You are not due to die yet for you talk with us as cheerfully as if you were in good health.' He died with a smile on his face.

Bede

A well-known writer once pointed out that God must have a sense of humour, otherwise why did God make the duck with such a funny looking bill?

It is the heart that is not yet sure of God that is afraid to laugh in God's presence.

George Macdonald

> Teach us good Lord
> To enjoy the fun of your creation
> Not to take ourselves too seriously
> And to allow the sense of humour
> Which is your gift to us
> To bubble over as it should.

Contentment with godliness is great gain.
1 Timothy 6:6

So I must accept with equanimity whatever befalls me, whether it be good or bad, and always give thanks to God, who taught me to trust in him always without hesitation. God must have heard my prayer . . . Daily I expect murder, fraud or captivity, or whatever it may be; but I fear none of these things because of the promises of heaven. I have cast myself into the hands of God Almighty, who rules everywhere. As the prophet says, 'Cast your cares upon the Lord, and the Lord will care for you.'

And if I have done any good for my God whom I love, I beg him that I may shed blood with those exiles and captives for his name, even though I should be denied a grave, or my body be torn to pieces. I am convinced that if this should happen to me, I would have gained my soul together with my body, because on that day we shall rise in the brightness of the sun, that is, in the glory of Christ Jesus our Redeemer, as children of the living God and joint heirs with Christ, to be conformed to his image; for of him, and by him, and in him we shall reign.

Patrick of Ireland

To live content with small means
To seek elegance rather than luxury
And refinement rather than fashion
To be worthy, not respectable
And wealthy, not rich
To study hard, think quietly, talk gently, act frankly
To listen to stars and birds, babes and sages, with open heart
To bear all cheerfully
Do all bravely
Await occasions, hurry never
In a word, to let the spiritual, unbidden and unconscious
Grow up through the common.
This is to be my symphony.

William Ellery Channing

Grant me, Lord, the serenity of knowing that I do your will
And contentment with my lot.
Grant me the courage to change what I can change,
The grace to accept what I cannot change
And the wisdom to know the difference.

God forbid that I should glory in anything except the cross of our Lord
Jesus Christ.
Galatians 6:14

The phrase 'the true Cross' has passed into the English language. What
does this mean, and what should it mean for us today?

The Emperor Diocletian divided the government of the expanding
Roman Empire between himself and Constantius, the Governor of
Britain, who had a Christian wife named Helena. But owing to
unforeseen circumstances, their son Constantine became Emperor of
both east and west. Before a major battle against the last of his rivals
Constantine had a vision of a cross in the sky, with the words 'In this
sign conquer' above it. Ever afterwards, Constantine encouraged the
church as an ally of a united Empire and the Cross became a popular
symbol, though it is doubtful whether Constantine knew what the
Cross meant in his own experience.

His mother Helena, however, became ever more devoted to Christ.
Christians had as yet no written Gospels and they no longer had the
test of persecution as a focus for their devotion. Helena went on
journeys to the Holy Land to find, as a focus for devotion, a fragment
of the Cross on which Christ had been crucified. The fragment she
believed she found did indeed excite the devotion of many.

The story of Helena and her discovery of the True Cross became the
subject of an epic medieval English poem. Some have attributed this to
Cynewulf, the 8th century Bishop of Lindisfarne. But Celtic Christians
realised that the 'true' Cross does not consist in the externals, but in the
experience of total self-giving and sacrifice: that is what Christians have
to prize and adopt as their own way. Millions are confused about this.
Muslims, for example, think that the Cross stands for the sword, which
Christians used in the Crusades in order to recapture the site of 'the
True Cross'.

The Celts loved another poem about the Cross, *The Dream of the
Rood*. In this poem (which some also attribute to Cynewulf) the poet
imagines that the cross-beam on which Christ was nailed (the Rood)
could express its feelings. When the Rood has finished speaking the
poet dreamer concludes, 'This is my heart's desire, all my hope waits on
the Cross.' That is 'the true Cross'.

Lord, make this my heart's desire also.

The Lord said to his people 'I scattered you in all directions . . . But now anyone who strikes you strikes the apple of my eye.'
Zechariah 2:6, 8

I did not go to Ireland of my own accord; not, that is, until I had nearly perished. This was for my good, for in this way the Lord purged me, and made me fit to be what I am now, but which once I was far from being – someone who cares and labours for the salvation of others. In those days I did not care for anyone, not even for myself.

On the occasion when several of my seniors rejected me God spoke to me personally. He did not say 'you have seen' but 'we have seen', as if he included himself. It was as if God was saying, 'Whoever touches you touches the apple of my eye.'

Therefore I thank God who has strengthened me in everything . . . After this experience I felt not a little strength, and my trust was proved right before God and people.

And so I say boldly, my conscience does not blame me now or in the future: God is my witness that I have not lied in the account I have given you.

Enough of this. I must not, however, hide the gift God gave me in the land of my captivity, because there I earnestly sought him, and there I found him, and he saved me from all evil because – so I believe – of his Spirit who lives in me.

Patrick of Ireland

> Father, you affirmed your Son at his baptism
> Before he entered a time of testing.
> Father, you affirmed your servant Patrick
> In the midst of his time of trial.
> Father, affirm me in my time of need.
> May I rest in the assurance
> That I am the apple of your eye.

I have done my best in the race, I have run the full distance, I have kept the Faith. And now the prize of victory is waiting for me.
2 Timothy 4:7, 8

Why were the saints saints? Because they were cheerful when it was difficult to be cheerful, patient when it was difficult to be patient; and because they pushed on when they wanted to stand still, and kept silent when they wanted to talk, and were agreeable when they wanted to be disagreeable. That was all. It was quite simple and always will be.

Anon

Wales's saint David is a fine example of somebody who persevered in and out of season. The wife of the local chief tried to get rid of his monastery, then to corrupt his monks, who pressed David to move it elsewhere even though God had clearly led them to that site. As we have seen, David stood firm, and in the end, due to this promiscuous woman over-reaching herself, she herself had to flee. David's biographer observed that his purpose, 'was neither dissolved nor softened by prosperity, nor terrified when weakened by adversity.'

The four securities of the children of Life: the wearing away of the passions, fear of the pains, love of the sufferings, belief in the rewards. If the passions were not worn away, they would not be left behind. If the pains were not feared, they would not be guarded against. If the sufferings were not loved, they would not be endured. If the rewards were not believed in, they would not be attained.

Colmán mac Béognae The Alphabet of Devotion

Never give up. Never, never give up. Never, never, never give up.
The entire speech Winston Churchill gave at a school prize-giving

> O God
> when we your servants are called upon
> to undertake any task
> whether it be small or great
> help us to know that
> it is not the beginning of the task
> but the continuing of it to the end
> which yields the true glory.
> *Inspired by words of Sir Francis Drake*

Because of what you have done the earth shall be cursed.
Genesis 3:17

The person who tramples the world tramples themself.
Columbanus

> The high, the low
> All of creation
> God gives to humankind to use.
> If this privilege is misused
> God's justice permits creation to punish humanity.
>
> *Hildegard of Bingen*

> I am Eve, great Adam's wife
> It is I that outraged Jesus of old.
> It is I that stole heaven from my children
> By rights it is I that should have gone upon the Tree,
> It is I that plucked the apple.
> It overcame the control of my greed
> For that, women will not cease from folly
> As long as they live in the light of day.
> There would be no ice in any place
> There would be no glistening windy winter
> There would be no hell, there would be no sorrow
> There would be no fear
> Were it not for me.
>
> *Early Irish lyrics*

Since the beginning of time our task has been to harmonise the spiritual and material realms. We were intended to be mediators between God and creation, but have been disobedient. In our failure, God, in human form, fulfils this task by uniting to himself his creation in the closest possible way, taking the form of that which he created.
Tim Cooper, Green Christianity

There is enough in the world for everyone's need but not for everyone's greed.

Mahatma Gandhi

> O one God, O true God, O chief God,
> O God of one substance, O God only mighty in three Persons
> truly pitiful, forgive.
>
> *Attributed to St Ciaran*

We all reflect like mirrors the glory of the Lord, and are being changed into his likeness from one degree of glory to another.
2 Corinthians 3:18

Whenever I give moral instruction, I first try to demonstrate the inherent power and quality of human nature. I try to show the wonderful virtues which all human beings can acquire. Most people look at the virtues in others, and imagine that such virtues are far beyond their reach. Yet God has implanted in every person the capacity to attain the very highest level of virtue.

But people cannot grow in virtue on their own. We each need companions to guide and direct us on the way of righteousness; without such companions we are liable to stray from the firm path, and then sink into the mud of despair. At first a companion who has achieved a high level of virtue can seem utterly different from oneself. But as friendship grows, one begins to see in the companion a mirror of oneself. The reason is that, in moral capacities, God has created us all the same: we are each capable of achieving the same degree of moral goodness. Once people perceive this truth, they are filled with hope, knowing that in the fullness of time they can share the moral virtue of Christ himself.

Pelagius Letter to Demetrius

The best thing we can do is to prepare for the five encounters we shall all have: an encounter with disappointments, an encounter with death, an encounter with God's people, an encounter with devils, an encounter with resurrection on Judgment Day.

Colmán mac Béognae The Alphabet of Devotion

> God, I am bathing my face in the sun
> In the nine rays of the sun
> As Mary bathed her Son
> In generous milk fermented
>
> Love be in my countenance
> Benevolence in my mind
> Dew of honey in my tongue
> My breath as the incense.

Carmina Gadelica

We have given up underhanded ways; we refuse to manipulate or to misconstrue God's word, but by the open statement of truth we commend ourselves to every person's conscience.
2 Corinthians 4:2

When Christianity became the official religion of the Roman Empire Christians fell into the temptation to adopt double standards. Aidan's example, however, was different from the model of Christianity that was being expressed in the church elsewhere. Integrity was a hallmark of Aidan and the Celtic saints.

The highest recommendation of (Aidan's) teaching to all was that he and his followers lived as they taught . . .
    Such was Aidan's industry in carrying out and teaching the divine commandment, his diligence in study and keeping vigil, his authority, such as became a priest, in reproving the proud and the mighty . . . To put it briefly, so far as one can learn from those who knew him, he made it his business to omit none of the commands of the evangelists, the apostles, and the prophets, but he set himself to carry them out in his deeds, so far as he was able. All these things I greatly admire and love in this bishop and I have no doubt that all this was pleasing to God.

Bede

I would be true, for there are those who trust me.
I would be pure, for there are those who care.
I would be strong, for there is much to suffer.
I would be brave, for there is much to dare.
Howard Arnold Walter

Sift me, O Lord.
Bring all that is false in me into the light
And take it away.
Give me strength to be true
In all I say and think and do.

The father asked his elder son to work in his vineyard that day. 'I don't want to,' he said; however, later he changed his mind and went. The father said the same thing to his second son, who replied 'Yes, I'll go,' but he did not in fact go. Which of the two did what his father wanted?
Matthew 21:28–31

After Cuthbert reluctantly agreed to become a bishop 'he continued with the utmost constancy to be what he had been before. He showed the same humility of heart, the same poverty of dress, and, being full of authority and grace, he maintained the dignity of a bishop without abandoning the ideal of a monk or the virtue of the hermit . . .

'His discourse was pure and frank, full of gravity and probity, full of sweetness and grace, dealing with the ministry of the law, the teaching of the faith, the virtue of temperance, and the practice of righteousness . . . He followed the example of the saints, fulfilling the duty of peace among the brothers; he held fast to humility also and the excellent gift of love without which every other virtue is worth nothing. He cared for the poor, fed the hungry, clothed the naked, took in strangers, redeemed captives, and protected widows and orphans.'

The Life of Cuthbert *by an anonymous monk of Lindisfarne*

The silent power of a consistent life
Florence Nightingale

Long obedience in the same direction.
Frederick Nietzsche

> I make Christ's Cross over my face.
> Each day and each night
> That I place myself under his keeping
> I shall not be overwhelmed
> I shall not be destroyed
> I shall not be imprisoned
> I shall not be cast down.
> Black thoughts shall not lie on me.
> Confusion shall not lie on me.
> No ill-will of enemy shall lie on me.

Do not abandon me and worship idols.
Leviticus 9:4

An idol is any thing which I put before God. It may be a car or a
custom, a person or a passion, a lottery or a horoscope. In Cuthbert's
day an idol often took the form of a power of nature that it was
thought could create a windfall or good luck.

After Boisil died Cuthbert was made prior of the Melrose monastery:
'He not only taught those in the monastery how to live . . . he also
sought to convert the neighbouring people far and wide from a life of
foolish customs to a love of heavenly joys. For many of them profaned
the creed they held by wicked deeds and some of them, too, in times
of plague, would forget the sacred mysteries of the faith into which
they had been initiated and take to the false remedies of idolatry, as
though they could ward off a blow inflicted by God the Creator by
means of incantations or amulets or any other mysteries of devilish art.
So he frequently went forth from the monastery to correct the errors of
those who had sinned in both these ways, sometimes on horseback but
more often on foot; he came to the neighbouring villages and preached
the way of truth to those who had gone astray . . .

'None of those present would presume to hide from him the secrets
of their hearts, but they all made open confession of their sins because
they realised that these things could never be hidden from him; and
they cleansed themselves from the sins they had confessed by fruits of
repentance. He used especially to make for those places that were far
away in steep and rugged mountains, which others dreaded to visit and
whose poverty and ignorance kept other teachers away. Giving himself
up gladly to this devoted labour, he instructed them with such devotion
that he would often leave the monastery for a week, and sometimes for
up to a month.'

Bede

Now
Robed in stillness
In this quiet place
Emptied of all I was
I bring all that I am
Your gift of shepherding
To use and bless.
          Cuthbert's Prayer,
          St Aidan's Chapel,
          Bradford Cathedral

Keep your head in all situations, endure hardship . . . discharge all the
duties of your ministry.
2 Timothy 4:5

Today is the autumnal equinox, when the hours of light and dark are
in equal balance. This is a good day to take stock of our lives in order
to make sure that we have a God-given balance, and a deportment that
reflects this.

This may seem a forlorn task, until we realise that Christ who is the
perfect specimen of a balanced human being, can calm our agitated or
overworked parts, heal our sick parts, and strengthen our weak parts.

Gildas, who has been nicknamed the Jeremiah of the early British
church, because he was so critical of its lax members, believed in fasting
and prayer; yet he was equally aware of the danger of going overboard,
and losing a sense of proportion:

There is no point in abstaining from bodily food if you do not have
love in your heart. Those who do not fast much but who take great
care to keep their heart pure (on which, as they know, their life
ultimately depends) are better off than those who are vegetarian, or
travel in carriages, and think they are therefore superior to everyone
else. To these people death has entered through the window of their
pride.

Gildas

Grant me the serenity
That comes from placing the different parts of my being
Under your harmonising sway.
Today may I grow in balance.

The Sovereign Lord has filled me with his Spirit. He has chosen me and sent me to . . . announce release to hostages and to set the prisoners free.
Isaiah 61:1

Adamnan, who died in September 704 as Abbot of Iona, won his spurs in Ireland where he helped secure the release of sixty hostages with the help of the Caim, the Celtic Circling Prayer.

Saxon raiders had taken the hostages from Meath, in Ireland. Adamnan and his team sailed to Britain to try and negotiate their release with King Aldfrith. When they hauled their boats on to the shore they walked in a circle round them, saying protective prayers out loud. Shortly, the sea surrounded the boats, but a dry circle of sand was left upon which the boats were beached. This created a healthy respect for the negotiators among the Saxons. By the close of the negotiations the Saxons had not only agreed to the release of the hostages, but also to cease raids altogether. Later, at a convention, Adamnan's proposal that women should be totally excluded from war was accepted nationally.

People in a religious habit were held in great respect, so that whenever a priest or a monk went anywhere he was gladly received by all as God's servant. If they chanced to meet him by the roadside, they ran towards him and, bowing their heads, were eager either to be signed with the cross by his hand or to receive a blessing. Great attention was paid to his exhortations, and on Sundays the people flocked eagerly to the church or the monastery, not to get food for the body but to hear the Word of God . . . They were so free from all taint of avarice that none of them would accept lands or possessions to build monasteries, unless compelled to by the secular authorities. This practice was observed universally by the Northumbrian churches for some time afterwards.

Bede

Lord, help us to be peace-makers.
Give us the statesmanship of the prayerful heart,
the willingness to move out towards others.
Give us the faith to do our bit
that we may contribute towards building a civilisation of love.

O Lord, don't stay away from me! Come quickly to my rescue!
Psalm 22:19

I am hated. What shall I do, Lord? I am most despised. Look, your
sheep around me are torn to pieces and driven away by those robbers
on the orders of the hostile Coroticus. Ravening wolves have devoured
the flock of the Lord which, in Ireland, was indeed growing splendidly
with the greatest care – I cannot count their number.

They have filled their houses with the spoils of dead Christians, they
live on plunder. They do not know, the wretches, that what they offer
their friends and sons as food is deadly poison, just as Eve did not
understand that it was death she gave her husband. So are all that do
evil: they work death as their eternal punishment.

Patrick of Ireland's letter to Coroticus

> I stand in the troughs of life's hard seas
> The Saviour from ill stands up to his knees.
>
> I stand and look at the wrecks of my time
> The Father of Time puts his hand in mine.
>
> I stand and behold a heart that is grim
> The gentle Spirit puts a smile within.
>
> I kneel before the fates above
> And I find the One whose name is Love.
>
> We weep for the hungry without any bread
> For children who need to be fed
> We weep for mistreated ones, strangers to love
> The oppressed by force from above.
>
> We pray against cruelty, hatred and pain
> Inhumanity and greed for gain
> We pray for hostages, may they go free.
> And forgive the sinners, starting with me.

Andrew Dick

Be happy with those who are happy, weep with those who weep.
Have the same concern for everyone. Do not be proud but accept
humble duties.
Romans 12:15, 16

Be helpful when you are at the bottom of the ladder and be the lowest
when you are in authority. Be simple in faith but well trained in
manners; demanding in your own affairs but unconcerned in those of
others. Be guileless in friendship, astute in the face of deceit, tough in
time of ease, tender in hard times. Keep your options open when
there's no problem, but dig in when you must choose. Be pleasant
when things are unpleasant, and sorrowful when they are pleasant.
Disagree where necessary, but be in agreement about the truth. Be
serious in pleasures but kindly when things are bitter. Be strong in trials,
weak in dissensions . . .

  Be friendly with people of honour, stiff with rascals, gentle to the
weak, firm to the stubborn, steadfast to the proud, humble to the
lowly. Always be sober, chaste, modest. Be discreet in duty, persistent
in study, unshaken in turmoil, valiant in the cause of truth, cautious in
time of strife. Be submissive to good, unbending to evil, gentle in
curiosity, untiring in love, just in all things. Be respectful to the worthy,
merciful to the poor. Be mindful of favours, unmindful of wrongs.
Love ordinary people, and don't crave for riches, but cool down
excitement and speak your mind.

  Obey your seniors, keep up with your juniors, equal your equals,
emulate the perfect. Don't envy your betters, or grieve at those who
surpass you, or censure those who fall behind, but agree with those
who urge you on. Though weary, don't give up. Weep and rejoice at
the same time out of zeal and hope. Advance with determination, but
always fear for the end.

Columbanus Letter to a young disciple

    For my shield this day I call
    Heaven's might, Son's brightness
    Moon's whiteness
    Fire's glory
    Lightning's swiftness
    Wind's wildness
    Ocean's depth
    Earth's solidity
    Rock's immobility.
    From Patrick's Breastplate

Haman, the enemy of the Jewish people, had cast lots (or purim as they are called) to determine the day for destroying the Jews; he had planned to wipe them out. But Queen Esther went to the king, and the king issued orders with the result that Haman suffered the fate he had planned for the Jews . . . The Queen wrote a letter directing the Jews and their descendants to always observe the days of Purim.
Esther 9:24, 25, 31

Have you ever had that awful feeling that somebody has got it in for you, and that there is nothing you can do about it? If so, take heart from the experience of Queen Esther, in the Bible, and of Samson of Dol.

Samson learned that a region of Britanny was in dire distress because an alien king, urged on by his evil wife, had killed the hereditary head of the estates, put his son Judual under sentence of death, and alienated the fearful population. Samson stayed at the palace in order to negotiate Judual's release, to the fury of the Queen, who tried one ploy after another to kill him. First, she pressed him to eat a meal before departing, and instructed her servant to take him a poisoned drink. As the servant gave him the glass, Samson made the sign of the cross over it and spilt it, saying calmly, 'this is not an appropriate cup for someone to drink.'

The King, softening after Samson had healed one of his staff, arranged for Samson to visit Judual: the Queen arranged for an unbroken, angry horse to be brought for his use. Samson made the sign of the cross again, this time on the horse, and calmly sat astride it. The horse, perhaps sensing the deep peace within Samson, became as timid as a mouse!

The Queen was determined that Samson should never return, so even when he was leaving to journey on by boat, she arranged for a hungry lion to be let loose at the port. Samson's biographer observed that the indomitable man of God invoked the name of Christ and discharged after the beast, 'his customary missiles as if from a catapult', saying, 'I charge you in the name of Jesus Christ who has given us power to tread under foot you and things like you, that your terrible power against the human race may from this day never rise again, but that you die quickly in the presence of all these people so that the people of this region may know that God has sent me here as a servant of Christ.' The lion died that hour, and everyone present, even the Queen herself, pledged to support both Judual's release and Samson's mission.

> Lord, help me always to believe
> that all things work together for good
> to those who love you.

The kingdom of heaven is right here, so turn away from your sins.
Mark 1:15

The safety first mentality which pervades most organised life today, is stifling the frontier mentality which is part of the nature God has given us. As David Adam reminds us in his book *Borderlands*, we are in danger of becoming safe people who have never been all at sea or experienced 'the cliffs of fall' (as the poet Gerard Manley Hopkins described the mind's mountain of grief). We avoid crossing frontiers in case we are shot at. Yet in reality life is ever taking us into the edge of things. Frontiers are exciting places and everyone should be encouraged to explore them.

Jesus was often in the border lands: between countries, between heaven and earth; he was on the fringes of society, with lepers, tax collectors, prostitutes, as well as with top people.

Columbanus described his fellow Irish people as 'inhabitants of the world's edge'. Celtic Christians were good at crossing borders, by foot or by coracle. Like St Brendan, some ventured into the great unknown, and possibly reached America. Others, like Patrick and Aidan, went out to a foreign people and became one with them for the love of God. Missionaries such as Columbanus founded Christian communities in the most unlikely locations, and hermits found their place of resurrection in the wildest of places.

Celtic Christians have also been able to keep an awareness of the 'other' more easily than many peoples. This was expressed in a beautifully simple way by a woman from Kerry in the south west of Ireland. When she was asked where heaven was, she replied, 'about a foot and a half above a person.' Such an awareness has us always treading exciting border lands.

> Great Spirit, Wild Goose of the Almighty
> Be my eye in the dark places
> Be my flight in the trapped places
> Be my host in the wild places
> Be my brood in the barren places
> Be my formation in the lost places.

Again I looked, and I heard angels, thousands and millions of them!
They stood round the throne.
Revelation 5:11

> I am weary and forlorn
> Lead me to the land of angels
> I think it is time I went for a space
> To the court of Christ
> To the peace of heaven.
>   *Carmina Gadelica*

In the Celtic as in the Orthodox understanding of life we are never
alone, and God is never alone. God likes company. And that is just as
true of the non-earthly realm as it is of earth. God has peopled the
unseen world with the bodiless beings we know as angels. They always
delight to do God's will, they are not weighed down with worldly
baggage.

Unlike the fanciful portrayals of angels in medieval times, there is an
earthy reality about angel encounters in the Bible. Six roles for these
bodiless servants of God can be discerned. They shield (e.g. Daniel
3:28; 12:1); they reveal God's message of salvation (e.g. Matthew 1:20);
they heal (Tobit 3:17 apocrypha); they carry out God's judgments
(Rev. 15:7, 8) they escort souls at death (Luke 16:22); and they praise
God (Luke 2:13).

On this eve of St Michael and All Angels Day it is good to turn our
thoughts towards angels. Michaelmas should be a significant time for us
as it was for Celtic Christians, who offer us a feast of angel stories.
Bede's writings brim with stories of encounters with angels, and one
third of Adamnan's *Life of Columba* consists of angel experiences.

> Have mercy on little ones abused
> May tender angels draw them to your presence.
> Have mercy on those in black trial
> May healing angels lift them into your presence.
> Have mercy on souls at death's door
> May holy angels escort them to your presence.
> Have mercy on we who remain
> May smiling angels radiate to us your presence.

Then Michael, one of the chief angels, came to help me, because I had been left there alone.
Daniel 10:13

In the New Testament Michael is named as the chief of the angels (Jude 9). The Book of Revelation depicts him as throwing down the dragon, a picture of Satan, who can come in the form of anti-Christ in any age. The first Celtic evangelists introduced Christianity to a society that was under the spell of many kinds of magical and unseen powers. They often built places of Christian worship on high places that had previously been dedicated to such powers; and these churches were often dedicated to Michael. Two well known examples of such Celtic foundations, built as a result of God giving direction to a Christian leader in the area, are Mont St Michel in Britanny and St Michael's Mount in Cornwall.

> Thou Michael the victorious
> I make my circuit under thy shield
> Thou Michael of the white steed
> And of the brilliant blades
> Conqueror of the dragon
> Be thou at my back
> Thou ranger of the heavens
> Thou warrior of the King of all
> O Michael victorious
> My pride and my guide
> O Michael the victorious
> The glory of mine eye.
>
> I make my circuit
> In the fellowship of the saint
> On the grass sward, on the meadow
> On the cold leathery hill.
> Though I should travel ocean
> And the hard globe of the world
> No harm can ever befall me
> Neath the shelter of thy shield
> O Michael victorious
> The jewel of my heart
> O Michael the victorious
> God's shepherd thou art
> > > *Carmina Gadelica*

Jesus said: Be careful that you never despise a single one of these little ones – for I tell you that they have angels who see my Father's face continually in heaven.
Matthew 18:10

Columba sat transcribing the Scriptures in his little cell at Iona. Two brothers who were near the open door were alarmed when his countenance suddenly changed and he shouted 'Help! help!'

'What is the matter?' they asked with consternation. Columba told them, 'A brother at our monastery at Oakwood Plain in Derry was working at the very top of the large house they are building there, and he slipped and began to fall. I ordered the angel of the Lord who was standing just there among you two to go immediately to save this brother.'

Later they learned that a man had indeed fallen from that great height, but nothing was broken, and he did not even feel any bruise. As they discussed this Columba said, 'How wonderful beyond words is the swift motion of an angel, it is as swift as lightning. For the heavenly spirit who flew from us when that man began to fall was there to support him in a twinkling of an eye before his body reached the ground. How wonderful that God gives such help through his angels, even when much land and sea lies between.'

> O angel guardian of my right hand
> Attend to me this night
> Rescue me in the battling floods
> Array me in your linen, for I am naked
> Succour me, for I am feeble and forlorn
>
> Steer my coracle in the crooked eddies
> Guide my step in gap and in pit
> Guard me in the treacherous turnings
> And save me from the harm of the wicked
> Save me from the harm this night
>
> Drive me from the taint of pollution
> Encompass me till Doom from evil
> O kindly angel of my right hand
> Deliver me from the wicked this night
> O deliver me this night.
>
> *Carmina Gadelica (adapted)*

LOOKING FORWARD

We are looking to the promise of glory that is set before us. It is a time of
waiting and praying and we are encouraged to keep true to the path by
the saints that have died in faith.

The angel told Daniel: Three more kings will appear in Persia, and then a fourth.
Daniel 11:2

Perhaps you have you been, or will be, involved in selecting or voting for someone to fill a vacant post? The Bible warns us against automatically choosing the person with the most charms. The story of the prophet Samuel choosing the future King David, who was regarded as the least of his large and talented family (see 1 Samuel 16) is a timely warning. The account of Columba's choice of Aidan mac-Gabran to fill the vacant throne of Dalriada not only warns us against presumption, it also encourages us to believe that God always has ways of guiding us to the right person.

When the king of Dalriada died in 574 the question of the succession involved Columba, who was related to the royal household, and who was the leader of the now dominant religion. Columba went into retreat on the island of Hinba to seek God's guidance. He felt that, since there were no sons, the eldest nephew of the deceased king should be chosen.

One night, however, Columba had a vision of an angel carrying a book which contained a list of the kings. Columba's candidate did not appear in it, but his younger brother, Aidan, did. Columba read in the book that he was to instal Aidan as king, but he refused. Suddenly, the angel stretched out its hand and gave Columba a mighty slap on his side which left a mark for the rest of his life. The angel told him. 'You must know for certain that I have been sent to you by God, and if you continue to refuse to install Aidan as king I shall hit you again.'

Columba was not amused by this vision, but it recurred three nights in succession. After the third time Columba got the point. He sailed to Iona, consecrated Aidan as King, gave him a heartfelt blessing, and prophesied as to the future of his dynasty. Aidan's reign proved to be a period of sound government and of peace between previously warring regions.

> O Michael militant king of the angels,
> Shield your people with the power of your sword.
> Spread your wing over sea and land
> And bring us to our goal.

After this I saw four angels standing at the four corners of the earth holding back the four winds . . . and I saw another angel coming up from the east with the seal of the living God. The angel loudly called to the four angels to whom God had given power to damage the earth and the sea, 'Do not harm them until we mark the servants of our God with a seal on their foreheads.'
Revelation 7:1–3

Despite the advances of medicine, many people still live in fear of a sudden catastrophe or epidemic such as AIDS. In the period of the Celtic saints the deadly plague would suddenly sweep through and decimate whole populations. In such situations it is easy to lose sight of the fact that God is still in overall control. We feel so powerless; what can we do?

Columba set aside a day in the Iona woods for sustained prayer combat. As he began to pray an oncoming wave of deathly black creatures relentlessly attacked with iron darts, desiring to wipe out him and many in the Iona community. Columba linked this experience with the threat of oncoming plague. His biographer, Adamnan, writes:

But he, single-handed, against innumerable foes of such a nature, fought with the utmost bravery, having received the armour of the apostle Paul. The contest was maintained on both sides during the greater part of the day, nor could the demons, countless though they were, vanquish him, nor was he able, by himself, to drive them out from his island, until the angels of God, as the saint afterwards told certain persons, came to his aid, when the demons in terror gave way.

On his way back Columba informed some brothers that Iona would now be spared the plague, but it would invade the monasteries in the region of Tiree. This came only too true. Two days later Columba added a postscript, whose lesson for us is: Don't leave the combat to somebody else. Baithen, the leader of one monastery in the Tiree region, had called his community to all-out fasting and prayer, and as a result only one brother there would die of the plague. This, too, came to pass exactly as Columba had foreseen.

> Good angels, messengers of God,
> Protect us from all that would plague our bodies
> Protect us from all that would plague our souls.

Praise the Lord from heaven, you that live in the heights above. Praise the Lord, all you angels and heavenly armies of the Lord.
Psalm 148:1, 2

If you pray truly, you will feel within yourself a great assurance, and the angels will be your companions. Know this, that as we pray, the holy angels encourage us and stand at our sides, full of joy, and at the same time interceding on our behalf.

Evagrius of Pontus

> He created good angels and archangels,
> the orders of Principalities and Thrones, of Powers and Virtues
> so that the goodness and majesty of the Trinity
> might not be unproductive in all works of bounty
> but might have heavenly beings in which he might
> greatly show forth his favours by a word of power.
>
> From the summit of the kingdom of heaven, where angels stand,
> from his radiant brightness, from the loneliness of his own form
> through being proud Lucifer had fallen, whom he had formed
> and the apostate angels also, by the same sad fall
> of the author of vainglory and obstinate envy,
> the rest continuing in their dominions.
>
> At once, when the stars were made, lights of the firmament
> the angels praised for his wonderful creating
> the Lord of this immense mass, the Craftsman of the Heavens,
> with a praiseworthy proclamation, fitting and unchanging
> in an excellent symphony they gave thanks to the Lord
> not by any endowment of nature, but out of love and choice.

Altus Prosator Attributed to Columba

> May the seven angels of the Holy Spirit
> And the two guardian angels
> Shield us this and every night
> Till light and dawn shall come.

Carmina Gadelica

Praise the Lord, sun, moon and shining stars. Praise the Lord highest heavens and the waters . . . Praise the Lord strong winds . . . all animals and . . . all peoples.
Psalm 148:3, 4, 8, 10, 11

Praised be you, my Lord, with all your creatures
Especially Sir Brother Sun
Who is the day, and through whom you give us light.
He is beautiful and radiant, with great splendour
And bears a likeness of you, Most High One.

Praised be you, my Lord, through Brother Wind
And through the air, cloudy and serene, and every kind of weather
Through which you give sustenance to your creatures.

Praised be you, my Lord, through Sister Water
Who is very useful and humble, precious and pure.

Praised be you, my Lord, through Brother Fire
Through whom you light the night
He is beautiful and playful, robust and strong.

Praised be you, my Lord, through our sister, Mother Earth
Who sustains and governs us
And who produces varied fruits with coloured flowers and herbs.

Francis of Assisi
translation based on that of Armstrong and Brady

Blessed Lord
as Francis found joy in creation, in beauty and simplicity
but perfect joy in sharing the sufferings of the world
so may we, abiding in your love
receive your gift of perfect joy
and by the power of your Spirit
radiate your joy
and find, even in suffering,
the glory of God.

A prayer at the Franciscan Priory, Almouth

God divided light from darkness by a circle.
Job 25:10

Flocks with shepherds' huts burgeoned around Ninian's community at Whithorn, for the brothers, pilgrims and poor people all needed to be fed. Ninian wanted to bless these as well as the monastery, so when the flocks were gathered in at night he would walk right round them, marking a circle on the earth with his staff. Then he would raise his hand and ask God's protection on everything within the circle.

On Michaelmas Day at Iona all the humans and even the animals walked sunwise around the Angels Hill to seek God's blessing on the island for the coming year. We know that abbots of Iona such as Columba and Adamnan practised the circling prayer. Adamnan tells us that when Columba sailed from Loch Foyle he blessed a stone by the water's edge and made a circuit round it sunwise. It was from that stone that he went into the boat. Columba taught that anybody going on a journey who did the circling prayer round the stone would most likely arrive in safety.

In Wales you can still see traces of the circles of stones that surrounded monasteries and other holy places. They marked a place dedicated to Christ like human sentries, protecting the inhabitants from evil forces.

What is the significance of the circle for Christians? Celtic Christians carried on the Druids' understanding that the Devil was frustrated by anything that had no end, no break, no entrance, because they knew that God is never ending both in time and in love, and the Three Selves within God form an ever encircling Presence. One of the chief rites of the sun-worship of pagan Celts was to turn sunwise in order to entice the sun to bless their crops. The Christians said to them, in effect, 'The Creator of the sun is now amongst us, we will continue to circle our crops, but now we do it in the name of the Sun of Suns. The Creator had built the circling of the sun into creation, which reflects something of its Creator, so it is good for us.' This is not magic, it is an expression of the reality of the encircling Presence of God. To say the Caim or Circling prayer, stretch out your arm and index finger and turn around sunwise calling for the Presence to encircle the person or thing you pray for.

> Circle me, Lord
> Keep love within, keep strife without
> Keep hope within, keep despair without
> Keep peace within, keep harm without.

I have given you the choice between a blessing or a curse.
Deuteronomy 30:1

By granting us the wonderful gift of freedom, God gave us the capacity
to do evil as well as do good. Indeed, we would not be free unless God
had given us this ability: there is no freedom for the person who does
good by instinct and not by choice. Likewise, as the holy Welsh monk
Pelagius taught, there is no freedom if it is impossible for us to do
good. In this sense the capacity to do evil is itself good; evil actions,
although God does not want them, are themselves signs of the goodness
of God in allowing them.

Some Christians developed the idea that 'original sin', which affects
us all, means that people who do not listen to God in nature or in
human beings, and who therefore damage them, are not responsible,
because only born again Christians can be expected to know God's
ways. Pelagius taught that each person is capable of both good and evil,
and is responsible for their choices. He was accused of also teaching that
human beings are born without sin, and fatalistic Christians thought that
ruled out the need for a Saviour. That certainly would not be a true
Christian belief, but the extracts from Pelagius in this book provide
sound Christian guidance.

A person might say that the world would be a better place if everyone
within it were always good and never evil. But such a world would be
flawed because it would lack one essential ingredient of goodness,
namely freedom. When God created the world he was acting freely; no
other force compelled God to create the world. Thus by creating
humans in his image, God had to give them freedom. A person who
could only do good and never do evil would be in chains; a person
who can choose good or evil shares the freedom of God.

Pelagius To Demetrius

> In the strength of the Warrior of God
> I oppose all that pollutes.
> In the eye of the Face of God
> I expose all that deceives.
> In the energy of the Servant of God
> I bind up all that is broken.

Count it all joy, my brothers and sisters, when all kinds of trials come your way, for you know that when your faith succeeds in facing such trials, the result is the ability to endure . . . so that you may be complete, lacking nothing.
James 1:2, 3, 4

There is no follower of Christ who is not at times perplexed by the suffering of good men and women. When we see a bad person suffer, we can interpret it as punishment for sin. So if an evil person contracts a painful and fatal illness while still young, if their house burns to the ground, if they lose their wealth in some dishonest transaction, we feel that justice is being done. But if a good person falls fatally ill in their youth, if an honest and hardworking person becomes destitute, we are indignant. We cannot understand how God can permit such injustice.

Our indignation arises from superficial knowledge. We look at pain and pleasure, sorrow and joy, in shallow, material terms. Yet a good person, even if undergoing great physical distress, still senses the serene peace of God deep within their soul. The loyal disciple of Christ who is compelled to live in poverty knows that they are sharing the poverty of Christ. And the Scriptures assure us that in poverty and in agony the soul of Christ knew the heavenly joy of God.

Pelagius

When a person who is both good and young is struck down it causes particular distress. One such person was the Northumbrian King Oswald. A generation after his death, when new Christians in the south of England were devastated by plague, God used his example to transform a dying boy and bring faith to bear on the problem of innocent suffering. The onset of plague prompted the monastery to begin a vigil of fasting and prayer. On the second day of the vigil two apostles appeared to this small boy and said, 'Do not let the fear of death trouble you. We are going to take you to the heavenly kingdom . . . Call the priest and tell him the Lord has heard your prayers and not one more person from the monastery or the estates linked to it will die of this plague; all sufferers will be restored. God has granted this in response to the prayers of the saintly King Oswald. It was on this very day that he was slain in battle and taken to heaven.' All this came to pass. The boy died in bliss, and the faith of the people grew stronger.

> Lord, help me offer to you
> The gift of deep but not bitter suffering

If you carry out the commands I give you today you will receive a blessing. If you turn away from these commands, to go after false gods, you will receive a curse.
Deuteronomy 11:27, 28

God created all human beings in God's image, to be like God. God has made animals more powerful than human beings, but we have been given intelligence and freedom.

We alone are able to recognise God as our maker, and therefore to understand the goodness of God's creation. We alone have the capacity to distinguish between good and evil, right and wrong. This means that our actions need not be compulsions, we do not have to be swayed by our immediate wants and desires, as are the animals. Instead, we can make choices. Day by day, hour by hour, we have to make decisions. In each decision we can choose either good or evil. This freedom to choose makes us like God. If we choose evil, that freedom becomes a curse. If we choose good, it becomes our greatest blessing.

Pelagius

There is no evil in anything created by God, nor can anything of His become an obstacle to our union with Him. The obstacle is in our 'self', that is to say in the tenacious need to maintain our separate, external, egotistic will.

Thomas Merton

Toothache starts in a rotten tooth,
Then the pain spreads through the jaw
Until one's whole head starts to throb.
Every thought is filled with toothache.

Sin starts with a rotten action,
Then the pleasure spreads through the body
Until the soul itself becomes enslaved.
Every feeling is filled with sinful desire.

Pull out the aching tooth.
Root out the sinful action.
       Robert Van de Weyer Celtic Parables

Why do you point out the speck in the other person's eye and pay no attention to the log in your own eye? . . . First, take the log out of your own eye, and then you will be able to see clearly to take the speck out of the other person's eye.
Matthew 7:3, 5

Even the best and holiest of people have stubborn areas in their lives. Perhaps a person eats or drinks to excess and refuses to restrain their appetite; perhaps a person has a quick and harsh temper and refuses to restrain their anger; perhaps a person needs to be the leader in every situation, and cannot take advice or criticism, nor defer to the better judgment of others.

    Compared with the other areas in which a person is good and holy, these stubborn areas may seem quite trivial. Yet if they remain unchecked they can corrode a person's soul and blot their record.

Pelagius To a mature Christian

O Saviour of the human race
O true physician of every disease
O heart-pitier and assister of all misery
O fount of true purity and true knowledge
Forgive.

O star-like sun
O guiding light
O home of the planets
O fiery-maned and marvellous one
Forgive.

O holy scholar of holy strength
O overflowing, loving, silent one
O generous and thunderous giver of gifts
O rock-like warrior of a hundred hosts
Forgive.

Attributed to St Ciaran (adapted)

My servant will not crush a bruised reed or quench a smouldering flame.
Matthew 12:20

In a world of right and wrong, in which we are free spirits, it would be foolish to ask Christians never to criticise. But think of the occasions when Jesus criticised; they were very few, always timely, and he never crushed a bruised reed. He always affirmed the people who needed it. Criticism should only be made on rare occasions, as a last resort, in a kindly spirit, after prayer and thought, to the person concerned, and only if it is both true and necessary.

The easiest sin to commit is to criticise a brother, calling him a fool. We are usually cautious about accusing a brother of a major sin; we feel we must have sufficient evidence before making such an accusation. But to accuse a brother of doing something stupid hardly seems to matter. So we lightly toss off such critical remarks.

Yet such criticism can wound deeply. It can stay with a person for years after the person who uttered it has forgotten about it. This is because so many people lack a sense of self-worth, and fear failure. So a critical remark can destroy their confidence completely, discouraging them so much that they may never again attempt the task that was criticised.

So we must be far more vigilant against committing this easy sin than against the more obvious and serious sins.

Pelagius To an elderly friend

Lord,
let our memory provide no shelter
for grievance against another.
Lord,
let our heart provide no harbour
for hatred of another.
Lord,
let our tongue be no accomplice
in the judgement of a brother.
Northumbrian Office

Pride comes before a fall.
Proverbs 16:18

A brother began to pester Abba Theodore with all sorts of questions
and opinions about aspects of God's work, none of which he had
seriously engaged in himself. The old Abba said to him, 'You have not
yet found the ship you are to sail in, or put your baggage in it, so how
is it that you seem to be already in the city you plan to sail to? When
you have first worked hard in the thing you talk about, then you can
speak from the experience of the thing itself'.

Three brothers came to an Abba in Scete. The first proudly told him,
'I have committed the Old and New Testaments to memory.' 'You
have filled the air with words,' the Abba told him. The second
informed him, 'I have transcribed the Old and New Testaments with
my own hands.' 'And you have filled your windows with manuscripts,'
was the reply. The third, who felt he had devoted so much time to
prayer and study that he had no time to spare for household jobs
announced that 'The grass grows on my hearthstone.' The Abba said,
'And you have driven hospitality from you.'

Sayings of the Desert Fathers

An Englishman is a self-made man and worships his maker.
English saying

Fools rush in where angels fear to tread
British proverb

Speak up to but not beyond your experience.
Frank Buchman

Almighty, I'm steeped in the 'I know best' mentality.
I invite your Holy Spirit to convict me of presumption,
To expose every lingering bit of it in any corner of my life
And to winkle it all out.
Give to me the wisdom of humility.

How young and old should regard one another

You elders . . . should not try and dominate those who have been put in your care, but you should be examples for them to follow . . . In the same way you younger people should give yourselves to the older ones. And all of you must put on the apron of humility, to serve one another.
2 Peter 5:3, 5

Old people often envy the vigour and good health of the young, their greater capacity to enjoy physical pleasures, and the length of years they have ahead of them. The truth is young people should envy the old.

Although old people have less physical and mental energy, they have greater spiritual reserves. Although they can enjoy fewer physical pleasures, they have greater capacity for spiritual enjoyment. Thus the old are better prepared for death, and for life beyond death. So the fewer years that are ahead of them should be a reason to celebrate, not to indulge self-pity.

Although a young person like yourself may assume that you have many years ahead of you, you cannot be sure. The soul is attached to the body by a fragile thread which can snap at any moment. So although you are younger than I am, you may die before me. Do not, therefore, merely envy old age: imitate its virtues. Direct your physical energies into spiritual matters, let these become your major source of pleasure. In this way you will be ready for death whenever it comes.

Pelagius To a young friend

> O God, to whom to love and to be are one
> Hear my faith-cry for those who are more yours than mine.
> Give each of them what is best for each.
> I cannot tell what it is.
> But you know.
> I only ask that you love them and keep them
> With the loving and keeping
> You showed to Mary's son and yours.
>
> *Collected by Alistair MacLean in* Hebridean Altars

I chose some of your people to be prophets, and some to be
Nazirites . . . but you made the Nazirites drink wine, and ordered the
prophets not to speak my message.
Amos 2:11, 12

Certain Christians, not just monks and nuns, follow what they call a
Rule or a Way of Life. This sets out the values and goals they choose
to make their priority, and a check-list, suited to their circumstances, of
practices which help them to live these. Some Christians argue that
they want to be rid of rules and regulations, and, since no two
situations are alike, all they need is the Holy Spirit to guide them. Here
is some advice to consider:

In a single day we make so many decisions, we cannot possibly
weigh up the good and evil consequences of each decision. We are
liable to make foolish and wrong decisions. For this reason we need a
rule, a simple set of moral principles that we can apply to each decision
we make. This will not be foolproof, but with a good rule, our
decision will far more often be right than wrong.

Another reason for a rule is this: Jesus tells us to pray always; yet
sometimes we love to devote much time to prayer whereas at other
times we are dry or feel far too busy to pray. A rule prevents us from
making excuses; it spurs us to pray at a particular time even when our
heart is cold towards God.

The teaching of Jesus must be the primary general guide for any
disciple, but Jesus himself did not give rules. The source of a rule is
inside your own heart. What we call conscience is a kind of rule which
God has written in your heart. If you wish to formulate a rule you
must listen to your conscience and write down on paper what God has
written on the heart.

Pelagius

> Eternal God
> our beginning and our end
> accompany us through the rest of our journey.
> Open our eyes to praise you for your creation,
> and to see the work you set before us.
> *Based on St Finbarr's Cathedral Midday Prayer, Cork*

Be ready at all times to answer anyone who asks you to explain the
hope you have in you, but do it with gentleness and respect.
1 Peter 3:15

You have a deep desire to appear wise, but you have no confidence in
yourself: you do not regard yourself as wise. So in the company of
others you remain silent; even when the conversation turns to spiritual
matters, where words of wisdom are most necessary, you remain silent.
You hope that people will interpret your silence as a sign of the depth
of your wisdom – so deep that mere words cannot communicate it.
Some people try to deceive others with dishonest words; you are trying
to deceive others with dishonest silence.

If you possess wisdom on particular matters, it is your duty under
God to express this wisdom to others, so they can benefit from it. If
you do not possess wisdom on matters of importance, it is your duty
under God to ask questions of those who do possess wisdom so you
can learn from it. In either case you must speak.

This does not mean that words must flow ceaselessly from your
mouth like a river. Use words sparingly, so that they express exactly
what you mean. But without words you will remain ignorant and
stupid.

Pelagius To a young friend

In Sophia, the highest wisdom-principle, all the greatness and majesty of
the unknown that is in God and all that is rich and maternal in his
creation are united inseparably, as paternal and maternal principles, the
uncreated Father and created Mother-Wisdom.

Thomas Merton

> Lord help me
> Never to pretend
> To know more than I do know,
> Always to be ready to speak out of my experience,
> Up to my experience
> But not to speak beyond it.

When working with the Jews I live like a Jew in order to win
them . . . when working with Gentiles, I live like a Gentile in order to
win Gentiles . . . Among the weak in faith I become weak like one of
them, in order to win them.
1 Corinthians 9:20, 21, 22

Someone asks, 'Surely a Christian should stand against current trends in
order to uphold the values of the Gospel rather than to go with the
flow?' Wherever contemporary values conflict with those of Jesus, that
is certainly true. But have we examined how much in our church ethos
is a matter, not of values, but of cultural taste? St Paul was the first
person to confront evil boldly, yet it was also he who gave a mission
model of becoming one with different groups and cultures (in all things
except sin) in order to win them to a relationship with Christ.

Celtic Christians, too, were clear about sin, but unlike Christians in
other parts, they sat loose to churchy culture if it was alien to their
people. They had their meetings at the places where the people
normally met; they built their places of worship on the places where
people had previously worshipped as non-Christians; they carried on
customs such as circling farms and homes, but now they did this in the
name of the One True God. In the years following Patrick in Ireland
the shape of church organisation reflected that of the clan. Instead of
organisation being imposed from outside, it was like a wheel, in which
the clan welcomed a Christian community as its hub.

Celtic Christians resisted the idea that Christians should cut off the
long, flowing hair which Celts felt was their glory, and for which Celtic
Christians could give glory to God. Evangelists such as Aidan and Chad
resisted pressure to use the form of transport that top people used but
which would have distanced them from ordinary people. They used
their feet, not a horse, to make visits. Aidan resisted pressure to impose
all the Christian laws on unchurched people before they had come to
know and love Jesus and the milk of his teaching. When groups of
Christians gathered at natural meeting places, they would often play folk
music, and would join in with other folk singers whether they were
Christian or not.

> Creator of diverse cultures
> Brother to all peoples,
> Flowing Spirit
> Help me to go with the flow
> Of all that is good and human around me.

'Master', Simon answered, 'we worked hard all night long and caught no fish. Nevertheless, if you say so, I will let down the nets.' Simon let them down and caught such a large number of fish that the nets were about to break.
Luke 5:5, 6

Simon Peter knew more about fishing than did Jesus, who had a background in carpentry. He knew where the fish were, and he knew that night was the right time to catch them. So it must have seemed daft when Jesus told him that if he pushed the boat out in the morning he would make a catch. But Simon was learning that Jesus was a channel of a wisdom higher than his own know-how. Each of us has to learn this lesson in our own way. This is how St Gall learned it:

Gall is the best known of Columbanus' followers, and accompanied him to Annegray and Luxeuil where they founded some of the first Celtic Christian communities on the continent of Europe. Gall was very bright, but he was also hot-headed, and needed to learn lessons of humility.

One day at Luxeuil Columbanus, who was the Abbot, asked Gall, who was a keen fisherman, to go to a particular river to catch fish. Gall took this as an opportunity to show his independence and his better knowledge of fishing; he went to a different river where he knew there were more fish.

It was true the fish were plentiful, for he could see them swimming all around his net. But for some reason, though he tried all day, not a single one would swim into the net! Rather sheepishly Gall returned to Columbanus. All Columbanus said, in a mild manner, was, 'Why not try doing what I told you?'

Next day Gall swallowed his pride and followed Columbanus' instruction. Sure enough, the moment he threw his net into the river the fish came in so fast that he could hardly pull them out. Gall got the point that although he was more clever than others, he was also more conceited, and that pride comes before a fall.

Lord take pride and false independence from my spirit.

It is better to trust in the Lord than to depend upon human leaders.
Psalm 118:9

One of the curses of our society is a condition the has been described
as 'the cycle of dependency'. Proud and false independence is wrong,
but dependency (as distinct from mutual inter-dependence) and failure
to take responsibility is also wrong; it is a subtle form of idolatry. We
can so easily put leaders on to pedestals, and expect them to do for us
what we can only do for ourselves. Certainly, we can only do these
things in the strength God gives, but God is as available to us as he is
to them. In fact there should never be a 'them'.

Celtic Christianity spawned close fellowships and delightful
friendships, but it did not spawn dependency. If someone wanted to
enter a monastery (and sometimes these became the only safe and
decent places around) they had to wait outside for days. They had to
show that they could take responsibility for their food, sleep and time,
that they could take their own decisions and that they could work hard.

Maedoc and Molaise were bosom friends. But they were open to the
possibility that they might be called to travel independent paths. 'Ah
Jesus,' they prayed one day at the foot of two trees, 'is it your will that
we should part, or that we should remain together to the end?' Then
one of the trees fell to the south, and the other to the north. They
knew then that it had been revealed to them that they must part.
Maedoc went south and built a monastery at Ferns. Molaise went north
and built a monastery in Devenish.

During a gathering of a large religious movement, someone begged
the leader, 'Our children are being murdered in the streets. Come and
help us.' The leader was thoughtfully silent. 'Brother,' he simply said,
'you are hurting, and I feel for you. Let me give you my address and
phone number. I'll do what I can to help you. But please – do not
look to me as a leader. I may be dead tomorrow. God wants to raise
up a leader in you.'

> Moment by moment you give me choices, O Lord.
> Help me to make those choices.

When you please the Lord you can make your enemies into friends.
Proverbs 16:7

Gall learned the hard way that he needed other people. When a hostile
ruler came to power the monks had to leave the region. But Gall
became too ill to travel with Columbanus, who left him behind,
believing that his illness was in some way connected with a weakness in
his character. After the others had left, Gall managed to get his fishing
nets and his few possessions on to a boat and get himself to a priest
who nursed him back to health.

It seems that Gall now realised he had made so many mistakes in the
way he related both to brothers and to local people. He had destroyed
their objects of worship before he had made friends with them. Now
he thought that the best thing he could was to serve God alone in a life
of prayer, and prepare for heaven.

Gall asked the priest to recommend a place where he could live as a
hermit. The priest replied that the mountains and valleys were too full
of wild beasts for this to be viable. 'If God be for us, who shall be
against us?' Gall replied.

So they came to a place by a river where Gall settled, and the wild
beasts became his friends. Other hermits joined him, for he had now
learned to be humble, to be like the humus, the earth. Columbanus
may have sensed this, and wanted to heal the divide that had come
between them, for before he died he sent Gall his Abbot's staff as a sign
that the past was over and that he believed in Gall's God-given calling.

Gall was in fact pressed to become Abbot of the monastery at
Luxeuil, but he had now no worldly ambitions, and refused. However,
the world flocked to his cell. The monastery which took the place of
his hermit's settlement became a centre of life and learning for Europe.
The town which grew up around, St Gallen, is now one of the great
industrial cities of Switzerland.

> Humble me Lord.
> May I be sensitive to other people whatever their background.
> May I be led, not by my self-opinionated will, but by you alone.
> And may this result in friendships.

You crown the year with your goodness.
Psalm 65:11

> O sacred season of autumn, be my teacher
> For I wish to learn the virtue of contentment
> As I gaze upon your full-coloured beauty
> I sense all about you an at-home-ness with your amber riches.
> You are the season of retirement
> of full barns and harvested fields.
> The cycle of growth has ceased
> and the busy work of giving life
> is now completed.
> I sense in you no regrets;
> you've lived a full life.
> I live in a society that is ever restless
> always eager for more mountains to climb
> seeking happiness through more and more possessions.
> As a child of my culture
> I am seldom truly at peace with what I have.
> Teach me to take stock of what I have given and received;
> may I know that it's enough,
> that my striving can cease
> in the abundance of God's grace.
> May I know the contentment
> that allows the totality of my energies
> to come to full flower.
> May I know that like you I am rich beyond measure.
>
> *Edward Hays*

I thank you for the wind
That clears the fog and clog of life,
For chimneys that allow air and warmth to move through our lives,
For the texture of the bricks and tiles.
I thank you for house tops and street lights
And for the sound of traffic moving.
I thank you for TV and satellite dishes.
These open the world up to people in their little dwellings.
So much energy, so much enterprise –
The friendly smiles of Sister Earth.

You know who your teachers were, and you remember that ever since you were a child you have known the Holy Scriptures . . . All Scripture is inspired by God and is useful for teaching the truth, rebuking error, correcting faults, and giving instruction for right living, so that the person who serves God may be fully qualified and equipped to do every kind of good work.
2 Timothy 3:14–17

When we are adolescent, it seems as if a thousand little ways of behaving are second nature to adults, but we ourselves are unsure and self conscious about how to react in different situations: how to converse, how to eat things, when and how to arrive and leave.

We need the freedom not to have to prove we know things, that it is OK to ask what is the appropriate thing to do, to take time to observe how others behave, gradually to get a sense of what is appropriate, yet to remain open to inspirations that are unique to us.

Once a group of brothers were enjoying a picnic by a riverside in Ireland, when a bard strolled by. He joined the brothers and they enjoyed conversation for some time, before he said it was time to go, and went on his way. It would have been considered appropriate for the brothers to have invited the bard to sing some of his songs, composed by himself, before he left them, so later the brothers asked Columba why he had not, on this occasion, given such an invitation. 'Because,' said Columba, 'that poor man has been killed; and since I sensed that this would happen, how could I have requested a happy song from someone who is about to meet such an unhappy end?'

> Lord of the shadows, Lord of the day
> Lord of the elements, Lord of the grey
> Lord of creation, Lord of the journey.
> I am unsure, weak and frail.
>
> Grant me sureness in the nearness of your clasp
> Father keep me in every steep
> Saviour reach me in every slip
> Spirit teach me in every fall.

Dear children, keep yourselves from idols.
1 John 5:21

The first things that come to mind when idols are mentioned are the carved figures of pagan faiths. Bear in mind, however, as you read the following story, that an idol is an expression of a universal tendency – to substitute some thing in the place of God. Behind all idolatry is the desire to control, to make God in our own image, to chase after illusions.

As Samson passed through the Hundred of Twigg, in Cornwall, he heard a group of people acting out a ritual in honour of a god. He stilled the brothers as he silently watched. In order not to appear threatening Samson took just two brothers with him and greeted their leader, Guedianus. Gently, he explained that it was not good to forsake the one God who created all things in order to worship one created thing. This brought varied reactions. Some jeered, some were angry, some argued that since it was tradition it surely could not be wrong, others simply told him to go away.

Circumstances, however, intervened, and Samson believed that God, unlike the idol, could use these circumstances. A lad who had been driving some horses far too fast, fell headlong from his horse, and twisted his head badly as he fell. He lay on the ground like a lifeless corpse; everyone gathered round, and as they realised they could do nothing, they began to weep. Samson took an initiative. 'You can see that your idol can do nothing for this fellow,' he said. 'If you promise you will destroy and cease to worship this idol, I, with God's assistance, will restore him to life.' The pagans agreed. Samson asked them to withdraw and prayed over the lad for two hours. At the end of that time he delivered him safe and sound. The pagans destroyed their idol, and gave their allegiance to Samson. He instructed and baptised them as Christians. On the hill, in place of the idol, Samson carved a cross on a standing stone in his own hand.

> The dearest idol I have known
> Whate'er that idol be
> Help me to tear it from thy throne
> And worship only Thee.
> *William Cowper*

When I remember you in my prayers I always thank my God because I hear of your love for all God's people and your faith towards the Lord Jesus . . . I have received much joy and encouragement from your love, because the hearts of God's people have been refreshed through you, my brother.
Philemon 4, 5, 7

Brendan of Birr was known as the chief of the prophets of Ireland, and he was a life-long friend of Columba. A church synod at Meltown, in Meath, had decided to ex-communicate Columba who belonged to a hostile clan. When Columba arrived at the synod only one person rose to greet him, Brendan. This took courage. Brendan told everyone, 'I dare not slight the man chosen by God to lead nations into life.'

The two men remained close even when they were far apart. Not only did Brendan have prophetic foresight of Columba's future ministry; Columba, on Iona, was aware of Brendan's death in the west of Ireland on November 29, and saw angels carrying his soul to heaven.

Have you taken to time to become aware of the souls with whom you have great affinity? Does God want you to move with that awareness? To be in touch through means of new technology, or just by carrying each other in prayer?

Friends are a little bit of heaven here on earth.

Anon

> Father I offer you these friends
> Jesus I thank you for these bonds
> Spirit I look to you for this rapport.

Righteousness exalts a nation.
Proverbs 13:34

Though the Celtic church and culture was wrecked by Viking
invasions, the Gaels triumphed in the end. They converted the
Norsemen to Christianity and even the kings of Norway craved the
honour of burial on holy Iona. The kings of Alban continued to be
buried there, for it had become home for the hearts of Pict and Scot
alike. Kenneth MacAlpin, the half-Pictish Scot who in 845 welded the
two people together . . . also was laid in the soil of Iona.

Columba's legacy was something more abiding than relics or
buildings. He left his people a vision of what God can do in and
through a person, if they were willing to go the whole way.

As a prince and an adviser to kings he was inevitably concerned with
politics and his work resulted in vast social, political and economic
consequences . . . But how did he do it? Not by political means but by
spiritual . . . His politics were to change the hearts of politicians.

The founding of Iona stands out like a divine intervention in history.
It was the decisive stroke in the war of Faith and it let loose the spirit
of the Peregrini (the wanderers for the love of God) which was to
transform Europe.

Reginald B. Hale

People must choose to be governed by God or they condemn
themselves to be ruled by tyrants.

William Penn 1644–1718

Some nation must give a lead. Some nation must find God's will as her
destiny and God-guided people as her representatives at home and
abroad. Will it be your nation?

Frank Buchman

May our nation find your will as her destiny.
May our nation find God-guided representatives at home and abroad.
May our nation find peace within itself
And become a peace-maker in the international family.

O Lord, here we are before you in our guilt.
Ezra 9:15 (The prayer of Ezra on behalf of his people)

A romantic idea gained credence that Celtic saints such as Cuthbert prayed in the sea all night and every night. There is no evidence for that, and, if they did, they would have been masochists.

It is true that Celtic Christians at times prayed in cold water as a form of penance. And there is no doubt, as we have learned, that Cuthbert was once seen praying in the sea at night during a visit to the monastery at Coldingham.

In this case, there may have been a particular reason. This is how I see it: The men and women in this mixed monastery had slid into immoral ways. Their Abbess, Ebba, though a good person, was ineffective. So she invited Cuthbert to visit the monastery, no doubt filling his mind with all the sleaze she had been unable to deal with.

Cuthbert, within himself, took authority over the situation. He made himself one with his brothers and sisters in the monastery. Then, acting as their representative, he went down into the pure, salt sea. The sharp cold of the water cooled their passions; the size of the ocean put their sins into perspective compared to the love and power of God. The immersion of their representative in the sea was a way of immersing this community in God. The chanting of God's praise in the psalms was an offering on behalf of the community, as well as a weapon that made its enemies – lust, lies, laziness – flee away.

It may be that your attention is drawn to a situation where immorality or dishonesty have taken a hold; it seems like a barrel of apples in which every apple threatens to become rotten. You ask, 'What can I do?'

Perhaps the example of people in the Bible such as Ezra, or of forbears in the Faith such as Cuthbert, will give us the resolve to take authority in prayer, and to make confession, petition and praise on their behalf. For, as the saying has it, As I am, so is my people.

Lord Jesus Christ
Who became the representative of the whole human race
In your name I represent this group of people
Which is in such a mess
And which you have put on my heart.
I bring them now to you . . .

The Lord gives sleep to his loved ones.
Psalm 127:2

Celtic Christians allow God to permeate every area of life, even the hidden or unconscious areas. Since one third of our lives is likely to be spent in sleep, it is important to invite God into our sleeping hours.

> I lie down this night with God
> And God will lie down with me
> I lie down this night with Christ
> And Christ will lie down with me
> I lie down this night with the Spirit
> And the Spirit will lie down with me.
> The Three of my love will be lying down with me.
> I shall not lie down with sin
> Nor shall sin or sin's shadow lie down with me
> I lie down this night with God
> And God will lie down with me.
>
> *Carmina Gadelica*

> Sleep, sleep, and away with sorrow
> Sleep in the arms of Jesus
> Sleep in the breast of virgin mother
> Sleep in the calm of all calm
> Sleep in the love of all loves
> Sleep in the Lord of life eternal.
>
> *Carmina Gadelica (adapted)*

> May the blessing of the Son
> help you do what must be done.
> May the Spirit stroke your brow
> as weary down to sleep you go.
> May the Father mark your rest
> empower you for tomorrow's test,
> May the Trinity rekindle
> the pure flames of your life's candle.
>
> *Ramon Beeching*

O God, you are my God, and I long for you from early morning; my whole being desires you. Like a dry, worn-out and waterless land, my soul is thirsty for you. Let me see you in the house of prayer . . . for your constant love is better than life itself.
Psalm 63:1, 2, 3

How happy are those who will be found on the look-out when the Lord comes. O happy look-out, in which they look for God the Creator of the universe, who fills and transcends all things.

I, too, though I am frail, desire to rise up from the sleep of idleness, to kindle the flame of divine love, the longing that is at the heart of divine compassion, and to rise above the stars, so that God's love ever burns within me. O that my life might be like a living flame that burns throughout the dark night in the house of God, giving light to all who come in from the cold.

Lord, give me that love which does not fail people; make my life like an open fire that you are always kindling, which nothing can quench. O Saviour most sweet, may I receive perpetual light from you, so that the world's darkness may be driven from us. O eternal Priest, may I see you, observe you, desire you, and love you alone as you shine in your eternal temple.

O loving Saviour, reveal yourself to us, so that knowing you we may love you, loving you we may desire you, desiring you we may contemplate you, you alone, by day and by night, and ever hold you in our thoughts.

Inspire us with your love, that it may possess all our inward parts, and all the different parts of our bodies, till this love is so huge that even the many waves of the world, the currents of air, sea or land cannot quench it.

Columbanus

Awesome Lord of earth and heaven
rule my heart.
My faith, my love to you be given
my every part

Early Irish

All things that exist were made by God the Word . . . and the Word is life.
John 1:3, 4

As we approach the close of the three months' harvest period, which the Celts felt it important to mark, it is customary to dwell on the theme of creation once again. Let us meditate on these reflections by the Celts' great mystical theologian, John Scotus Eriugena:

All things, even what seems to us to be without vital movement, live in the Word.

If you want to know how all things subsist in God-the-Word, choose some examples from created nature and think about them . . . Consider the infinite, multiple power of the seed – how many grasses, fruits, and animals are contained in each kind of seed; and how there surges forth from each a beautiful, innumerable multiplicity of forms. Contemplate with your inner eye how in a master the many laws of an art or science are one; how they live in the spirit that disposes them. Contemplate how an infinite number of lines may subsist in a single point, and other similar examples drawn from nature. 'For in Him', as the Scripture says, 'we live and move and have our being.'

But . . . human nature, even if it had not sinned, would not have been able to shine by its own strength. Although human nature is capable of wisdom, it is not itself wisdom. Just as the air does not shine by itself, yet is able to receive the light of the sun, so the Word wishes to teach us, 'It is not you who shine; but the Spirit of your Father shines in you.' You are not a light in yourselves, you are only able to participate in the divine light.

John Scotus Eriugena
Homily on the Prologue to the Gospel of St John (abridged)

> Creator, we are contained in you,
> And we are connected to all else that is contained in you.
> Help us not to rebel against our connectedness.
> Light-giver, we are reflectors for you,
> And, as we connect with others, we become rays of light.
> Help us not to shut out your light.
> Shine, Jesus, shine in us today.

At sunset Jacob came to a holy place and camped there. He lay down to sleep . . . and dreamed.
Genesis 28:11, 12

A sunset speaks of an ordinary day's work completed well, of a year moving towards its climax, transfigured by glory. It is a gift. It cannot be won by restless striving. It is a glory; it makes the body tingle and the spirit serenely soar. The tiresome or clashing features of the day become silhouettes — beautiful, harmonious. Their darkness speaks of a mysterious but deep meaning.

The evening of our years is meant to be lived in such a dimension. Hear God saying to us, 'Let me have my way among you. Do not strive, and I will crown your life with glory.'

On that night when St Columba, by a happy and blessed death passed from earth to heaven, while I and others with me were fishing in the valley of the river Find, we saw the whole vault of heaven become suddenly illuminated. Towards the east there appeared something like an immense pillar of fire, which seemed to illuminate the whole earth like the summer sun at noon. After that the column penetrated the heavens, darkness followed, as if the sun had just set.

Adamnan

We welcome the Sun of suns who dispels the shades of sin.
The sun rises daily only because you command it;
Its splendour will not last, created things all perish.
Christ the true Sun nothing can destroy;
The Splendour of God, he shall reign for ever!

I praise you for the sun
The face of the God of life
As the sun sets in peace
May I settle in with you

You are set free from the ruling spirits of the universe.
Colossians 2:20

The belief is common in some country areas that there are people who
can cast an evil eye on anything they please; for example, if they cast an
evil eye on you, you may miscarry a baby or have a miscarriage of
justice. There are modern forms of this belief which have an almost
universal and a malign influence. Many of us go through life
conditioned by what someone has said about us. Perhaps a parent told
us that we would never be any good at something; maybe we are into
'channelling' or we are always reading horoscopes. We accept an image
of ourselves that is distorted by other people's perceptions; we act out
the false information that has been fed to us. We live a lie. We are not
free to rise to our God-given destiny.

The Christian discovers that no one need be the prisoner of fate.
The eyes of Jesus's mother Mary were able to look upon the awful
agony of her son, and share something of his sacrificial love. This spurs
us to believe that we can ask Jesus to cast his eyes, with those of his
mother, upon us. Their eyes of love, which want only what is true and
best for us, have power to override any spell that a lesser and evil eye
has cast upon us.

> When Mary saw him, as she stood,
> High on the cross, all torn and rent,
> Rained from her eyes three showers of blood
> And at its foot she made lament.
>
> An Evil eye has me undone
> Paling my face in dule and dree
> I cry to Mary and her Son
> Take the ill eye away from me.
> > *From the* Religious Songs of Connacht
> > *collected by Douglas Hyde*

Lord, I want to name those of my reflex actions
That spring from what others have put upon me
Through their looks or their words.
I give these to you.
Help me to see myself as you see me.
Set me free to be your child, your adult,
Moving freely as a person under the influence of your Spirit.

Death is swallowed up in victory.
1 Corinthians 15:54

Soon you and I will die. We do not know the day or the hour of
death; God alone has such knowledge. But we can be certain that many
more years have elapsed since birth than will pass between now and
death. You say that you have no fear of death. I fear death because I
fear having to account for my evil deeds before God. You say that you
fear the process of dying. I do not fear dying because I know that God
will not force me to suffer pain beyond my capacity to endure it.
Elderly people like ourselves frequently make attempts to amend their
behaviour, hoping that God will forgive them past sins and judge them
on present goodness. God will not be swayed by that kind of
calculation. It is the heart, not the mind, that needs to change: we must
learn to love God more fully. And love coming from the heart makes
no calculation. If a person loves God with his whole heart, he will
entrust himself to God's love, without seeking to sway God's judgment
by displays of good behaviour. If my heart could change in such a way,
my fear of death would disappear.

Pelagius' letter to an elderly friend

Alone with none but you, my God,
I journey on my way.
What need I fear, when you are near,
O King of night and day?
More safe am I within your hand
Than if a host did round me stand.

My life I yield to your command,
And bow to your control,
In peaceful calm, for from your arm
No power can snatch my soul.
Could earthly foes ever appal
A soul that heeds the heavenly call!

Attributed to St Columba

The Lord Almighty says, 'My people are oppressed, but the One who will rescue them is strong – his name is the Lord Almighty. He will take up their cause but will bring trouble to Babylon . . . Babylon will be haunted by demons and evil spirits.'
Jeremiah 50:33, 34, 39

Winter draws near, nights draw in, and something within us draws back and is afraid. Hallowe'en (that is, the evening of All Hallows, meaning all the holy ones or saints of God) is a day when, in the past and today, people focus on the darkness that is encroaching, and on the spirits, fears and powers which seem to 'appear' at this time. The idea of wearing masks and witches hats was not to imitate evil spirits, it was to frighten them off! Today many older people are frightened to go out after dark, or to open the door, not because of evil spirits, but because of youngsters taking 'trick or treat' too far.

Some people think that dressing up as witches etc. at Hallowe'en parties is harmless fun; however, it would be foolish to underestimate the reality of the occult forces, which are reviving, not declining. The Celtic Christians understood that our world is like a good land that is temporarily under occupation by malign forces. Their responsibility was to expel evil forces in the name of the Owner, and to claim back the land for God. In order to do this they used protective prayers like a coat of armour. Today it is good to focus on Christ's victory over evil, to circle in prayer the places that attract fears or forces of darkness; to light a candle to symbolise Christ, the Light of the world, whom no darkness can quench, and to use prayers such as these:

> Compassionate God of heaven's powers
> Screen me from people with evil intentions.
> Compassionate God of freedom
> Screen me from curses and spells.
> Compassionate God of the saints
> Screen me from bad deeds, bad words, bad thoughts.
> Compassionate God of eternity
> Screen me from bad influences here in the past.
> May your cross be between me
> And all things coming darkly towards me.

Therefore since we have this great cloud of witnesses around us, let us rid ourselves of everything that gets in the way, and of the sin which holds on to us so tightly, and let us run with determination the race that lies before us.
Hebrews 12:1

Christians replaced Samhain, the dismal Celtic New Year which marked the coming of darkness, with All Saints' Day, the glorious celebration of believers who had gone into the dazzling light of God's presence.

O most dear ones, I can see you, beginning the journey to the land where there is no night nor sorrow nor death . . . You shall reign with the apostles and prophets and martyrs. You shall seize the everlasting kingdoms, as Christ promised, when he said: 'They shall come from the east and the west and shall sit down with Abraham and Isaac and Jacob in the kingdom of heaven.'

St Patrick's letter to Coroticus.

When in the Acts of the Apostles the apostles came together in one place, Solomon's Porch, which became a focus of peace and unity, crowds came who were made whole from diseases even by the shadow cast by the apostles. And truly, up to this day, wherever Christians gather together for the yearly festival of an individual, the Lord never ceases to perform mighty works.

On this splendid festal day of St Samson, at God's inspiration, mighty works of God that are just as great have without doubt been witnessed. For this reason we recognise that God has endowed Samson with an everlasting quality and an unhampered freedom. As we celebrate the heavenly kingdom on his day we perceive the next life with a clear, keen insight. For we firmly believe that he is engaged in another, better, unending life among the saints of God, whom we see shining forth among us, strong and mighty in the Lord.

From The Life of Samson of Dol

Eternal Friend, as I thank you
For your cloud of witnesses who shine so brightly,
And who beckon to us so eagerly
Help me to grow strong and holy like them
That I may live more fully and boldly for you
And keep my eyes on the eternal kingdom.

They are yours, O Lord, you lover of souls.
Wisdom 2:26

God has put within us a need to recollect, from time to time, those people who, though now dead, have loved or influenced us: to remember them, to savour them, to talk to God about them, and perhaps to complete a grieving process. Today, why not remember these in a few moments of silence, thank God for them, and keep them in mind throughout the day?

What a comfort it is if we know that these dear ones died united to Christ. But what of those who gave no sure sign of this, whose faith at the moment of death was known to God alone? Celtic Christians believed, as the Bible teaches, that God's attitude towards all dead people is like the attitude an earthly mother takes to all her children – she longs to draw them close to her. This still leaves the decision whether to reject or respond to that love to the person concerned, but it means that when we think about the dead in our prayers we picture God wooing them.

Hail, sister! May you live in God.

On a 4th century tombstone at York.

Since it was you, O Christ, who bought this soul –
At the time it gave up its life
At the time of pouring sweat
At the time of returning to clay
At the time of the shedding of blood
At the time of severing the breath
At the time you delivered judgment –
May your peace be on your ingathering of souls
Jesus Christ, Son of gentle Mary
Your peace be upon your own ingathering.

High king of the holy angels
Take possession of the beloved soul
And guide it home to the Three of limitless love
Yes, to the Three of limitless love.

Carmina Gadelica (adapted)

Life after death

I know a man who was snatched up to Paradise (I do not know whether this actually happened or whether it was a vision), and there he heard things that cannot be put into words . . . I will boast about this man.
2 Corinthians 12:3,4,5

In 696 Drithelm died one evening in Northumbria, but came back to life early in the morning, causing panic amongst his grieving family. He gave away his estate and joined a monastery at Melrose. When people asked him what had caused him to make such a dramatic change of lifestyle this is what he told them, 'A shining figure led me north east to a valley. On one side there was a gale, and on the other a great fire. Both sides were full of souls which seemed to be tossed from one side to the other. The wretches could never find rest. I began to believe this must be hell. But my guide told me it was not that. He took me slowly to the farther end of the valley, which was gradually filled with thick darkness. Huge black flames suddenly arose and subsided into a pit. Each time this happened I noticed that the flames were filled with human souls, and there was a revolting stench. Then a gang of spirits dragged these howling souls laughingly first into the darkness, and then into the burning pit. Some of them threatened to drag me there too. In my extremity a bright star drew near behind me, which caused these spirits to run away. The bright star turned out to be my heavenly guide, who brought me back into the light. However, in front of us was a seemingly infinite wall. I wondered why we approached it, since there was no way through, but somehow, we found ourselves inside it, in a large and fragrant garden. Here were innumerable souls in white, all rejoicing. I wondered if this was the kingdom of heaven, but my guide said that it was not.

We passed on towards a place of exquisite scents and singing and brightness. I was eager to enter, but just then my guide led me back the way we had come. The guide explained that we had been to the place of trial and discipline. Though their purging was terrible, they were to repent before their final death and heaven was to be opened to them. Many people are spared their torment through the prayers of God's people. The delightful place is where souls who have led lives full of good works go; though they are not yet ready to see Christ face to face. At the day of judgment they shall all see Christ. As for you who are about to go back to the earth, if you live a life that is simple and right with God, you will be able to join those joyful troops of the Lord.'

Based on Bede

Lord, have mercy upon me.

Lord, you raised me up from the gates of death so that I may recount your praises before your people and tell of your deliverance.
Psalm 9:13,14

The radical new lifestyle that Drithelm adopted after his near death experience had twin peaks.

The first peak was voluntary poverty. Following a day of prayer after his recovery he divided his estate into three. The first third he gave to his wife, the second third to his children, and the last third to himself. That third he promptly distributed to people in the neighbourhood who were in greatest need. Is that a model worth considering when we make our wills?

The second peak was the singing of God's praises in and out of season. His hut was on the edge of the monastery grounds, by the river Tweed. He frequently, as a penance, stood in the water, sometimes up to his waist and at other times up to his neck, reciting scriptures or singing psalms for as long as he could endure it. He did this even in winter, standing in the river with bits of ice floating about him! Bystanders would say, 'It's wonderful that you can stand such cold,' and Drithelm would reply, 'I have seen it colder.' And when they asked, 'How can you endure such austerity?' Drithelm dryly replied, 'I have seen more austerity.'

This man of Melrose became a talking point in the region, and many people were influenced for God by his example.

> November is a 'no' month. It is easy to allow ourselves to be pulled down.
> So I decided to make it a 'yes' month. Each day I make sure there is something for which I can say 'yes' to God.
> *Margaret Burns of Northumberland*

> Champion, save me from being a fair-weather Christian.
> When I get cold feet
> Remind me of the example of people such as Drithelm.
> May the praises of God be in my mouth
> Whatever I feel like
> Today and every day.

Build houses and settle down.
Jeremiah 29:5

This is the time of year when the cold and the dark seem set to take over, a time when our instinct is to withdraw. It is the Celtic season of Samhain, when those cattle which had to be brought down from the hills, and which could not be accommodated, were slaughtered. The bonfires which we associate with this season get their name from the 'bone fires', in which the inedible parts of the carcasses were destroyed. The fires are also associated with the idea of clearing the decks for winter; the leaves and the excess things of summer are swept up and burned. Something in the human psyche, too, needs to clear the decks, and to accept a reduction in the number of choices that are available to us, and to settle down.

Our ego resists the idea of accepting limits. Some people get depression at this time of year. Others flout what God is saying through nature by indulging in a reckless lifestyle throughout the winter. Yet think of the animals who hibernate. Think of the wonders of spring flowers – they would not be able to burst forth if they had not first lain still in the wintry earth.

So how should a Christian respond to this time of year? In two ways. First, by fighting against the darkness of fear, despair, self-concern and evil spirits. We expel these in the name of Christ and receive his strength, faith, and selfless love. Second, by not fighting against the God-given rhythm of the season, but by going with its flow. November's grey days, dark nights, cold rains, thick fog help me to accept that I am mortal. This means that I will take more time to be inside, alone, still with God; I will take more time for study and the inner life. I will spend less time dashing around, purchasing, starting schemes.

> Father, Saviour, Sustainer
> As this cold, dark month encroaches
> Give to us the stability of the deep earth
> And the hope of heaven.

Jesus said to the robber: This day you will be with me in paradise.
Luke 23:43

How often have we known Christians pray mutually exclusive things
for a person who is near death? This happened with Columba.

Columba prayed that the Lord would release him into heaven on the
thirtieth anniversary of his ministry in Britain. On that day he saw two
shining beings approach, en route to escort him to heaven and his face
was wreathed in smiles. Two monks then observed Columba's
expression suddenly darken. They drew out of him the reason: although
these angels had come in answer to his prayers, Christians in other
places had been praying too – that God would spare Columba more
years yet. Columba told the monks that, though he was disappointed,
God would grant him four more years in answer to the prayers of the
churches. The result was that Columba saw these angels withdraw
beyond Iona.

Four years later, Columba knew the time of his departure had surely
now come, and carefully prepared his farewells. He went round the
island on a cart blessing the people and crops. He issued this statement
from the store barn, 'I heartily congratulate the monks of my
community because although I have to depart from you, you have
enough bread for the year.'

He sat on a seat as he returned to the monastery. His pack horse,
sensing he was to leave earth, laid its head on Columba's lap and began
to weep like a human being. Columba told an attendant who wanted
to shoo it away: 'No. My fellow humans would have known nothing
about my dying if I had not revealed this to them, yet God has clearly
revealed to this dumb animal that its master is about to depart.'

Later, in a final spurt of energy Columba ran into the church. His
attendant lifted his arm and Columba left this world blessing his
brothers with the sign of the cross.

Almighty God, Father, Son, and Holy Spirit,
to me the least of saints, to me allow that I may keep a door in
  Paradise.
That I may keep even the small door that is least used, the stiffest
  door.
If it be in your house, O God, that I can see the glory even afar,
and hear your voice, and know that I am with you, O God.
Columba

Soul friends at death

Saul and Jonathan – in life they were loved and gracious, and in death they were not parted. They were swifter than eagles, they were stronger than lions.
2 Samuel 1:23

Ciaran was young, handsome, and had been much used of God to establish many churches in Ireland when he became a sudden victim of plague. Knowing that he was soon to die, Ciaran asked to be carried to a small mound where he looked at the vast open sky. His monks then carried him to the little church where he blessed them; he then asked that he should be shut in and left there alone until his soul friend, Kevin, arrived from Glendalough.

Ciaran, however, died before Kevin arrived, though the brothers kept his corpse in the church until Kevin arrived.

As soon as Kevin entered the church Ciaran's spirit re-entered his body, so that he could have fellowship with Kevin.

After a day together Ciaran blessed Kevin, and Kevin blessed water and gave Holy Communion to Ciaran. Ciaran gave his bell to Kevin as a sign of their lasting unity, and then he finally went to heaven.

> When the soul separates
> From the perverse body
> And goes in bursts of light
> Up from out its human frame
> O holy God of eternity
> Come to seek me and to find me.
>
> May God and Jesus aid me
> May God and Jesus protect me
> May God and Jesus eternally
> Seek and find me.
> *Carmina Gadelica*

For we know that if the 'earthly tent' we live in is destroyed, we have a 'building' from God, an eternal home not made with hands.
2 Corinthians 5:1

> I have not many friends of influence upon earth; they have
>   journeyed on
> from the joys of this world to find the King of Glory;
> they live in heaven with the High Father, they dwell in splendour.
> Now I look day by day for that time when the cross of the Lord
> which once I saw in a dream here on earth
> will fetch me away from this fleeting life
> and lift me to the home of joy and happiness
> where the people of God are seated at the feast in eternal bliss,
> and set me down where I may live in glory unending
> and share the joy of the saints.
> May the Lord be a friend to me,
> He who suffered once for the sins of all
> here on earth on the gallows tree.
> He has redeemed us; He has given life to us and a home in heaven.
>   *From* The Dream of the Rood *trans. Kevin Crossley-Holland*

> Saviour and Friend, how wonderful art Thou,
> My companion upon the changeful way,
> The comforter of its weariness,
> My guide to the Eternal Town,
> The welcome at its gate.
>
>   *Hebridean Altars*

> I am going home with you, to your home, to your home;
> I am going home with you, to your home of mercy.
> I am going home with you, to your home, to your home;
> I am going home with you, to the place of all the blessings.
>   *Carmina Gadelica (adapted)*

Since we believe that Jesus died and rose again, so will it be for those who have died: God will bring them to life with Jesus.
1 Thessalonians 4:14

A certain brother one night, hearing that Fintan was keeping vigil in prayer, desired to know in what place he prayed. He searched for him on this side and that, until at last he came to the Christian burial ground. It was a night of darkness. This brother gazed at Fintan face to face, and witnessed an extraordinary light spreading far and wide. This light was so bright that his eyes were almost blinded, but God preserved him through that same grace that was upon Fintan.

> Before he leaves on his fated journey
> No one will be so wise that he need not
> Reflect while time still remains
> Whether his soul will win delight
> Or darkness after his death-day.
> *Bede's Death Song*

Lord of the sunrise, source and ground of my being
you know me in my mother's womb.
As my first day begins, heal me of the pain and hurt I receive.

Lord of the dawn, you see me grow strong as I learn to walk and
   talk, heal me of tears of separation and loss.

Lord of the high noon, you accompany me along life's journey,
guide me in choice and strengthen me in adversity.

Lord of the dusk, as my life declines,
help me to surrender all that I have and all that I am into your hand.

Lord of the sunset, as I go to my eternal home
strengthen me on my last journey with you
that I may entrust my soul into your hands in faith and hope.
Michael Halliwell

You have come to the city of the living God, the heavenly Jerusalem, with its thousands of angels. You have come to the joyful gathering of God's first-born children, whose names are written in heaven.
Hebrews 12:22, 23

The day came when Ninian, full of years, was himself stricken with a wasting disease, and racked by pain. Yet even while he was beset with illness, his mind soared above the sky. The revered lover of justice spoke as follows, 'The potter's kiln shakes the pots with the force of the flame, but cruel burdens are the trials of just people. I should like to suffer dissolution and see Christ face to face.' When he had uttered these words, his spirit departed his pure body and passed through the clear heights of the star-studded heavens.

Then when the breath of life had left his dying limbs, he was immediately surrounded by the shining host, and now blazing bright in snow-white vestment, like Phosphorus in the sky, he was carried in angel arms beyond the stars of heaven. Passing through the companies of the saints and the everlasting hosts, he rejoiced to visit the innermost shrine of the King throned on high. He clearly perceived, united as he was with the celestial hosts in the halls of heaven, the glory of the Trinity, the hymns of gladness, together with the supreme denizens of the Holy City on high.

From The Miracles of Bishop Nynia *translated by Winifred MacQueen*

> O being of brightness, friend of light
> From the blessed realms of grace
> Gently encircle me, sweetly enclosing me
> Guarding my soul-shrine from harm this day.
> Keep me from anguish
> Keep me from danger
> Encircle my voyage over the seas.
> A light will you lend me
> To keep and defend me
> O beautiful being, O guardian this night.
> Be a guiding star above me
> Illuminate each rock and tide
> Guide my ship across the waters
> To the waveless harbour side.
>
> *Collected by Caitlin Matthews*

The glory of the nation lies slain upon the high places! How the
mighty have fallen! Weep . . .. How the mighty have fallen!
2 Samuel 1:19, 24, 25

Today we remember those untold millions who have lost their lives in
war. We mourn for the goodness and the wisdom, the life and the
laughter, the potential and the passion that perished with them

It is also a day when we re-dedicate ourselves to help fashion a world
of peace that they died to bring. How can we do this? How can
Remembrance be more than a wistful evaporation of hopes?

In the early church only those who had shed their blood for the faith
were formally pronounced saints. Until Martin of Tours. He, who gave
up being a soldier in order to create the peace of the kingdom of
heaven on earth, was the first non-martyr to be so recognised. His feast
day is in three days time.

His father, a senior Roman army officer, named him Martin, which
means warrior, and trained him to become a soldier. While Martin was
playing as a boy, in Italy, a thunderstorm struck. He ran for shelter and
found himself in a church service. He listened to the stories of Jesus and
was captivated. He accepted a new kind of training, to become a
soldier of Christ. Before Martin had completed his instruction in the
Christian faith and been baptised, his father presented him to the
Emperor. Although he was only fifteen years old, he was tall and
strong, and he was sent to begin military service in France. On his
arrival at Amiens he met a beggar. Moved with compassion, Martin
took off his own fine cloak, cut it in half, and gave one half to the
beggar. That night he had a dream. Jesus stood by his bed and said,
'Martin, you have done a great act of love for me. I was cold and you
gave me half your cloak.' He dressed, went to the nearest church, woke
the priest, and asked to be baptised. After two more years in the army,
Martin went to the Emperor, and braving the Emperor's anger,
persuaded him to release him from the army so that he could serve
God without any pay, and begin to build a Christian community of
peace.

> Peace between victor and vanquished.
> Peace between old and young.
> Peace between rich and poor.
> The peace of Christ above all peace.

Even though I walk through the valley of deepest shadow I will fear no evil, for you are with me.
Psalm 23:4

November is a time of advancing shadows. Celtic Christians did not run away from these, they went alone into places of shadow, and there they faced the shadows inside themselves. They learned the importance of doing this from the desert Christians.

Just as it is impossible for a person to see their reflection in a pool whose water is disturbed, so, too, the soul, unless it is cleansed from alien thoughts, cannot pray to God in contemplation.
Sayings of the Desert Fathers

The psychiatrist Carl Jung gave the name 'Shadow' to that part of our inner life that is unacceptable to us. Jesus drew the distinction between the surface life and the shadow life when he likened some proud church people to sepulchres that were painted white outside but full of rot inside.

In his book *Why do Christians break down?* William Miller admits, 'I break down because I am afraid to admit that evil, unacceptable, inappropriate tendencies still exist within me, even though I have committed myself to the way of Christ, and I cannot accept them as being truly part of me.'

The qualities that we bring to the surface when we interact with the outer world are subtly adapted in order to get the approval of others. The opposite qualities to these get buried in our subconscious, and lie there unattended. Subconsciously we don't want to know these parts of ourselves for fear that they will damage ourselves or others.

Take time to get in touch with your shadow. Make a list of the things that most often make you angry with other people. That may give clues as to your shadow. Once you have become real about your vices, make a conscious effort to replace each vice with its opposite virtue; that was how Celtic Christians approached this matter. And then invite in God's light.

> Holy Three, help me to stay with you
> While I stay with the darkness in myself.
> Throw your light upon this darkness.
> Give me strength to know, to bear pain
> And to journey through into a greater wholeness.

All the people of the world come from one stock.
Acts 13:26

I am sure that the exploration of this Celtic world will be prophetic for
the future as we try to break down the barriers so that we may reach
out to one another. This discovery of my own Celtic roots has meant
that I have also become more aware of the riches of many other
traditional peoples. Here, instead of the highly individualistic,
competitive, inward-looking approach common in today's society . . .
everyone sees themself in relation to one another.

Esther de Waal The Celtic Way of Prayer

At the root of all war is fear.
Thomas Merton

Only love – which means humility – can cast out the fear which is the
root of all war.

> All humankind are one vast family
> this world our home.
> We sleep beneath one roof,
> the starry sky.
> We warm ourselves before one hearth,
> the blazing sun.
> Upon one floor of soil we stand
> and breathe one air
> and drink one water
> and walk the night
> beneath one luminescent moon.
> The children of one God we are
> brothers and sisters of one blood
> and members in one worldwide family of God.
> *From* The Book of Remembrance
> *Cathedral of St Paul the Apostle,*
> *Los Angeles, California*

> Christ, victim of barriers
> Christ, vanquisher of barriers
> Christ, linking us across the shores
> Of treachery and time
> Be with us all this day.

For everything there is a season, and a time for everything that happens
in this world . . . I can see that there is nothing better than that a
person should enjoy their lot.
Ecclesiastes 3:1, 22

Do not too easily escape from a dull day.
It is natural to turn from the cold to the heat of indoors.
It is natural to turn from the dusk to the electric light.
It is natural to turn from the damp to a dry house.
There is a time to do these things
but there is also a time to shake the hand of a November day.
November days are a necessary part of life.
They correspond to something in the 'shadow' side of my being.
Part of me is damp, or wet, or grey.
Learn to accept this.
Accept that life is a journey that passes through the seasons.
Do not renege on the journey.
Drabness in nature is not boring, it is different.
It is a post-mortem on a fruitful season, a prelude to a spring-time,
a pause for taking stock, a time to reflect.
It also has its special charisms.
For example, the rows of bare trees become a salute
Once they are uncluttered by green foliage.

God before me, God behind me
God above me, God below me.
I on the path of God
God upon my track.

Who is there on land?
Who is there on wave?
Who is there on billow?
Who is there by door-post?
Who is along with us?
God and Lord.

I am here abroad
I am here in need
I am here in pain
I am here in straits
I am here alone.
O God, aid me.

Carmina Gadelica

Who through faith conquered kingdoms, administered justice, obtained
promises, shut the mouths of lions . . . won strength out of weakness.
Hebrews 11:33, 34

When the Emperor released Martin from the army, he had to walk all
the way home. It took him weeks. His mother joyfully became a
Christian, but his father, whose pride was hurt, turned him out. So
Martin walked all the way back to France. There, he offered his help to
Hilary, Bishop of Poitiers, who ordained him a deacon.

Martin wanted to live in solitude, so after a time he went to the
quiet village of Liguge and built himself a little cell – the first in
Europe. He was not alone for long. He would rise from prayer to
respond to human needs. One day he tended a leper; another day he
prayed for hours over a man who had hanged himself, whose life
returned; a madman was cured. God's power was mightily at work in
him, so it was not surprising that, when the local Bishop of Tours died
in 572 all the people were determined to make Martin their next
bishop.

As Bishop, Martin made evangelistic visits to pagan villages. One
pagan priest challenged him to be bound to a tree as it was felled, to
test whether His God could save him. The tree turned away from
Martin as it fell and the whole population turned towards Christ.
Martin used his privilege of being a guest at the Emperor's table to ask
for the release, before he ate anything, of innocent prisoners in Tours.
The Emperor deeply respected Martin's Christian example.

Martin did not live in a comfortable palace, he lived like a monk. He
inspired many young men to live like this, and they built a large
monastery, with individual cells cut into the rock, large gardens, fields
stables and chapel. They only spoke when necessary.

Martin has an honoured place in the Celtic calendar for two reasons.
He pioneered an informal monasticism which, following the Eastern
model, combined individual freedom of movement with a framework
of common fellowship. The second reason is that Martin did not stay in
the towns only; he healed and evangelised even in moors and
mountains all over France until he died at the age of eighty.

Great God, thank you for Martin, soldier, servant and soul-winner.
Inspire us by his example
To live lives of discipline and compassion
And to have an eye for building others up.

We brought nothing into the world, and we take nothing out.
1 Timothy 6:7

Remembrance of the dead is given importance in the Sayings of the
Desert Christians:

If there are graves in the area where you live, go to them constantly,
and meditate on those lying there . . . And when you hear that a
brother or sister is about to leave this world to go to the Lord, go and
stay with them in order to contemplate how a soul leaves the body.

A truly philosophical work (says an Abba to visiting philosophers) is
to meditate constantly on death.

The Desert Christians referred to death as 'The Great Passage'. Like
the Celtic Christians after them, they knew that death was, in some
cases, very painful; yet even then, they experienced it fundamentally as
a celebration, as the following story illustrates:

The brothers said to Abba Moses (the former brigand), 'Let us escape
since the barbarians are coming.' 'I'll stay here,' Moses replied, 'I have
been waiting so long for this day so that the word of my Lord Jesus
Christ may be fulfilled, "All those who have used the sword will die by
the sword."' There were seven brothers there. Before any of them
could escape, the barbarians arrived and slew them all.

However, a brother who was not with them in that hut hid under
some palm fronds and saw everything. He saw seven crowns coming
down to rest on the heads of Abba Moses and the six brothers killed
with him.

> Lord of the Great Passage,
> You hold a crown ready in your hand.
> If I trust in my own will
> I cannot receive it.
> I trust in you alone
> And I am eager to come to you.

Wisdom calls out at the crossroads: Take my instruction, for wisdom is better than jewels, and all that you desire cannot compare with her. I hate pride and arrogance. I have good advice. By me, rulers rule, and all who govern rightly.
Proverbs 8:1, 10, 11, 13–15

Hilda was born in 614 a pagan. In 627 she was baptised by Paulinus, a missionary sent from Rome. She nobly served God for the first half of her life as a laywoman within a large royal household. She was motivated for service by Aidan and his friends, who, 'visited her frequently, instructed her assiduously, and loved her heartily for her innate wisdom and her devotion to the service of God.'

It seems that in 635 she decided to enter a monastery in France. Aidan acted swiftly, and persuaded her to use her gifts in Britain. After a trial period at a small community house by the river Wear, Hilda ruled over the monastery at Hartlepool for some years, where she established the Rule of Life that Aidan had taught her, no doubt based upon the Rule Columba had introduced at Iona. Here she showed such qualities of leadership that she was called upon to establish or reform a community at Whitby.

At Whitby they lived by the same Rule. These Christ-like qualities particularly made an impression upon people: peace, love, respect for every person, purity and devotion.

After the example of the primitive church, no one was rich, no one was in need, for they had all things in common and none had any private property. So great was her prudence that not only ordinary people, but kings and princes sometimes sought and received her counsel when in difficulties.

Bede

Wisdom on High, help me to learn from the likes of Hilda:
To be reliable
To grow in prudence.
To study, work and pray hard, but not too hard;
To treat every person with courtesy and none with contempt;
To maintain resolute faith,
Balanced judgment, and outgoing friendships.

For like the jewels of a crown they shall shine on his land.
Zechariah 9:16

All who knew Hilda used to call her mother because of her outstanding
devotion and grace. She was not only an example of holy life to all
who were in the monastery but she also provided an opportunity for
salvation and repentance to many who lived far away and who heard
the happy story of her industry and virtue. This was bound to happen
in fulfilment of the dream which her mother had when Hilda was an
infant. She dreamed that her husband was taken away and, though she
searched, no trace of him could be found (he was, in fact killed by
poisoning). Suddenly in the midst of her search she found a most
precious necklace under her garment and, as she gazed closely at it, it
seemed to spread such a blaze of light that it filled all Britain with its
gracious splendour. This dream was truly fulfilled in her daughter Hilda;
for her life was an example of the words of light, blessed not only to
herself, but to many who desired to live uprightly.

Bede

Hilda trained a stream of leaders who went out to establish Christ's way
in places far and near; five of these became bishops.

Trade with the gifts God has given you.
Bend your minds to holy learning that you may escape the fretting
    moth of littleness of mind that would wear out your souls.
Brace your wills to actions that they may not be the spoils of weak
    desires.
Train your hearts and lips to song which gives courage to the soul.
Being buffeted by trials, learn to laugh.
Being reproved, give thanks.
Having failed, determine to succeed.

Homily of St Hilda *Anon*

Sacred Three, as we thank you for the life of Hilda,
A jewel in your church who lit up a dark land
Release the hidden treasures in the lives of women
And in the lives of all your people today
That we too may come to shine for you.

If you remember that your brother or sister has something against you,
first be reconciled to them.
Matthew 5:23, 24

Hilda stands as a symbol of reconciliation. She was host to the deeply
divided Roman and Celtic parties who gathered at Whitby for the
Synod of 664. Some of the Irish monks resigned from their monastery
and departed to Ireland after the synod agreed to impose Roman
regulations upon the Celtic churches. They were devastated. Other
Celtic monks stayed, but were hostile. Hilda maintained friendships
with people on both sides. Even on her deathbed, as we have seen, she
urged her sisters and brothers to maintain peace and unity with all
people, not just with those of their own party.

This is not an easy peace I would give you, my children. It cost me the
cross to reconcile you to my Father. You must humble yourselves
before each other, listen to each other's pain, share your brother's
burden, seek his forgiveness, if you would really be reconciled in my
love and my way.
    A prophecy received by Myrtle Kerr of Rostrevor Christian Renewal Centre,
                                                            Northern Island

God give to me by grace what you give to my dog by nature.
                                            Mechthild of Magdeburg

It is not our differences that really matter; it is the meanness behind that
is ugly.

                                                        Mahatma Gandhi

        Peace between parties,
        Peace between neighbours
        Peace between lovers
        In love of the King of life.

        Peace between peoples
        Peace between traditions
        Peace between generations
        In love of the Lord of all.

Jesus said, 'Whoever loves their father or mother more than me is not fitted to be my disciple.'
Matthew 10:37

Columbanus was born in the south of Ireland. He grew to be tall, fair and handsome, a darling of a close and loving family. He received a superb education, and he dressed, like others of his rank, in a fine silk tunic bordered with gold. He had, in fact, everything the world could offer. But Columbanus wanted something more than the world could offer, he wanted to give his whole life to God. Since he did not know how to do this, he consulted a wise old hermit. She told him there was only one way for him: he had to leave all forms of human security behind – even his beloved family – and make life-long vows of service to God. In those days that meant becoming a monk. His mother was against this, so much so, that on the day Columbanus was due to leave home she lay down across the doorway to try to prevent him leaving. It was to no avail. Columbanus was clear; perhaps he had reflected upon those words of Jesus quoted above; he knew that, though we are to honour our mothers, we are never to put them first, for that place belongs to Jesus alone. So Columbanus joined the monastery at Bangor, and went on to become its most famous pupil.

A friend of mine once returned to live with her mother in order to help her recover from alcoholism. She did this because God told her to. But after a time, she realised that her mother was becoming as dependent upon her as once she had been dependent upon alcohol. As she prayed about this, she felt God was telling her it was time to move on, though she was to maintain caring contact. Mature Christian friends agreed this was right.

However, on the day she was to leave, her mother went berserk, and threatened to commit suicide if her daughter left. The younger woman wondered if she should stay after all, and went aside to pray. God clearly said: 'Go now, I will look after your mother.' So she did leave, and God did look after her mother, who became creative, at times vigorous, and even radiant.

> O Mighty One, may I put no one on a pedestal.
> Help me to honour my parents
> But never to put them in the place
> That only you should have.

He will persist until he causes justice to triumph, and in him all people will put their trust.
Matthew 12:20, 21

Columbanus trained at the Irish monastery at Bangor, which was rich in its enterprises. Yet he felt impelled to go out to the great continent, where so much of the Christian heritage was being swept away, and eventually he was given permission to leave with twelve other monks. They travelled across what is now France, through the ruins of former Roman cities. The poor people who lived in the shadow of these ruins welcomed the brothers and their faith was transplanted.

When they reached northern Gaul several local kings welcomed them, since, whatever their personal lifestyle, they held men of God in respect. Columbanus told King Sigebert, 'He who seeks nothing has need of nothing. My sole ambition is to follow Christ.' The king was so struck by this that he offered Columbanus land; he, however, was shrewd enough to realise that kings slaughtered one another, so he chose some land for a monastery on neutral territory in the Vosges mountains. Although winter was approaching, they set aside their own needs for comfort and built a place of prayer before they built their own beehive shaped cells.

Starvation threatened them, but a man whose wife had been cured in response to their prayers gave them food supplies. Crowds began to flock to them, and guest accommodation had to be built. The number of monks increased, so another monastery was built, at Luxeuil, and then a third.

Once a service to the people of the kingdom had been established, Columbanus turned his attention to the king, Theodoric. He tried to wean him away from his many mistresses and to persuade him to marry, which he did. The power behind the throne, however, the king's grandmother, Brunhilda, soon sent the new queen packing, and declared unofficial war on Columbanus' monasteries. Eventually Columbanus was ordered out of their territory, but on their way to the port crowds flocked to the monks. Moreover, the boat on which they were to be transported back to Ireland struck a sandbank, and the captain discharged his passengers. So the monks became free again.

> Faithful God, teach me that defeat, if given to you,
> Is your opportunity for a new advance.
> Help me to remain faithful in every setback today.

People will stumble and fall, but we will rise and stand firm.
Psalm 20:8

Columbanus and his monks made their weary way to the courts of several kings as they travelled north, stopping for a time by the shores of Lake Zurich, which was under the jurisdiction of their friend, King Theodobert. There they established a community which was to grow into the Swiss town of Bregenz.

Columbanus made a long journey south to pass on some prophetic words to King Theodobert. 'You will lose your life and your soul unless you become a monk now,' he told him. 'If you do not do this voluntarily you will be made to do it against your will.' Sadly, Theodobert disregarded Columbanus' advice His army was completely destroyed in battle; he was taken captive and forced to wear a monk's habit as a sign of submission. This defeat meant that Theodobert's lands returned to the jurisdiction of relatives who were hostile to Columbanus, so he said farewell to his monks, and moved on to Italy accompanied by just a small band of brothers, one of whom, Gall, they left behind on the way. The Lombard King and Queen welcomed him, and they built their last monastery at Bobbio. There he died on November 23 615.

After his death the sternness of Columbanus' original Rule gave way to the gentler system of Benedict. This may have been what was needed over the long term, but tough times call for tough measures, and the Celtic monks had been called to a task tougher even than breaking virgin ground – they had to win back lost territory. Only people with an overmastering faith could have seen why it was worth doing. Only men who trained their bodies to stand up to unbelievable physical hardships, and their souls to battle through seemingly impossible situations, could have survived.

We can learn this key lesson from Columbanus: he trained his team to depend upon God alone. They were not put off their calling by the way other people treated them, however harsh. They used the spiritual armoury of prophetic direction, and faith-directed mission so that they overcame all things in Christ's power, and stood firm in all circumstances.

> Toughen me, Lord.
> Give me a heart of love
> But a backbone of steel.

Respect all people.
1 Peter 2:17

Leaders from Scotland, England and Ireland assembled at a great convention on the plains of Birr in 697 and accepted the Law of Adamnan which guaranteed protection of women, children and other civilians.

Adamnan, whom we remember today, was born into the same royal family as Columba. Abbot of Iona, diplomat, writer, peacemaker, he was respected for his wisdom and knowledge of the Scriptures, and near the end of his life he achieved this major advance in social justice.

His mother Ronnat first turned his thoughts towards the plight of women in the 7th century. Then he received divine guidance to make, 'a law in Ireland and Britain for the sake of the mother of each one, because a mother has borne each one, and for the sake of Mary, the mother of Jesus Christ.'

This law protected women from offences ranging from murder and rape to impugning the good name of a married woman. Penalties were exacted and fines had to be paid to the communities established by Columba which were known to be honest.

This law came to be known as Cain Adamnain or The Law of the Innocents. The attitude that fuelled this legislation was expressed thus, '. . . great is the sin when anyone kills the one who is mother and sister to Christ's mother'. What a contrast to the horrific descriptions of women in war in those days, 'On one side of her she would carry her bag of provisions, on the other her babe . . . her husband behind her flogging her on to battle . . . for at that time it was the head of a woman or her two breasts which were taken as trophies.'

> High King, Creator of all
> Remind us that every human life is sacred
> Whether it belongs to a woman in a war-torn land
> Or to a handicapped person next door
> To an unborn infant or a terminally ill patient.
> Remind us that whatever a person's age, race or creed
> Each individual has been made in your likeness
> And Christ has given his all for them.
> This makes them precious in your sight.

Do not neglect to show hospitality to strangers, for by doing that some have entertained angels without knowing it.
Hebrews 13:2

We came from Palestine to one of the Abbas in Egypt, who gave us generous hospitality. So we asked him, 'When the monks in Palestine give hospitality to visitors they keep to their own Rule of fasting; why don't you do that?' The Abba gave us this reply, 'I am always fasting, but I can't keep you here always. Although fasting is useful and necessary, it is a matter of my personal choice. But whether I show love to you is not a question of choice, it is the law of God. So, to receive Christ in you I must be fully present to you, and be sharing with you. When I have sent you on your way I can take up fasting again.' The Abba also quoted the words of Jesus, 'The friends and family of a bridegroom do not fast while he is with them; they wait until he has left before they fast.'

Cassian

We saw a stranger yesterday
We put food in the eating place
Drink in the drinking place
Music in the listening place
And with the sacred name of the triune God
He blessed us and our house
Our cattle and our dear ones.
As the lark says in her song:
Often, often, often goes the Christ
In the stranger's guise.

A Celtic rune of hospitality

Bless, O Lord, the food we eat
and if there be any poor creature
hungry or thirsty walking along the road
send them into us that we can share the food with them
just as you share your gifts with all of us.

*From an Irish grace
collected by Mount Melleray Monastery, Ireland*

The Lord told Isaiah to go back to King Hezekiah and say to him, 'I have heard your prayer and seen your tears . . . I will let you live fifteen years longer.'
2 Kings 20:4–6

God extended Hezekiah's life as a result of his prayers. Some early Irish Christians asked their beloved Saint Moninna to pray that her life would be extended, too. But in her case God had something else in mind.

Moninna was one of the earliest saints of Ireland about whom we have reliable information. She was a contemplative linked to a community, and much loved by her own people throughout the region. When they learned that she was on her death-bed, the local rulers and many others gathered round, and appealed to the local bishop to give this message to her. 'We appeal to you as those who are linked to you by blood and by the spirit, that you will give just one more year of your earthly presence with us. For we know that God will give you whatever you ask. In fact any of us who has a slave girl will set her free to the Lord, and every man employed as a fighting man will give away a cow in its prime in exchange for your life.'

Moninna gave these good folk the following reply through the bishop: 'May God bless you for bothering yourselves with my weak self. If you had asked before yesterday I would have granted your request. But from today I cannot do so. You see, the apostles Peter and Paul have been sent to guide my soul to heaven and they are here with me now. I see them holding a kind of cloth with marvellous gold and artwork. I must go with them to my Lord who sent them. God hears your prayers. He will give a life to one of you. I pray God's blessing on your wives, children, and homes; I leave you my badger skin coat and my garden tools. I have no doubt that if you carry these with you when enemies attack God will deliver you. Do not be sad at my leaving you. For I truly believe that Christ, with whom I now go to stay, will give you whatever I ask of Him in heaven no less than when I prayed to Him on earth.'

> Saviour and Friend,
> May I leave this life with my loved ones around me.
> May I leave this life united with your dear ones in heaven.
> May I leave this life with oil and with gladness.
> May I leave this life in order to give more blessings.

Why are you cast down, O my soul, and why are you disquieted within me? Hope in God, for I shall again praise my Helper and my God. *Psalm 42:11.*

As nights draw in dark depression settles upon many of us to a greater or lesser degree. In some cases it is clinical depression. Treatment may include prescribing the right chemicals, vitamins and so on. For others the depression, though not clinical, is still bad enough. There is less sun, less exercise, less fresh air, less stimulus, less relaxation, less fun, less travel – and we become stale and cast down.

What can we do about this? We can't help a slump in our spirit, but we can choose not to yield to self pity, to selfishness, and we can choose not to hide from depression in hyperactivity which only builds up future trouble. We can follow the example of the Celts, and tell stories of the heroes. Then we can raise our downcast spirits in these two ways:

First, through constant praise. Some people do this by singing hymns or in tongues. As we have seen, Columba linked our praise with the eternal praise being offered to the Trinity:

By the singing of hymns eagerly ringing out
by thousands of angels rejoicing in holy dances
and by the four living creatures full of eyes with the twenty four
    elders
casting their crowns under the feet of the Lamb of God
the Trinity is praised in eternal three-fold exchanges.

Columba Altus prosator

Second, we can respond to depression by praying over the depressed person within us. Talk to it, and cherish it, be gentle towards it and give it a treat. Let the love of Jesus come to your depressed inner being.

Put oil or water on your face and repeat this prayer:

I will bathe my face
In the nine rays of the sun
As Mary washed her Son
In the rich fermented milk.

Now place your hand over your heart and pray:
The love that Mary gave to her one Son
May all the world give me.
The love that Jesus gave to John the Baptist
Grant that I give to whoever meets me.
Both prayers are from the Carmina Gadelica

Make the best of the little you have here on earth and you will be given a big opportunity in the eternal homeland.
Luke 16:9

Have you sometimes wondered what heaven is like? Some people project on to it inadequate, boring, fading images from human life. The opposite is the truth. The unknown author of this fourteenth century account of the death of St David knew that heaven was a wow!

After David had given his parting blessing to everyone who had gathered, he spoke to them, 'Take care that you guard your faith and do the little things which I have taught and shown you. Good bye. Be good. For we shall never meet again.' The people broke out in a great crying.

From the Sunday to the Wednesday after David's death they ate and drank nothing; they just prayed. On Tuesday night the whole town and the sky were filled with singing and joy of angels. In the morning Jesus Christ came, accompanied by nine orders of angels, and the sun shone with brilliance. That day, the first day of March, Jesus Christ bore David's soul away in great triumph and gladness and honour.

The angels bore his soul to a place where there is rest without labour, joy without sadness, an abundance of good things, victory, brilliance, and beauty: a place where Christ's champions are commended and the undeserving wealthy are ignored, where there is health without sickness, youth without old age, peace without dissension, glory without vain ostentation, songs that do not pall, and rewards without end.

From The Book of the Anchorite of Llanddewibrefi, 1356 (adapted)

> Faithful vigil ended
> watching, waiting cease.
> Master, grant your servants
> their discharge in peace.
> *Timothy Dudley-Smith,*
> *based on words from Luke 2*

The time has come for you to wake up out of your sleep.
Romans 13:11

Do not consider what you are but what you will be. What you are lasts for a mere moment; what you will be is eternal. Do not be lazy, but acquire in a short time what you will possess for ever. Overcome the dislike of exerting yourself now by thinking of the reward to come. Why do you chase after vain things? Remember, life's joys disappear like a dream in the night. So wake up . . .

Columbanus

We sleep when we think that the world is as it always was.
It is high time to awake to the truth that Jesus has come.
His summons is urgent in our midst.
Nearer than we know he is coming in judgement.
He might come in judgement this Christmas.

We confess that we sleep
when we think that power is still of this world.
It is high time to awake
to the truth that his power alone is working permanently.
All the civilisations built in scorn of his power
are as if they had never been.
And our civilisation with them will equally go down.
Nearer than we know he will be seen coming in power.
He might even come in power this Christmas.

Give us grace to wait in spiritual expectancy his coming again
to practise true humility
to be exercised in the ways of real power, to express his glory
that we may recognise the kingship of a cradle
the royalty of being ruled, the seniority of service
so that should he come this Christmas
his body bloody but his head crowned
we would be found among those who worshipped
and not among those who would kill.
If these things would be
it is high time to awake out of sleep.

George McLeod,
founder of the 20th century Iona Community

The man who had had the demons went all through the Ten Towns, telling what Jesus had done for him. And all who heard it were amazed.
Mark 5:20

'The Church is the only organisation that exists for those who are not its members,' said Archbishop William Temple. The lives of Jesus's first apostles demonstrate great zeal to spread the Good News to others. We learn of their mission journeys in the Bible, and through tradition, which tells, for example, of Thomas founding a church in India. Britain's own early apostles had a similar zeal.

When Samson first landed on the beaches of Britanny he brought with him a large crew to help begin the great mission there. But God's first lesson for them was this: no amount of evangelistic organisation is a substitute for a prayed for, God-architected, God-timed healing encounter. Such an encounter can have a domino effect which influences a whole region before the organisation has even begun to get into gear.

As they were mooring their boat they saw a hut not far from the harbour, and a man weeping, and gazing out towards the sea. Samson went to him and asked what was the problem. 'I have now waited here three days and three nights', the man told him, 'for someone to come and help me from across the sea.' He was a devout man of prayer, who had a leprous wife and a deranged daughter, and as he had prayed for them, God had given him the assurance that he was to wait at the harbour for such a man who would heal them.

Samson went to the man's home and poured forth prayers over the sick women, who were restored to health. This was the start of a wonderful ministry, and from there Samson established Christian communities throughout the region, one of which, at Dol, became the most famous of all.

> God of healing
> God of strategy
> Help me pray like that weeping man;
> Help me act like that heroic apostle.

Prepare the way of the Lord.
Mark 1:3

> In the wasteland may the Glory shine
> In the land of the lost may the King make his home.

For Celtic Christians the time before Christmas (known as Advent, which means the Coming) is a period of preparation, as we repent and wait in hope for the coming return of Christ. This period used to be known as a second Lent. Fasting was less severe, but people carved out time to go apart and wait on God. Could we make it our aim to dispel the spirit of restlessness and acquisition, and to instil the spirit of wonder, warning and waiting during this period?

What did those Celtic Christians focus their minds on during these weeks, and what should we focus our minds on? God prepared for the birth of Christ within his people, through prophets. Many of them lived in simplicity as a sign that they were waiting for God to fulfil his promises. As we meditate on their lives and words we, too, hear the call to live lives of simplicity as a sign. Then we think about the witnesses at the time of Christ's birth, Mary and Joseph, Elizabeth and Zechariah, Anna and Simeon, whose waiting was joyful and humble.

This is also a time for thinking about what the universe, humanity, and ourselves are coming to, and about the four last things of death, giving account, eternal bliss, and separation.

At heart, this should be a time of waiting in contemplation of the presence of Christ within us; for we are called, like Mary, to be bearers of Christ now and into the future.

In the coming days the readings will focus on these things.

> Calm us to wait for the gift of Christ;
> Cleanse us to prepare the way for Christ;
> Teach us to contemplate the wonder of Christ;
> Touch us to know the presence of Christ;
> Anoint us to bear the life of Christ.

You know my heart. You have come to me at night . . . reveal your
wonderful love and save me.
Psalm 17:3, 7

> We wait in the darkness, expectantly, longingly, anxiously,
>   thoughtfully.
> The darkness is our friend.
> In the darkness of the womb, we have all been nurtured and
>   protected.
> In the darkness of the womb
> the Christ-child was made ready for the journey into light.
> It is only in the darkness that we can see the splendour of the
>   universe – blankets of stars, the solitary glowings of the planets.
> It was the darkness that allowed the Magi to find the star
> that guided them to where the Christ-child lay.
> In the darkness of the night, desert people find relief
> from the cruel relentless heat of the sun.
> In the blessed desert darkness Mary and Joseph were able to flee with
>   the infant Jesus to safety in Egypt.
> In the darkness of sleep, we are soothed and restored,
>   healed and renewed.
> In the darkness of sleep, dreams rise up. God spoke to Joseph and
>   the wise men through dreams. God is speaking still.
> Sometimes in the solitude of the darkness our fears and concerns,
> our hopes and visions rise to the surface. We come face to face with
>   ourselves and with the road that lies ahead of us.
> And in that same darkness we find companionship for the journey.
> In that same darkness we sometimes allow ourselves to wonder and
>   worry whether the human race is going to survive.
> And then, in the darkness we know that you are with us, O God,
> yet still we await your coming.
> In the darkness that contains both our hopelessness and our hope,
> we watch for a sign of God's hope.
> For you are with us, O God, in darkness and in light.
>
> *Presbyterian Church of Aotearoa, New Zealand (abridged)*

> O God of life, darken not to me your light
> O God of life, close not to me your joy
> O God of life, shut not to me your door
> O God of life, refuse not to me your mercy
> O God of life, soften to me your anger
> And O God of life, crown to me your goodness.
>
> *Carmina Gadelica*

Clear a way for the Eternal through the waste . . . every valley must be filled up, every mountain and hill lowered, rough places smoothed.
Isaiah 40:3, 4

We can prepare the way for Christ by drawing up a list of things we would need to clear up if Christ was to make a personal royal visit to our area. I recall a local person saying, as a team of people cut the hedges and grass verges the day before a royal visit, 'A royal visit is the the only way we'd have got some of these things done. Without it we would have waited for ever.' Once you have made such a list, why not pick out one or two things that you can begin to do something about now?

Three most basic ways we can clear the way is by honesty, reconciliation, and preparing for our own death. Honesty: so many shop-lifters deceive themselves that they are not thieves that stores have to put up signs saying 'Shop Lifting is Theft'. Do we deceive ourselves that tax evasion, or withholding rightful information from another person is not theft?

Reconciliation: is there someone who is upset with us to whom we can give the gift of love this season?

Preparing our own death: am I ready to be 'called home' today? Are my affairs in order? Have I done those things that I ought to have done? Can I get rid of clutter that prevents me fulfilling the heart's desires God has put within me?

> Christ, Light of the world
> Meet us in our place of darkness,
> Journey with us
> And bring us to your new dawning.
> *RJS*

> Heaven, shed your dew
> Clouds, rain down salvation
> Earth bring forth the Saviour
> *Praise in all our days*
> *Common Prayer at Taizé*

You are my friends if you do what I command you. I do not call you servants any longer, because a servant does not know what his master is doing.
John 15:14, 15

The Celtic church was composed not only of outstanding individuals such as Patrick, Columba and Brigid, it also had indigenous movements which shaped and re-shaped its life. In the 8th century a reform movement began within monasticism in southern Ireland which over time spread to northern Ireland and Scotland, and inspired new bursts of holiness and literature. The monks of this reform were known in Gaelic as Celi De, which roughly means Friends of God.

These Christians, like the prophets who cleared away wrong things so that God could move in, tried to clear up certain abuses that had crept into the monasteries. The leadership of monasteries was often hereditary, but as the generations passed some descendants of founders were far from God. This meant that truly holy monks were shut out and corrupt practices flourished. It created a feeling of vengeance among the people and among some monks, and there were violent attacks on abbots and monasteries, not all of whom deserved it.

The reforms were not brought in by force or rebellion, so much as by example and persuasion. Monks were encouraged to withdraw from worldly affairs in order to concentrate on 'the three profitable things': prayer, work and study. The Anamchara or Soul Friend played a particularly important role in this renewal.

This concentration on holiness produced many inspired writings: lists of martyrs, accounts of the saints, guidelines for making restitution (known as 'Penitentials'), liturgy such as *The Stowe Missal*, and early Irish nature and hermit poetry.

Each generation has to learn that 'God has no grandchildren'. We each of us have be to born anew of God's spirit, brought to our knees in penitence and wonder at the presence of God. Are you hiding behind Christians who have gone before you, or are you flowing in the life of the Holy Spirit that is ever fresh?

> Lord, take from me all that is mere human accretion.
> Give to me a
> Broken spirit and a humble heart
> That I may be intent on you alone.

They asked Jesus, 'Why do you eat and drink with tax collectors and other outcasts?' Jesus answered them, 'People who are well do not need a doctor.'
Luke 5:30, 31

Jesus lived life with the marginalised – the lepers, prostitutes and tax-collectors. Jesus was edged out of the synagogue, out of the temple, out of the city, out of society and out of life – yet remained totally in touch with the heart of life.

Celtic Christians have a strong sense of living on 'edges' or 'boundary places' between the material world and the other world. Dr George MacLeod, founder of the 20th century Iona Community, spoke of Iona as a 'thin place' where the membrane between this world and the other world, between the material and the spiritual, was very permeable.

This sense of living in a 'between place' enabled Celtic Christians to make connections between the physical and the intangible, the seen and the unseen, this world and a permanent 'other' world.

Philip Sheldrake Living Between Worlds

Many ancient Celtic sites are on the edge – Iona, Lindisfarne, Whitby, Jarrow, Burgh, Bradwell, Whithorn.
At the edge we see horizons denied to those who stay in the middle.
Walking along a cliff-top our bodies and souls face each other and that is how we grow.
The edge is in fact always the centre of spiritual renewal.
We are called to mould the kingdoms of the earth so that they reflect the Kingdom of Heaven.
Any Christian movement that becomes respectable risks being brought from the edge to the centre – and so risks being given the kiss of death.
How will I keep myself on the spiritual edge?

Reflections from Martin Wallace

Lead me from that which fades to that which endures
Lead me from day's dawning to Light eternal
Lead from tide's turning to heaven's ocean of Love
Lead me from the shore's edge to eternal life
Lead me from serving the weakest to finding the Highest.

I saw the dead, great and small alike, standing before the throne . . . the dead were judged according to what they had done, as recorded in the books . . . whoever did not have his name in the book of the living was thrown into the lake of fire.
Revelation 20:12, 15

The day of the Lord, most righteous King of Kings, is at hand:
a day of anger and vindication, of darkness and of cloud
a day of wonderful mighty thunders
a day also of distress, of sorrow and of sadness
in which the love and desire of women will cease
and the striving of men and the desire of this world.

We shall stand trembling before the Lord's judgement seat
and we shall render an account of all our deeds
seeing also our crimes placed before our gaze
and the books of conscience thrown open before us.

Columba *Altus prosator*

Fierce winter winds seem like an onslaught. Everything that is not secure and in place is swept away: loose tiles from the roof, stray items left lying around. Yet what seems an enemy is in truth a good thing. Winds remind us that we are mortal, that things need to be put in place and made secure. This is even more true of eternal things. The idea of God's judgement can seem pitiless: in truth it is all mercy. God longs for us to be right, to be true, for things to be in place in our lives, so that we can endure and live with him in the world that is indestructible.

Holy God, holy and mighty,
Strip from me all that is false and out of place
Strengthen my roots in you
Bring me to that place
Where I desire you alone.

When the Lord comes, he will bring to light the things now hidden in darkness, and will disclose the purposes of the heart.
1 Corinthians 4:5

Suppose that in the next life you see two doors in front of you. Over one door are the words 'What I want'. Over the other door are the words 'What God wants'. Which door will you choose to go through? In this life we may fudge the issue and try (unsuccessfully) to go through both doors. But it is not possible in fact to go through both doors. The time will come when we have to choose one or the other.

Suppose you walked through one or other of these doors. Looking back, the name written over the first door is 'hell'. The name written over the second door is 'heaven'.

Christ's wondrous figure, the form of the noble king, will come from east from out of the skies, sweet to the minds of his own folk, bitter to those steeped in sin, strangely diverse and different towards the blessed and the wretched.

To the good he will be gracious in appearance, beautiful and delightsome to that holy throng, attractive in his joy, affectionate and loving; agreeable and sweet it will be for his cherished people to look upon that shining form, to look with pleasure upon the mild coming of the Ruler, the mighty King, for those who had earlier pleased him well in their heart with words and with works.

To the evil he will be fearsome and terrible to see, to those sinful people who come forth there condemned by their crimes. It may serve as a warning of punishment to one who is possessed of the wise realisation, that he indeed dreads nothing at all who will not grow terrified in spirit with fear for that figure, when he sees the actual Lord of all created things journeying amid mighty marvels to judgement of the many, and round about him on every side journey squadrons of celestial angels, flocks of radiant beings, armies of saints, teeming in throngs.

Christ 3 The Judgement from The Exeter Book, 10th century

O Christ, deliver me from the ways of darkness
So that, holding firmly to your Word
The gate of glory may be opened to me.

What is crooked shall be made straight.
Luke 3:5

We talk about crooks or perverts as bent people; but the truth is that all of us are bent in some way, and not one of us can move into a state of bliss, into our ultimate fulfilment in God, unless every crooked thing is straightened out. We can prepare the way for the Lord by putting straight what is crooked. Crooked things include tax evasion, gossip, 'shortcuts', dishonest use of money, abuse, wilful failure to communicate, manipulative techniques, false fronts.

What things then are good? Those which have remained whole and uncorrupted as they were created, which God, according to the apostle, 'has prepared that we should walk in, the good works in which we are created in Christ Jesus'. These are: goodness, integrity, devotion, fairness, truth, mercy, caring, peace, spiritual joy, with the fruit of the Spirit; all these with their fruits are good. The opposites of these are the evil things: malice, irreverence, discrimination, lying, greed, hatred, discord, bitterness, with all the many fruits they bear. For the fruits of both good and evil are innumerable.

True discernment is the inseparable companion of Christian humility and opens the way to perfection to the true soldier of Christ.

If we all weigh our actions in the just balance of true discernment we shall not be hijacked into crooked ways. If we walk by the divine light we 'shall not go astray either to the right or to the left' but we shall always keep on the straight way, chanting with the conquering Psalmist 'O my God, light up my darkness, for through you I shall be delivered from temptation.'

The Rule of Columbanus

Lord Spirit, show me the things that are crooked in my life
Lord Judge, spare me from things that could be crooked in my life
Lord Christ, straighten out the things that are crooked in my life
O my God, light up my darkness
And deliver me this day from temptation.

Go to the Lord and you will live. If you do not go, he will sweep
down like fire on the people. The fire will burn up the people . . . and
no one will be able to put it out.
Amos 5:6

When Fursey (in an out-of-the-body vision) had been taken up to a
great height, he was told by the angels who were conducting him to
look back at the world. As he looked down, he saw some kind of dark
valley immediately beneath him and four fires in the air which were to
kindle and consume the world. One of them is falsehood, when we do
not fulfil our promise to renounce Satan and all his works as we
undertook to do at our baptism. The second is covetousness, when we
put the love of riches before the love of heavenly things; the third is
discord, when we do not fear to offend our neighbours even in trifling
matters; the fourth is injustice, when we think it a small thing to
despoil and defraud the weak. Gradually these fires grew together and
merged into one vast conflagration. As it approached him, he cried out
in fear to the angel, 'Look, sir, the fire is coming near me.' But the
angel answered, 'That which you did not kindle will not burn you; for
although the conflagration seems great and terrible, it tests each person
according to their deserts, and the evil desires of everyone will be
burned away in this fire.'
   . . . the angel then went on to give helpful advice as to what should
be done for the salvation of those who repented in the hour of death.
When Fursey had been restored to his body, he bore for the rest of his
life the marks of the burns which he had suffered while a disembodied
spirit; they were visible to all on his shoulder and his jaw. It is
marvellous to think that what he suffered secretly as a disembodied
spirit showed openly upon his flesh.
   An aged brother who is still living in our monastery relates that a
truthful and pious man told him that he had seen Fursey in East Anglia
and that, although it was during a time of severe winter weather and a
hard frost, and though Fursey sat wearing only a thin garment, yet as he
told his story, he sweated as though it were the middle of summer,
either because of the terror or else the joy which his recollections
aroused.

Bede

From deceit, greed, strife and dishonesty
Good Lord deliver us.

Then the Lord thundered from the heavens, and the voice of the Most
High was heard.
Psalm 18:13

There was a time when a famous British newspaper was known as 'The
Thunderer'. In those days it was the mouthpiece, not of Money or
Power so much as of Moral Truth. When that newspaper thundered,
people in high places, or wrong places, shook. That experience gives us
a clue to an aspect of God's nature.

Chad was greatly filled with the fear of the Lord and was mindful of
his last end in all he did. If a high wind arose, he would immediately
stop whatever he was doing and pray God to have mercy on the
human race. If the wind became a gale he would lie prostrate in earnest
prayer. If there was a violent storm, lightning or thunder he would go
to the church and devote himself to prayers and psalms until it passed.

When people asked him why he did this he replied, 'Have you not
read "The Lord also thundered in the heavens and the Most High gave
voice. Yes, the Most High sent arrows and scattered the people, shot
out lightnings and discomforted them?" For the Lord moves the air,
raises the winds, hurls the lightnings, and thunders forth from heaven in
order to rouse earth's inhabitants to revere him, to remind them of
future judgement in order to scatter their pride and confound their
presumption. The Lord does this by calling to their minds the time
when he will come in clouds in great power and majesty to judge the
living and the dead, while the heavens and the earth are aflame.'

Chad concluded, 'And so we ought to respond to God's heavenly
warning with due fear and love, so that as often as he disturbs the sky
and raises his hand as if about to strike, yet spares us still, we should
implore his mercy, examining our consciences, turning from our sins,
and thereafter behaving with such care so that we do not deserve to be
struck down.'

Told to Bede by one of Chad's fellow monks, Trumberht

God of the storm, God of the stillness
Of squalls of power and of shimmering calm
Into life's troughs and into life's billows
Come with the reach of your long right arm.

Jesus was indicating the way Peter would die and bring glory to God.
John 21:19

Here is an example of the hermit poetry which the Culdee renewal
inspired. It takes as its theme Death, one of the 'four last things' which
Christians reflect upon during Advent:

> Alone in my little oratory
> Without a single human being in my company
> Dear to me would such a pilgrimage be
> Before going to meet death.
>
> A hidden secret little hut
> For the forgiveness of every fault
> A conscience upright
> And untroubled intent on holy heaven.
>
> Let the place which shelters me
> Amid the monastic enclosures
> Be a beautiful spot hallowed by holy stones
> And I all alone therein.

Few of us have the opportunity to reach our end in such an
untrammelled, untroubled fashion. Peter the apostle had no such
opportunity; tradition says that he was crucified upside down. Yet he
teaches us that, whatever the circumstances of our death, we may die
intent on heaven alone. Here is a prayer that we may say over our
friends, or pray, in advance, for ourselves:

> In the name of the all-powerful Father
> In the name of the all-loving Son
> In the name of the pervading Spirit
> I command all spirit of fear to leave you
> I break the power of unforgiven sin in you
> I set you free from dependence upon human ties
> That you may be free as the wind
> As soft as sheep's wool
> As straight as an arrow
> And that you may journey into the heart of God.

God will complete his mysterious work.
Isaiah 28:21

Mist makes my spirit aware that everyday things are only one
dimension of life. Another, less static Presence can envelop my world.
This is a living presence. It is beautiful, yet not frolicsome like Spring.
There is something mysterious, sombre, about it. December mist is
God's outer aura, a prelude to something sharper and nearer God's
heart. In it I can be lost in wonder, love and praise. Behind the mist
are treasures waiting to be discovered – a bright month of advent and
nativity; the hope that a new year will kindle the heart flame ever
anew.

> Now I command you, my loved man,
> to describe your vision to all people:
> tell them with words this is the tree of glory
> on which the Son of God suffered once
> for the many sins committed by humankind,
> and for Adam's wickedness long ago.
> He sipped the drink of death, yet the Lord rose
> with his great strength to deliver humanity.
> Then he ascended into heaven. The Lord himself,
> Almighty God, with his host of angels
> will come to the middle world again
> on Domesday to reckon with each mortal.
> Then He who has the power of judgement
> will judge each one just as they deserve
> for the way in which they lived this fleeting life . . .
> Then folk will be fearful and give
> scant thought to what they say to Christ.
> But no one need be numbed by fear
> who has carried the best of all things in their breast;
> each soul that has longings to live with the Lord
> must search for a kingdom far beyond the frontiers of this world.
>   *From* The Dream of the Rood *trans. Kevin Crossley-Holland*

> > O Jesus, Son of David
> > you have given us to see the light of day.
> > May you carry us home with you
> > to the city of grace.
> >   *Anon, Mount Melleray Monastery, Ireland*

I could ask the darkness to hide me, or the light round me to turn into night, but even darkness is not dark for you.
Psalm 139:11, 12

Stars are distinct, fixed points. Navigators steer by them. Yet they twinkle.

God's standards are like stars. They are distinct, fixed sky marks by which all people can steer their lives.

God's standards are absolutes – truth, fairness, love, purity, unselfishness.

Yet these are also qualities that bring a sparkle to life. The person with these qualities is transparent and glows.

> Risen Christ we welcome you.
> You are the flowering bough of creation.
> From you cascades music like a million stars
> Truth to cleanse a myriad souls.
>   A Celtic Eucharist *The Community of Aidan and Hilda*

We know that night is not dark with you, O Lord.
But a great deal of me is not yet one with you.
In the night the things I fear come to the surface.
The unacknowledged parts of my personality
Poke through the shadows to haunt me.
It helps me to know that the blackness will lift
As surely as the dawn follows night.
But before that there is work to do.
Night has a purpose of its own.
My task is to acknowledge the shadows
And bring them to you who are the Morning Star.
You are author of light and dark.
The morning star would be nothing to us
Without its prelude, the night.
So thank you, Lord, for the night.

God hung the stars in the sky – the Great Bear, Orion, the Pleiades, and the stars of the south.
Job 9:9

The greatest contribution any of us can make to the coming of the King is to allow a sense of wonder to grow. 'To foster a sense of wonder' – this should be written into the aims of every school and of every home.

> My eyes like to see
> The lovely stars in the sky
> Shining like diamonds and crystals
> And the sun above my head
> And the moon shining and shining.
>
> Eyes are shiny, too,
> And the golden water shines.
>
> My eyes like to see candles
> And the light in the sky.
>
> God will give me a new heart
> That shines with happiness inside me.
>   *Angus aged 6*

> O star of wonder, star of light,
> star with royal beauty bright
> westward leading, still proceeding
> guide us to the perfect light.
>   *J. H. Hopkins*

Let the flowers close and the stars appear
Let hearts be glad and minds be calm
And let God's people say Amen, Amen
  Creation Liturgy of the Iona Community

> Open my eyes to your scenery
> Open my ears to your call
> Open my heart to your coming
> Great king, born in a stall.

Mary had been engaged to Joseph, but before they lived together, she was found to be pregnant by the Holy Spirit. Her husband, Joseph, being a good man and not willing to expose her to public disgrace, planned to put her away quietly.
Matthew 1:18, 19

It is hard, in our 'anything goes' society, to grasp the feelings of deep shock that engulfed Joseph when his fiancee, who had committed herself to him as a virgin, informed him that she was pregnant. A poet in ninth century Mercia, who writes in the style of Caedmon, tried to 'get under the skin' of Joseph and Mary. These extracts help us to see how they communicated their feelings to one another, and how they brought their feelings to God, both of which are vital to a good relationship:

Mary: O my Joseph, do you mean to divide us who are one, and to disdain my love?

Joseph: All at once I am deeply troubled, robbed of dignity.
I have endured hurtful abuses because of you, bitter insults; people mock me with acid words.
I must shed tears, full of sorrow.
Yet God can easily heal my grieving heart's wounds.
Everyone knows that I willingly received an innocent virgin.
Now where is her chastity?
And which is best, to keep quiet or to confess?
If I tell the truth, David's descendant will be stoned to death.
Even so, it is worse to conceal her crimes;
A perjurer is despised for as long as he lives.

Then the virgin revealed the miracle and spoke thus:

Mary: By the Son of God, saviour of souls, I speak the truth when I say that I have not embraced any man.
The archangel of heaven appeared to me and and said that the heavenly spirit would fill me with radiance,
that I should bear the Triumph of Life, the bright Son,
the mighty child of God, of the glorious Creator.
Now I am made his immaculate temple, the Spirit of Comfort resides in me – now you may set aside your sorrow.

From Advent Lyrics *9th century Mercia*

Today, O Lord,
As I contemplate Mary and Joseph
May I live in the wonder of your divine conceiving
May I live in the wonder of our divine receiving.

Christ always had the nature of God . . . but
of his own free will he gave up all he had and took the nature of a
servant.. He became like a man and appeared in human likeness.
Philippians 2:6, 7

The Gaelic race see the hand of God in every place, in every time and
in every thing.

Douglas Hyde

> He was imprisoned by his Jewish flesh and bones
> Within the confines of his country
> But he gave them as living planks to be nailed
> And raised from the grave, despite the guarding,
> A catholic body by his Father.
>
> And now Cardiff is as near as Calvary
> Bangor every inch as Bethlehem.
> The storms in Cardigan bay are stilled
> And on each street the deranged
> Can obtain salvation at the edge of his hem.
>
> He did not hide his Gospel among the clouds of Judea
> Beyond the eye and tongue of man.
> But he gives the life that will last for ever
> In a drop of wine and a morsel of bread
> And the Spirit's gift in drops of water.
>
> *Gwenallt translated by C. Davies*

Those whose faces are turned always towards the sun's rising
See the living light on its path approaching
As over the glittering sea where in tide's rising and falling
The sea beasts bask, on the Isles of Farne
Aidan and Cuthbert saw God's feet walking
Each day towards all who on world's shores await his coming.
That we too, hand in hand, have received the unending morning.

Kathleen Raine Lindisfarne

> Let the rumble of traffic diminish
> and the song of the birds grow clear
> and may the Son of God come striding towards you
> walking on these stones.
>
> *St Aidan's Chapel, Bradford Cathedral*

The law of sin is at work in my body. What an unhappy person I am! Who will rescue me from this body that is taking me to death? . . . our Lord Jesus Christ!
Romans 7:23–25

The glory of the human race is God; but it is the human race which receives the benefit of God's actions, God's wisdom and power.

Just as a doctor proves herself in her patients, so God is revealed in human beings. That is why Paul states, 'God has imprisoned all in unbelief, in order to have mercy upon all.' God is speaking here of the human race, which was excluded from immortality as a result of disobedience to God, but then obtained mercy by being adopted through the Son of God.

Without pride or boasting, human beings should truly value created things and their creator, that is, God, the all-powerful. We should live in God's love, willingly, thankfully; if we do, we will receive a greater glory from God and will go on to become like the one who died for us.

He, like us, was made of frail human flesh, in order to expel sin from human flesh. He came to invite us to become like himself, commissioning us to imitate God, placing us under obedience to the Father so that we might see and know God. He who did this is the Word of God, who lived in and became Son of humankind in order to accustom humans to live in God and to accustom God to live in humanity.

That is why he is a sign of our salvation, Immanuel, born of the Virgin, a sign given us personally by the Lord.

Isaiah makes the same point as St Paul, 'Be strong, weak hands and feeble knees; pluck up your courage, faint hearts. Be strong, do not be afraid. See, our God is coming with justice and to settle up; God is personally coming to save us.' It is not by ourselves but by the help of God that we are saved.

Irenaeus Against the Heresies

Dear Son of God, change my heart
You took flesh to redeem me
Dear Son of Mary, change my heart.

The one who is holy and true has the key of David, and when he opens a door no one can close it; when he closes a door no one can open it . . . The great Son of David has won the victory.
Revelation 3:7; 5:5

As Christians reflected over the centuries on the nature of the coming King, they were given awesome insights. These were expressed in 'The Prayer of the Great O's', known as the Advent Antiphons, which were said from December 17. This prayer expresses two great truths about Christ. First, that he was the eternal Son of God, the second person of the Trinity, the eternal Wisdom who had always been guiding God's people. Second, that the great representatives of God's people, such as Moses and King David, prefigured Christ. Jesus was perceived as living to the full what these characters lived in a measure. In the 14th century a monk from the Durham monastery became a hermit on the island of Farne, just as had their monastery's founding saint, Cuthbert. As this unknown hermit meditated on this vein, his imagination ran riot, and he wrote this prayer to Christ:

> You are David who scattered with strong arm your foes
> and shattered death's barred gates to free your own people;
> You slew the giant vaunting
> and the sons of Jacob taunting
> though you had but a sling.
> You like worm-wood undermining, armed and battle not
>   declining
> victory did nobly gain.
> Philistinian ranks were saddened
> Saul and his retainers gladdened
> by the trophies of the slain.
> Warfare for us waging blithely
> to the cross-top leaping lithely
> hell's great might you overthrew.
> Wondrous tones from your harp ringing
> – your wounds were in painful stringing –
> yield a tune folk did not know.
> Kindest Jesus then uphold us
> when death's darkness does enfold us
> be our comfort and our stay.

> *A monk of Farne*

> Give to us Christ's strength blithely to surmount life's ills.
> Give to us, O God, strong love
> And that beautiful crown of the King.

The Word of God became a human being and, full of grace and truth,
lived among us. We saw his glory, the glory which he received as the
Father's only Son.
John 1:14

> On the face of the world
> There was not born
> His equal.
> Three-person God
> Trinity's only Son
> Gentle and strong.
> Son of the Godhead
> Son of humanity
> Only Son of wonder.
> The Son of God is a refuge, Mary's Son a blessed
>   sanctuary
> A noble child was seen.
> Great is his splendour
> Great Lord and God
> In the place of glory.
> From the line of Adam
> We were born. From David's line
> The fulfilment of prophecy,
> The host was born again. By his word he saved the
>   blind and the deaf
> From all suffering
> The ragged.
> Foolish sinners
> And those of impure mind.

12th or 13th century Welsh
(Davies in Celtic Christian Spirituality)

> Child of glory
> Child of Mary
> Born in the stable
> King of all
> You came to our wasteland
> In our place suffered
> Happy we are counted
> Who to you are near
> Strengthen our hope
> Enliven our joy
> Keep us valiant
> faithful and near.

Carmina Gadelica (adapted)

This was how the birth of Jesus Christ took place. His mother Mary was engaged to Joseph, but before they were married, she found out that she was going to have a baby by the Holy Spirit.
Matthew 1:18

> Mary nurtures the Son of tenderness,
> God, supreme ruler of every nation:
> Her father, her strengthener, her brother.
>
> Mary nurtures a Son on whom dignity rests:
> None can violate his boundaries
> Whose words are beauty, who is neither young
> Nor grows old.
>
> The unwise can never perceive
> How Mary is related to God:
> Her Son, her Father, her Lord.
>
> But I know, though I be but frail and earthly,
> How Mary is bonded in the Spirit to the Trinity:
> Her Son and brother in the flesh,
> Her Father, her Lord, blessed almighty.
>> *Early or Middle Welsh (trans. Paul Quinn)*

Medical experts tell us that getting fit to have a baby takes time. If a mother's body is full of addictive substances from smoking, alcohol or drugs, or if it is lacking in vitamins, three to six months are needed for it to provide a healthy womb. Research now also confirms that stress, or lack of harmony, harms the unborn baby. Parents who pray for the child in their womb, who sing to it, feel it, and love it, are following in the path of Mary. Celtic Christians often imagined that they were present when Mary gave birth to Jesus, and they made beautiful prayers for the children they themselves bore.

> Help me to nurture your life in myself
> Help me to nurture your life in others.

The royal line of David is like a tree that has been cut down; but from the stump fresh shoots will sprout, and a new king will arise from among these.
Isaiah 11:1

Big doors swing on little hinges; God's people learned that after their capital city, their temple and their kings were destroyed. Out of the rubble prophet voices spoke. They said that, like shoots coming from the stump of a tree that has been cut down, a creative minority would arise, and would swing history God's way once again. Jesus's parents were nobodies, but they had slender links with the great King David. God used them to bring into being a new Person, and a new people, that transformed the Roman Empire. The creative minority of Celtic saints did the same in the period of the Dark Ages. Think of cradle places such as Llantwit Major, Iona, Lindisfarne. Will you be part of God's creative minority for the third millennium?

If five per cent of any body of people are wholly convinced about anything, they can swing the rest.

J. C. Smuts

As we, the Romans of the twentieth century, look out across our Earth, we see some signs for hope, many more for despair. Technology proceeds apace, delivering marvels . . . the conquering of diseases . . . revolutions in crop yields . . . the information highway . . . that would dazzle those who built the Roman roads, the first great information system. But that road system became impassable rubble, as the empire was overwhelmed by population explosions beyond its borders. So will ours . . .
    The future may be germinating today not in a boardroom in London or an office in Washington or a bank in Tokyo, but in some antique outpost or other . . . an orphanage in Peru . . . a house for the dying in Calcutta . . . in some unheralded corner where a great-hearted being is committed to loving outcasts in an extraordinary way . . . If our civilisation is to be saved – forget about our civilisation which, as Patrick would say, may pass 'in a moment like a cloud or smoke that is scattered by the wind' – if we are to be saved, it will not be by Romans but by saints.

Thomas Cahill How the Irish Saved Civilisation

Make me one of your dedicated minority, wholly given
to let you bring in your new era of love.

The Lord almighty says that he will send this curse out, and it will enter the house of every thief and the house of everyone who tells lies under oath. It will remain in their houses and leave them in ruins.
Zechariah 5:4

How often, after we have been robbed, have we prayed that God will convict or deal with the thief, but our prayers have seemed powerless? An experience of Samson's may fortify us.

A thief stole a beautiful jewelled crozier from the monastery where Samson was based. Within an hour the thief was so overwhelmed with the enormity of what he had done that he fell prostrate to the ground as if half dead. Nevertheless, he hardened his heart, and continued his life of crime, carrying round his waist a cloth in which he kept the jewels he had extracted from the crozier. On the night of the winter solstice he was crossing an iced-over pond, when the ice cracked under him and he drowned.

The following day a brother from the monastery was going for a stroll. He saw the cloth with its contents lying on the ice, and the stiffened corpse standing rigid in the middle of the ice. The lessons the brothers drew from this incident were that it is not possible to hide anything from God, either good or evil, and that God can work things out for his friends even in traumatic, depressing situations.

> Christ at the yearly turning
> Christ at every bend.
> Christ at each beginning
> Christ at every end
>
> Christ in every break-in
> Christ in shades of death
> Christ in icy waters
> Christ in wintry earth

Lord, when anyone does something to damage or diminish me,
Help me to place them into your hands
To trust you to deal with them
And to guide me in my responses.

I will give you treasures from dark, secret places.
Isaiah 45:3

> The darkest and the coldest time
> is also the brightest time:
> O Christmas Christ
> The radiance around the moon
> is not as fair
> as the radiance
> around your head.
> O Holy One
> the majesty of the winter sea
> is not as glorious as your majesty.
>
> At the departing times
> the coldest times
> of our lives;
> at the times of excitement
> and the times of expectancy;
> at the times of intersection,
> when hard choices
> have to be made
> be with us
> Prince of Peace.
>
> *Kate McIlhagga*

Now begin the twelve long nights of yule. One night soon will be born Jesus, Son of the King of Glory, creation's Joy. You will gleam to him moon and furthest star. You will gleam to him hills and housetops afar.

> Lord of the solstice, on this day of briefest light
> Help us to be at home with the treasures of the dark.
> As the days have drawn in
> Help us to flow with the ebb tides of life.
> At the turning of the year
> Help us to welcome the Dawn from on high.

The angel said to Mary, 'Do not be afraid, God has been gracious to you. You will become pregnant and give birth to a son, and you will name him Jesus. He will be great and will be called the Son of the Most High God.'
Luke 1:30–32

> Forget not, Trinity, holy and glorious
> That heaven's bright prince came down to bestow on us
> His love, as babe, into Mary's fair womb.
> For nine months he who is angels' Lord
> Was hidden, love's furnace, in a little room
> Humbler than all, whom all adored.
> A pure lamb, he stole down to earth
> To free us from our sin so blind.
> No city home will shield his birth
> His mother a stable for bed must find;
> There poorest of the poor she lay
> Nor wine nor meat for hunger's sting
> In the rude confines of the cattle bay
> Where God was born, apostles' king.
> Cold and exile he did not scorn
> In the donkey's manger, that holy morn.
>
> *Tadg Gaelach O Suilleabhain*

May the trust of Mary troubled by her strange call
And Joseph's encouragement beside her through all
Be God's gift to us.

May the radiant brightness and light of the Star
The hope and longing of searchers travelling from afar
Be God's gift to us.

May the wonder of shepherds surprised by God's love
The joy of the angels who came from above
Be God's gift to us.

May the peace of the Christ-child in carved trough of stone
Sounding the word 'Saviour' fashioned by Grace alone
Be God's gift to us.

Crawford Murrey

An angel of the Lord appeared to the shepherds, and the glory of the
Lord shone round about them.
Luke 2:9

> This night is the long night
> It will snow and it will drift
> White snow there will be till day
> White moon there will be till morn
> This night is the eve of the Great Nativity
> This night is born Mary Virgin's Son
> This night is born Jesus, Son of the King of Glory
> This night is born to us the root of our joy
> This night gleamed the sun of the mountains high
> This night gleamed sea and shore together
> This night was born Christ the King of greatness
> Ere it was heard that the Glory was come
> Heard was the wave upon the strand
> Ere 'twas heard that his foot had reached earth
> Heard was the song of the angels glorious
> This night is the long night
>
> Glowed to Him wood and tree
> Glowed to Him mount and sea
> Glowed to Him land and plain
> When that His foot was come to earth.

Carmina Gadelica

> Babe of Heaven, Defenceless Love
> In order to come to us
> You have to travel far from your home.
> Come to strengthen us
> On our pilgrimage of trust on earth.
> Your birth will show us
> The simplicity of the Father's love
> The wonder of being human.
> Help us to live fully human lives for you.

Mary gave birth to her first son . . . and laid him in a manger – there was no room for them to stay in the inn.
Luke 2:7

> The night the star shone
> Was born the Shepherd of our flock
> Of the Virgin of the hundred charms
> The Mother Mary.
>
> The Trinity eternal by her side
> In the manger cold and lowly.
> Come and give tithes of your means
> To the Healing Man
> The foam-white breastling beloved
> Without one home in the world
> The tender holy Babe driven forth
> Immanuel!
>
> The three angels of power
> Come you, come you down
> To the Christ of the people
> Give salutation.
>
> Kiss his hands
> Dry his feet
> With the hair of your heads
> And O! You world-pervading God
> And you, Jesus, Michael, Mary
> Do not forsake us.
>
> *Carmina Gadelica*

Your gift to us this day is more than we could ask or think – your very life.
This day may my gift to you be nothing less than my very life.

> Hail King! hail King! blessed is He! blessed is He!
> Hail King! hail King! blessed is He! blessed is He!
> Hail King! hail King! blessed is He
> The King of whom we sing
> All hail! let there be joy!
>
> *Carmina Gadelica*

The shepherds said to one another 'Let's go to Bethlehem and see this thing that has happened, which the Lord has told us.' So they hurried off and found Mary and Joseph and the baby lying in the manger.
Luke 2:15, 16

Once when I was living alone in my island, some of the brothers came to me on the holy day of the Lord's nativity, and asked me to go out of my hut so that I might spend with them this day so sacred, yet so joyful. I yielded, and we sat down to a feast. In the middle of the meal I said, 'Let us be careful not to be led into temptation through recklessness.' They answered, 'Let's be joyful today because it is the Lord's birthday.' After a time, while we were still indulging in feasting, rejoicing and story-telling I again began to warn them that we should always be alert to any approaching temptation. They said, 'You give us excellent instruction, but let us rejoice, for the angel, when the Lord was born, gave the shepherds glad tidings of the great joy that was to be observed by all the people.' I said, 'All right,' but later, for a third time, while they were still feasting, I gave a warning. This time they understood that I was not making this suggestion lightly, and they responded, 'Let's do as you say. We do actually now feel compelled to guard against temptations and the snares of the devil, keeping our minds alert.' When I said this, I did not know, nor did they, that any new trial would attack us, I was warned by instinct alone. However, when they got back to Lindisfarne the next morning, they found that the plague had struck and one of their number had died. This pestilence grew worse and worse, and nearly all that great company of spiritual fathers and brothers departed to be with the Lord. So will you, too; please always watch and pray.

Cuthbert, as recorded in Bede's Life

O Saviour Christ
You existed before the world began.
You came to save us and we are witnesses of your goodness.
You became a tiny child in a cot
Showing us the simplicity of our parent's love.
You chose Mary as your mother
And raised all motherhood to a divine vocation.
May all mothers be bearers of life and grace
To their husbands, their children and to all who come to their
   home.

The star went ahead of them until it stopped over the place where the young child was. They went into the house, and when they saw the child with his mother Mary, they knelt down and worshipped him.
Matthew 2:9, 11

The Virgin was beheld approaching
Christ so young on her breast
Angels bowing lowly before them
And the King of life was saying, "Tis meet.'

The Virgin of locks most glorious
The Jesus more gleaming-white than snow
Seraphs melodious singing their praise
And the King of life was saying, "Tis meet.'

O Mary Mother of wondrous power
Grant us the succour of thy strength
Bless the provision, bless the board,
Bless the ear, the corn, the food.

The Virgin of mien most glorious
The Jesus more gleaming-white than snow
She like the moon in the hills arising
He like the sun on the mountain-crests.
Carmina Gadelica

Cheers, the Gift; clap, the Gift
Cheers, the Gift on the living.
Son of the dawn, Son of the clouds
Son of the planet, Son of the star

Son of the flame, Son of the light
Son of the spheres, Son of the globe

Son of the elements, Son of the heavens
Son of the moon, Son of the sun

Son of Mary of the God-mind
And the Son of God first of all news.
Cheers, the Gift; clap, the Gift
Cheers, the Gift on the living.
Carmina Gadelica

King Herod gave orders to kill all the boys in and near Bethlehem who were two years old and younger. In this way what the prophet Jeremiah had foretold came true: A sound of mothers weeping is heard.
Matthew 2:16–18

> Why do you tear from me my darling son, the fruit of my womb?
> It was I who bore him, my breast he drank.
> My womb carried him about, my vitals he sucked, my heart he filled.
> He was my life, tis death to have him taken from me
> My strength has ebbed, my speech is silenced, my eyes are blinded.

> Then another woman said:
> . . . Infants you slay,
> The fathers you wound,
> The mothers you kill.
> Hell with your deed is full,
> Heaven is shut,
> You have spilt the blood of guiltless innocents.

> And yet another woman said
> O Christ, come to me!
> With my son take my soul quickly!
> O great Mary, mother of God's Son,
> What shall I do without my son?
> For your Son my spirit and sense are killed.
> I am become a crazy woman for my son.
> After the piteous slaughter
> My heart is a clot of blood
> From this day till Doom.

> *11th century, Anon*

The vivid Celtic imagination transposed the agony of the Bethlehem killings into their own breasts. Which situations in our world demand that we do the same? Who are the weak whom we need to defend against the tyranny of the strong in our sphere of action?

> High King of the universe
> By choosing to be born as a child
> You teach us to reverence every human life
> May we never despise, degrade or destroy it.
> Rather, help us sustain and preserve it.

When Joseph and Mary had finished doing all that they were required, they returned to their home in Nazareth. The child grew and became strong; he was full of wisdom, and God's blessings were upon him. *Luke 2:39, 40*

> To come into thy presence
> Thou Virgin of the lowly
> To come into thy presence
> Thou mother of Jesus Christ
>
> To come into thy presence
> Thou dwelling of meekness
> To come into thy presence
> Thou home of peace
>
> To come into thy presence
> Beauteous one of smiles
> To come into thy presence
> Beauteous one of women.
> *Carmina Gadelica*

We pray for people who have no decent house to live in
For those who provide foster homes
For parents to keep their marriage vows
For parents to think deeply about their child's character and calling

May our sons grow up strong and straight like young trees.
May our girls have the beauty of inner serenity.
May our farms and industries overflow.
May the voice of complaining cease from our streets.
Happy are the people from whom such blessings flow
Who put their trust in God.

Inspired by Psalm 144

I came from the Father, and I came into the world; and now I am
leaving the world and going to the Father . . . It is better for you that I
go away, because if I do not go away the Helper will not come to you.
John 16:28; 16:7

King Edwin informed the missionary Paulinus that he was willing to
accept the Christian faith for himself, but he first wished to consult with
his pagan advisors; if they agreed, they would together be consecrated
in the waters of life. Coifi, the chief of the pagan priests told the king:
  'I frankly admit that the religion which we have hitherto held has no
virtue nor profit in it.' Another of the king's advisers added, 'This is
how the present life of human beings on earth appears to me, King.
You are sitting feasting with your staff in a hall warmed by a fire, while
outside the wintry storms rage; then a sparrow flies across the hall. It
enters at one door and quickly flies out through the other. For the few
moments it is inside the wintry storm cannot touch it but after its brief
moment of calm it departs from your sight. Out of the wintry storm
and into it again – that is what human life is like. We know nothing of
what comes after it, or what went before it. If this new teaching brings
us more information, it seems right that we should accept it . . .' So
King Edwin, with all the nobles of his race and a vast number of the
common people received the faith, and were baptised at York in 627.

Bede

When the time came for Alexander Carmichael to bid a final farewell
to the friends he had made in the western parts of Scotland, Mor
MacNeill, who was 'poor and old and alone', sent him on his way with
this prayer:

> And you are now going away
> and leaving your people and your country
> dear one of my heart!
> Well, then, whole may you be
> and well may it go with you
> every way you go and every step you travel.
> And my own blessing go with you
> and the blessing of God go with you
> and the blessing of Mary Mother go with you
> every time you rise up and every time you lie down,
> until you lie down in sleep upon the arm of Jesus Christ
> of the virtues and of the blessings.

Carmina Gadelica

All things are possible to the person who believes.
Mark 9:23

I said to the man who stood at the gate of the year, 'Give me a light that I may tread safely into the unknown.' And he replied: 'Go out into the darkness and put your hand into the hand of God. That shall be better to you than light, and safer than a known way.'

The Desert by M. Louise Haskins

Suppose we find again the faith in God our forbears knew! The richest year of miracles in our history awaits those who are ready to follow God's leading without checks or conditions. Journey on with God. What blessings await you!

> May the blessing of light be on you
> light without light and light within.
> May the blessed sunlight shine upon you
> and warm your heart
> till it glows like a great peat fire
> so that the stranger may come and warm herself at it
> as well as the friend.
> And may the light shine out of your eyes
> like a candle set in the windows of a house
> bidding the wanderer to come in out of the storm.
> And may the blessing of the rain be on you
> the sweet soft rain.
> May it fall upon your spirit
> so that all the little flowers may spring up
> and shed their sweetness on the air.
> And may the blessing of the great rains be upon you
> that they beat upon your spirit and wash it fair and clean
> and leave there many a shining pool
> where the blue of heaven shines, and sometimes a star.
> And may the blessing of the earth be on you
> the great round earth.
> May you ever have a kindly greeting
> for people you pass as you go along the roads.
> And now may the Lord bless you
> and bless you kindly.
>
> *An old Irish Blessing translated by B. O'Malley*

Index of People

Adam, David Jan 30, May 11, Aug 24, Sept 27

Adamnan Feb 14, Apr 18, May 19, June 19, Sept 23, 28, Oct 2, 5, 28, Nov 23

Aidan Jan 5, Feb 21, Apr 3, June 18, 29, July 13, 21, Aug 20, 31, Sept 1–3, 19, Oct 15, Nov 17

Antony Jan 17, 18, 23, Feb 15, 21, Apr 18, July 20

Arthur (King Arthur) Jan 8, 9

Ashe, Geoffrey July 31

Attracta, July 30

Baudoin, King of the Belgians Aug 5

Bede Jan 22, Feb 14, 21, 27, Mar 19, May 27, June 5, 18, 28, 29, July 7, 12, 16, 20, 26, Sept 2, 12, 19, 21, 23, 28, Nov 9, 17, 18, Dec 8, 26, 30

Blake, William July 14

Boisil May 15, July 7, Sept 21

Bradley, Ian Feb 24

Branwalader (Brelade) Jan 19

Brendan Jan 4, May 16–18, July 16, Sept 27

Brendan of Birr Oct 22

Brigid Feb 1, 3–16, Apr 20, Aug 22

Brynach Aug 13

Buchman, Frank Jan 8, Apr 16, June 13, 30, Oct 11, 23

Burns, Robert July 11

Cahill, Thomas May 12

Chambers, Oswald July 14

Churchill, Winston Sept 16

Chad Mar 2, Oct 15, Dec 9

Caedmon Feb 11, Sept 12

Cassian, John Feb 14, Nov 24

Ciaran of Clonmacnoise Sept 9, 10, Nov 7

Climacus, John Feb 27

Colmán mac Béognae Apr 26–29, May 26, July 10, 12, Sept 16, 18

Columba Jan 3, 12, 28, Feb 14, 26, Apr 18, 29, May 19, June 2, 7–14, 16, 22–25, 27, 29, July 4, 22, Aug 10, 19, Sept 8, 11, 28, 30, Oct 1, 2, 3, 5, 20, 22, 23, 28, 30, Nov 6, 26, Dec 5

Columbanus Jan 4, 11, 20, Feb 16, 26, Apr 14, 15, 19, 25, May 1, June 19, 29, July 21, 29, Aug 9, Sept 17, 25, 27, Oct 16, 18, 26, Nov 20–22, 28, Dec 7

Comgall Jan 11, June 5, 18

Cuthbert Jan 22, Feb 12, 14, 15, 17, 19, 20, 27, Mar 11, 19, 20, 22, 31, Apr 4, 12, 20, 24, May 15, June 5, 30, July 1, 7, 12, 15, 16, 20, 26, Aug 21, Sept 7, 12, 20, 21, Oct 24, Dec 15, 17, 26

David of Wales Jan 22, Feb 9, 13, 19, 28, Mar 1, 3, 4, 6–10, 18, Apr 10, 11, May 13, 19, July 2, 3, 27, Sept 16, Nov 27

Desert Christians Jan 17, 18, 22, 23, 30, Feb 15, 18, 21, 23, 25, 26, Mar 12, 15, Apr 14, 15, May 20, July 14, 20, Sept 6, 7, 12, Oct 11, Nov 12, 16, 24

Dick, Andrew Sept 24

Drake, Francis Sept 16

Drithelm Nov 3, 4

Edwin Dec 30

Faustus of Riez Feb 27

Feheily, Tom May 31

Finbarr Apr 10

Francis of Assisi Oct 4

Fursey Jan 16, Dec 8

Gall Jan 11, Oct 16, 18, Nov 22

Gandhi Sept 17, Nov 19

George, Chief Dan Aug 9

Gildas July 31, Sept 22

Gwenallt (David G. Jones) July 27, Dec 15

Hale, Reginald Jan 15, Oct 23

Halliwell, Michael July 26, Nov 9

Helena Sept 14

Hilda Jan 22, Feb 11, June 28, Nov 17–19

Hildegard of Bingen May 22, Aug 7, 8 Sept 17

Hopkins, Gerard Manley Apr 19, Sept 27

Illtyd June 15, July 2, 3, 9, 18 28

Ignatius Loyola Feb 27

Irenaeus May 30, June 17, Dec 16

Ita Jan 11, May 23

Jerome   Feb 10, Aug 12

John Scotus Eriugena   Oct 27

Julian of Norwich   July 1

Kagawa   May 15

Kentigern (Mungo)   Jan 13, 15, 25–28, July 11, 18, 21

Kevin of Glendalough   June 3, July 19, Aug 3, 11, Nov 7

Lawrence, Brother   May 13

Lubich, Chiara   June 26

MacLeod, George   June 12, 17, Aug 6, Nov 28, Dec 4

McIlhagga, Kate   Mar 18, 20

Malo   Aug 18

Marban the hermit   Aug 3

Martin of Tours   Feb 10, June 12, Aug 26, Nov 14, 15

Mary, Virgin   Mar 25, May 14, July 21, Oct 29, Nov 30, Dec 14, 19, 23–27

Melangell   Aug 14

Merton, Thomas   Jan 22, 24, May 30, June 1, Oct 8, 14, Nov 13

Milne, Marjorie of Glastonbury   Aug 6, 24

Mitton, Michael   Apr 30, June 13

Modomnoc   Feb 13

Molaise   Sept 5, Oct 17

Moling   July 19

Molua   Aug 4

Monk of Farne   Dec 17

Moninna   Nov 25

Mungo (Kentigern)   Jan 13, 15, 25–28, July 11, 18, 21

Ninian   Jan 25, Apr 2, 5, 16, Aug 26–30, Oct 5, Nov 10

Oswald   Apr 3, June 18, Aug 5, 7, Sept 4, Oct 7

Oswin   Aug 20

Patrick   Mar 13–18, Apr 8, 11, 23, May 12, 30, July 16, 21, 30, Sept 13, 15, 24, 27, Oct 15, Nov 1, Dec 20

Pelagius   Feb 24, May 4, July 23, Sept 18, Oct 6–14, 30

Penn, William   Mar 10, Oct 23

Petroc   June 4

Polycarp   Jan 26

Raine, Kathleen   Dec 15

Samson   Jan 2, 10, 12, 19, Feb 7, 9, 22, 29, June 15, July 2, 9, 18, 28, Aug 17, Sept 26, Oct 21, Nov 1, 29, Dec 21

Samthann   May 25

Chief Seattle   May 8, Aug 8

Sellner, Edward C.   Apr 14

Seraphim   Apr 22–29

Shakespeare, William   May 15, July 4

Taylor, Hudson   June 29

Teilo   Feb 9, May 19

Teresa, Mother   Apr 15

Teresa of Avila   Feb 26, Sept 4

Waal, Esther de   May 4

Wallace, Martin   Dec 4

Wesley, John   May 24

Index of Subjects

Advent Nov 30–Dec 9, Dec 17, 20

Angels Sept 28–Oct 3

Anger Feb 18

Animals Jan 15, July 23, Aug 3, 8–22

Art May 12

Authority Mar 9, Oct 24

Balance July 3, 20, Sept 22, Nov 17, Dec 7

Baptism Jan 14, Apr 19, May 9, Aug 26, Dec 8

Beltane May 1

Bible Study July 9, Sept 2

Births Jan 7, 10, 11, 13

Blessing Feb 13, Dec 31

Breath May 3

Celi De (Friends of God) Mar 21, Dec 4

Celtic Psalter, The Aug 9

Circling (Caim) prayer Oct 5

Channel Isles Jan 2, 19

Christmas Dec 22–27

Children Jan 2, Mar 11, Apr 4, June 1, Nov 18

Church Jan 17, 19, 22, 25, 28, Mar 9, Apr 10, May 15, July 13, 18, Nov 29

Community of Aidan and Hilda May 10, 16, 17, July 9, Aug 6, Dec 12

Creation Jan 14, Feb 1, 11, Mar 10, 23, 26, Apr 1, May 4, 11, 12, 22, 28, June 4, July 23, 26, Aug 6, 7, 25, Sept 17, Oct 4, 27

Cross, the Mar 22–29 Sept 14

Death, dying Mar 30, Nov 3, 6–10, 13, 14, 16, 19, 25, 27

Depression Nov 5, 26

Detachment Jan 14, Feb 26, July 5, 10, Sept 13

Divine Plan Jan 12, 25, Apr 16, May 10, 15

Dream of the Rood, The Mar 26, 27, Nov 8, Dec 11

Dreams Jan 7, 10, 12, Feb 11, 22, 23, 24, 28, May 23, June 15, July 2, 7 Oct 28, Nov 14, Dec 1

Earth Apr 21, May 8, Aug 2, 7, 8

Easter Mar 29–Apr 7

Elements Jan 14, Apr 19–21, May 8, 19, Aug 7

Epiphany Jan 6, 7, 14

Evangelism Jan 28, Mar 3, 20, Aug 26, 31, Sept 1, Nov 29

Evil Jan 2, 27, Feb 18, 27, 28, Mar 6, 23, July 15, 19, 27, Oct 6, 8, 29, 31

Faith Mar 1, May 25, July 11, Oct 21

Families June 15, Dec 28, 29

Fathers Jan 10, 12, 13, 21, Feb 4, 28, Mar 7, 13, May 6, June 15, July 28, Aug 28, Nov 14, 15

Forgiveness Feb 8, 28, June 1, 16, 27, July 2, 3, 27, Aug 12, 20, 21, 27, Sept 17, Oct 9, Nov 19

Friendship Feb 17, Mar 8, Apr 22, 26, June 23, July 11, 21, Aug 19, Sept 6, Oct 22, Nov 7

Generosity Feb 5, 13, Apr 5, June 11, 25, 29, Aug 18, 30, Nov 24

Gentleness Jan 5, Feb 9, 24, June 18, July 13, 19, 28, Aug 4, Sept 1, Nov 26

Glastonbury July 31

God's Plan Apr 16, May 10

Hallowe'en Oct 31

Healing Feb 5, 6, Mar 3, June 11, July 15, Aug 27, Oct 2, 21

Heaven Nov 1–4, 6–10, 27

Holy Communion Feb 22, June 5

Holy Spirit Apr 21–May 19, June 7

Hospitality Jan 22, Feb 6, May 27, 29, June 25, Sept 7, Oct 11, Nov 24

Humility Mar 2, 9, July 13

Humour May 25, June 1, July 19, Sept 12

Imbolc Feb 1

Incarnation May 8, Dec 13–19, 24, 25

Integrity Jan 26, Mar 2, July 6, Sept 2, 13, 18–20

Iona June 11, 12, 16, Oct 23

Iona Community May 26, June 12, December 10, 12

Jesus Prayer, The Feb 12

Journeys Jan 1–7, May 16–18, June 23, July 5

Justice June 12, July 11, Aug 5, 20, 22, Sept 23, Nov 23

Lammas Aug 1

Leadership Jan 5, 8, 9, June 14, 24, 25, Dec 20

Listening Apr 12–16, May 10–14, May 26

Love Jan 2, 11, May 26, 29, 31

Martyrdom Jan 26, Feb 10

Mission Jan 25–28, Mar 3, 17, May 20–31, Sept 4, 21, Oct 14, Nov 29

Moderation July 20, July 5, Aug 22

Mothers Jan 12, 15, 25, 26, Feb 4, Mar 9, Apr 21, July 21, Aug 28, Sept 9, Oct 29, Nov 20, 23, Dec 27–29

Nations Jan 8, May 27, June 13, July 13, 27, Aug 20, Oct 23

New Year Jan 1, 2, 3, 4, Dec 31

Northumbria Community Jan 29, Oct 10

Peace Jan 22, Mar 31, Apr 25, May 27, July 12, Aug 24, Oct 1, Nov 14, 19

Penance Feb 10, May 19, June 11, 20, 27, July 4, Oct 24, Nov 4

Pentecost May 18, 27, 29 (See also Holy Spirit)

Prayer Jan 4, 9, Feb 7, 25, Apr 15, May 2, 31, June 8, 15, July 9, 11, 13, Aug 21, 22, Sept 3, 5, Oct 2, 5, 7, 13, 24 Nov 26, 29, Dec 9

Prophecy Jan 10, 11, Apr 10, June 12,

26, July 28, Aug 20, Nov 19, Dec 18

Rainbow June 26

Re-incarnation May 21

Remembrance Nov 14, 15

Resurrection Mar 31, Apr 1–7, May 21

Resurrection, place of Apr 7, 10, Sept 27

Rhythm Mar 7, 30, Aug 9, 24, Nov 5

Sanctity of life Dec 28

Samhain Nov 1

Signs and wonders Jan 11, 15, Feb 6, Apr 24, June 14, July 16, Aug 5, 10, 17, 26–29

Silence Feb 14, 23, Apr 13, 15

Simplicity Mar 10, July 5

Sleep Oct 25

Solstice June 21, Dec 21, 22

Sorrow Feb 8, 16, 19, Mar 24, 26, 28

Spiritual warfare Feb 17, 27, Mar 6, July 15, 26, 30

St Patrick's Breastplate Feb 3, Mar 17, Sept 25, Nov 29

Stowe Missal Dec 3

Suffering Jan 6, Mar 28, July 2, 14, Aug 6, 14, Oct 4, 7

Taizé Community Mar 7

Temptation Mar 12, July 26, Sept 6, Dec 26

Trinity May 29–June 2, July 29

Wandering Thoughts Aug 2

Water Jan 14, May 9, 19

Work Mar 4, 7, May 1

Young People Mar 13, 14, 19

Index of Bible Texts

Genesis
1:1, 2 Apr 30
1:10, 24; 2:7 Aug 7
1:26 May 31
2:7 Aug 8
3:17 Sept 17
7:13, 14 Aug 16
9:16 June 26
12:1 Jan 3
22:14 June 30
28:11 Oct 28
37:8, 18 Feb 24
49:25, 26 May 6

Exodus
3:8 Feb 13
3:14 May 28
15:22–26 Sept 8
32:10 Jan 8
35:31 May 12

Leviticus
9:4 Sept 21
19:18 Feb 9

Numbers
35:13, 15 Aug 14

Deuteronomy
6:5 Mar 19
6:6, 9 Feb 1
11:26–28 Oct 8
30:1 Oct 7
32:2 Jan 5, Sept 1
32:4 July 4
33:26 June 4

Judges
13:24, 25 July 28

1 Samuel
13:14 Aug 5

2 Samuel
1:19, 24, 25 Nov 14

1:23 Nov 7
21:3 June 27

1 Kings
17:12, 15 July 11
18:21 June 25
19:13, 15 Mar 15

2 Kings
2:8, 9 Sept 3, Dec 4
20:4–6 Nov 25

2 Chronicles
6:14 July 10
31:21 May 1

Ezra
9:15 Oct 24

Nehemiah
9:20, 21 Mar 16

Esther
9:24, 25, 31 Sept 26

Job
6:24 Aug 2
9:8, 10 Aug 10
9:9 Dec 13
25:10 Oct 5
37:1, 5, 21 May 22
38:25–30 Aug 2

Psalms
8:2 Mar 11
9:13, 14 Nov 4
17:3, 7 Dec 1
18:13 Dec 9
18:32–34 Jan 30
20:8 Nov 22
22:19 Sept 24
23:4 Nov 12
24:1 May 8, Aug 8
32:8 Apr 16

32:12 Mar 17
33:18, 19 Mar 22
39:5, 12 Jan 2
42:11 Nov 26
45:1 Aug 23
46:10 Aug 9
51:17 Feb 16
59:16 June 23
63:1–8 Oct 26
65:11 Oct 19
78:67–70 Mar 4
84:7 Jan 16
97:1 May 18
103:14, 15 Apr 21
104:12, 13 May 7
106:4–7 Jan 4
107:22 Feb 11
113:1, 3 ?
18:9 Oct 17
119:9, 10 Mar 13
122:6 July 31
127:2 Oct 25
131:2 July 12
133:1 Jan 21
134:10 June 9
139:7, 9, 10 May 4
139:11, 12 Dec 12
148:1, 2 Oct 3
148:3, 4, 8, 10, 11 Oct 4
148:13, 14 July 24
150:6 Mar 21

Proverbs
8:1 Mar 20
8:1, 10, 11 13–16 Nov 17
11:28 June 20
13:14 July 3
13:34 Oct 23
14:22 Mar 5
14:34 June 13
15:1 Aug 4
16:7 Oct 18
16:18 Oct 11

17:17 Mar 8
17:22 Sept 12
24:26 Jan 24

Ecclesiastes
3:1, 22 Nov 11
4:12 May 29
7:18 July 20
7:29 Mar 10
9:10 May 3

Song of Songs
1:3, 4 Feb 29
3:5 Aug 13
8:6 May 26

Isaiah
6:8 Aug 31
11:1 Dec 20
11:6 Aug 15
11:7 Aug 12
11:9 Mar 1
28:21 Dec 11
31:6–7 Jan 2
30:15 Jan 9
40:3, 4 Dec 2
40:31 Apr 13, Aug 9
42:7 Aug 22
45:3 Dec 22
53:6 Mar 24
53:4, 5 Mar 28
61:1 Sept 23
64:5 June 23

Jeremiah
1:4 Jan 13
6:16 Jan 19
29:5 Nov 5
31:33 Apr 29
50:33, 34, 39 Oct 31

Lamentations
3:23 Mar 31
3:28 Apr 15

Daniel
10:13 Sept 29

11:2 Oct 1
12:3 Aug 26

Hosea
2:17, 18 July 23

Joel
2:12 Feb 19
2:28, 29 May 23

Amos
2:11, 12 Oct 13
5:6 Dec 8

Zechariah
2:6, 8 Sept 15
5:4 Dec 21
9:16 Nov 18
10:11 May 16

Malachi
3:10 Feb 4

Matthew
1:18, 19 Dec 14
2:10–11 Jan 6
2:12 Jan 7
2:10, 11 Dec 27
2:16, 17, 18 Dec 28
5:5 Sept 10
5:6 Aug 30
5:23, 24 Nov 19
6:6 July 8
6:13 July 15
6:19–20 Feb 6, Aug 19
6:22 June 10
7:1 Feb 23
7:3, 5 Oct 9
7:28, 29 Mar 9
10:37 Nov 20
10:38, 39 June 12
11:5, 6 June 6
11:15 Apr 14
11:29 June 18
12:20 Oct 10, Nov 21
16:18, 19 Feb 22
17:2 Aug 6
18:10 Sept 30

21:21, 22 Sept 5
21:28–31 Sept 20
25:8, 9 Apr 22
25:21 Jan 28
25:37, 40 Apr 3
28:19 June 2

Mark
1:3 Nov 30, Dec 4
1:9–11 May 9
1:10, 11 May 30
1:12 Feb 7
1:15 Sept 27
1:35 Feb 15
5:20 Nov 29
6:2, 3 Sept 9
6:46, 47 June 3
8:19–21 Apr 2
9:23 Dec 31
9:40 May 20
10:46, 47, 52 Aug 27
10:48 Feb 8
12:1 July 1
15:47 Mar 30
16:17, 18 Aug 17

Luke
1:26, 31, 32 Dec 23
1:30, 35 Mar 25
2:7 Dec 25
2:9 Dec 24
2:15, 16 Dec 26
2:76–79 Jan 10
2:39, 40 Dec 29
2:40 Jan 15
3:5 Dec 7
3:16 Apr 26
3:21 Jan 14
4:42, 43 Mar 3
5:5, 6 Oct 16
5:30 Feb 7
6:36 Aug 18
6:38 Feb 5
7:26, 28 June 24
8:49 Apr 9
9:58 Jan 29
10:3 Jan 5

11:46 Sept 2
12:6, 7 Aug 11
12:27 May 5
12:49 Apr 20
13:20, 21 Feb 3
14:8, 10 Mar 16
16:9 Nov 27
16:10 May 13
18:13 Feb 25
19:31 Aug 3
23:43 Nov 6
25:53, 55, 56 Mar 29

John
1:2, 4 Jan 31, Oct 27
1:14 Dec 18
2:8 Apr 18
4:6, 7, 14 May 19
5:19; 8:28 Apr 12
7:38, 39 Apr 19
10:10 June 21
13:4, 5 Sept 7
14:12 Aug 29
15:14, 15 Dec 3
16:28; 16:7 Dec 30
17:21 Jan 20
19:17, 19 Mar 26
20:11, 16, 17 Apr 10
21:19 Dec 10

Acts
2:1, 7, 10, 11 May 27
4:24, 30 Apr 17
5:3, 4 Aug 28
5:12 July 16
7:59 Jan 26
8:36–38 May 9
10:44, 45 June 7
12:7, 10, 12, 14 May 25
13:26 Nov 13
17:11 July 9
20:9–11 Apr 5
20:35 June 29
22:14 Jan 25

Romans
1:16 July 6

1:20 Aug 25
4:16–17 Jan 11
7:23–25 Dec 16
8:26, 27 Mar 14
11:36 Aug 1
12:5 Jan 22,
12:5, 27 Sept 4
12:7, 10 May 14
12:11 Apr 23
12:15, 16 Sept 25
12:21 Mar 6
13:11 Nov 28

1 Corinthians
1:26, 27 July 17
4:5 Dec 6
6:15, 20 May 10
9:20, 21, 22 Oct 15
11:24 June 5
14:1 July 7
14:15 July 14
14:40 July 22
15:22 Apr 7
15:42–44 May 21
15:54 Oct 30
15:58 June 16

2 Corinthians
3:12 Mar 18
3:18 June 17
4:2 Sept 14
4:8, 9 July 21
4:10, 11, 14 Apr 8
5:1 Nov 8
6:17 Jan 17
6:10 Feb 26
7:2 July 13
12:2, 3, 5 Nov 3
13:7, 8 Apr 11
13:14 June 1

Galatians
3:28 July 27
4:19, 26, 31 July 18
5:16, 17 Sept 6
5:22 Apr 24, 25
5:29 July 24

6:9, 10 June 8
6:14 Sept 14

Ephesians
2:13, 19 May 24
3:17, 18, 19 Apr 28
4:6 Feb 18
4:10 May 11
4:29 June 15
5:16 Jan 27
5:18 Apr 27
6:7 May 2
6:13 Feb 27
6:14–17 July 26

Philippians
2:2 Jan 18
2:6, 7 Dec 14
3:13–14 Jan 1
4:12, 13 July 5, July 30

Colossians
1:27 Jan 12
2:7 June 28
2:20 Oct 29
3:1 Apr 6
2:20; 3:1, 9, 10 Apr 1

1 Thessalonians
4:14 Nov 9

2 Thessalonians
3:10 Mar 7

1 Timothy
3:16 July 29
4:8 Feb 20
6:6 Sept 13
6:7 Nov 16

2 Timothy
1:8 Feb 12
2:3, 4 July 2
3:14–17 Oct 20
4:5 Sept 22
4:7, 8 Sept 16

Titus
1:15 July 19

Philemon
4:7 Oct 22

Hebrews
2:18 Mar 12
3:19 Sept 11
11:33, 34 Nov 15
11:37, 39 Feb 10
11:35 Apr 4
12:1 Nov 1
12:23 Sept 28
13:2 Nov 24

James
1:2 Feb 17
1:3, 4 June 19
1:26; 2:6 Feb 21
2:1 Aug 20
3:7, 8 Aug 21

1 Peter
2:17 Nov 23
2:24 Mar 27
3:15 Oct 14

2 Peter
5:3, 5 Oct 12

1 John
1:5 Feb 2
4:1, 5, 19, 20 Feb 28,
    June 11
5:21 Oct 21

Revelation
3:7, 5:5 Dec 17
5:11 Sept 28
7:1–3 Oct 2
13:18 Mar 23
20:12, 15 Dec 5

Sources and Acknowledgments

The compiler and publisher are grateful for permission to reproduce copyright material. Great care has been taken to trace rights holders and to clear copyright permissions. This process is complicated, and if any required acknowledgments have been omitted, or any rights overlooked, it is unintentional and forgiveness is requested. Please notify the publishers who will include any omissions in future reprints.

Quotations from the Bible are selected from a variety of sources: New International Version copyright (c) 1973, 1978, 1984 by International Bible Society, used by permission of Hodder & Stoughton, a member of the Hodder Headline Group. All rights reserved.

The Good News Bible published by The Bible Societies/HarperCollins Publishers Ltd., UK, (c) American Bible Society, 1966, 1971, 1976, 1992.

The New Revised Standard Version (Anglicised Edition) copyright 1989, 1995 by the Division of Christian Education of the National Council of the Churches of Christ in the United States of America.

The author's own translation.

Geoffrey Ashe for the extract from his *Avalonian Quest*.

Ramon Beeching, Janet Donaldson, Michael Halliwell and Craig Roberts for their prayers as printed in *Pocket Celtic Prayers* compiled by Martin Wallace, Church House Press.

Juliet Boobbyer and Joanna Sciortino for extracts from their *Columba, the Play with Music*, Fowler Wright Books.

Boydell and Brewster Ltd. for extracts from *The Dream of the Rood*.

Thomas Cahill for the excerpt from his *How the Irish Saved Civilisation*, Doubleday.

Cambridge University Press for excerpts from *Two Lives of Saint Cuthbert* trans. Bertram Colgrave, 1985.

Ted Carr for an extract of the spoken words to his song *I Am*: part of the album *Mystic Prophet*, 1994.

The Central Board of Finance of the Church of England for the extract from *The Promise of His Glory*, Church House Publishing and Mowbray, 1991.

T. & T. Clark Ltd., 59 George Street, Edinburgh EH2 2LQ for the extracts from the translation of *St. Patrick's Breastplate* in *Introduction to Celtic Christianity*, Mackey (ed.).

Darton, Longman and Todd Ltd. for the extract taken from *Living Between Worlds* by Philip Sheldrake, published and copyright 1995 by Darton, Longman and Todd Ltd. and used by permission of the publishers.

Oliver Davies and Fiona Bowie for excerpts from *Celtic Christian Spirituality*, SPCK 1995.

The Dean and Chapter of Durham Cathedral for prayers from their booklet *The Spirit of the Cathedral*.

Edinburgh University Press 1994 for excerpts from *Iona, The Earliest Poetry of a Celtic Monastery*, Thomas Owen Clancy and Gilbert Markus; and from *St. Nynia* by John and W. MacQueen, Polygon, 1990.

Msg Tom Fehily for an extract from his leaflet on Christian Meditation.

Tomas O Fiaich (trans.) *Columbanus in his own Words*, Veritas Publications, 1974.

Forest of Peace Publishing, Inc., 251 Muncie Road, Leavenworth KS 66048, USA for an extract from *Prayers for a Planetary Pilgrim* by Edward Hays.

Brian Frost for excerpts from his *Glastonbury Journey*, Becket Publications, 1986.

Gomer Press for the excerpt from *Eples* by David Gwenallt Jones.

Michael Halliwell for extracts from his booklet *Thou my Whole Armour*.

HarperCollins Publishers Ltd., for the extract from *Mother Teresa: Spiritual Counsel*.

Hannah Hopkin, *The Living Legend of St Patrick*, Grafton Books, 1990.

Stephen Lawhead for an extract from *Arthur: Book III of The Pendragon Cycle*, Lion Publishing, Copyright 1989, Stephen Lawhead.

Llanerch Publishers, Felinfach, Lampeter for excerpts from *The Life of Samson of Dol*, Thomas Taylor (trans.); from *Life of Saint Columba* by Adamnan; from *Two Celtic Saints: The Lives of Ninian and Kentigern*; and from *Lives of Saints from the Book of Lismore*, Whitley Stokes (trans.).

Kate McIlhagga for prayers from *Seasons and Celebrations* published by N.C.E.C. 1020 Bristol Road, Selly Oak, Birmingham B29 6LB.

The Northumbria Community Trust for an extract from *A Way of Life, Rule of Life of the Northumbria Community* written by, published and copyright The Northumbria Community Trust; used with permission; also for a prayer taken from *Celtic Night Prayer – Cuthbert – into a desert place* published by HarperCollins Publishers Ltd., copyright 1996, by The Northumbria Community Trust and used with permission.

Brendan O'Malley for extracts from his *A Pilgrim's Manual, St David's*.

The Very Revd. J.S. Richardson, Bradford Cathedral, for two prayers from the Cathedral's *St Aidan Chapel Booklet*.

Oxford University Press for excerpts from Bede's *The Ecclesiastical History of the English People*, ed. Bertram Colgrave and R.A.B. Mynors, 1969. Copyright and reprinted by permission of Oxford University Press.

Richard Sharpe for extracts from Adamnan of Iona's *Life of St Columba* published by Penguin Books, 1995.

SPCK for excerpts from *The Open Gate* and *Borderlands* both by David Adam; and from *St. Seraphim of Sarov* by Valentine Zander, St. Vladimir Seminary Press, New York.

The Rev. Dr. Patrick Thomas for extracts from his *Candle in the Darkness*, Gomer Press, 1993.

University of Wales Press for extracts from Rhigyfarch's *Life of Saint David*, J.W. James (trans.) 1967.

Martin Wallace for an extract from his booklet, *Celtic Reflections*, Tim Tiley Prints.

Robert Van de Weyer for extracts from his *Celtic Parables*, DLT, 1997; *Celtic Fire*, DLT, 1996 and *The Letters of Pelagius: Celtic Soul Friend*, Arthur James, 1995.

Wild Goose Publications for extracts from *The Whole Earth Shall Cry Glory* by George MacLeod; *Iona Community Worship Book* and *The Wee Worship Book*.

LLOYD

PEOPLE AND PLACES IN THE BRITISH ISLES